Conditions of Music

LANGUAGE, DISCOURSE, SOCIETY
Editors: Stephen Heath and Colin MacCabe

Published

VISION AND PAINTING: The Logic of the Gaze
Norman Bryson

ALICE DOESN'T: Feminism, Semiotics, Cinema
Theresa de Lauretis

CONDITIONS OF MUSIC
Alan Durant

FEMINISM AND PSYCHOANALYSIS: The Daughter's Seduction
Jane Gallop

ON LAW AND IDEOLOGY
Paul Hirst

JAMES JOYCE AND THE REVOLUTION OF THE WORD
Colin MacCabe

THE TALKING CURE: Essays in Psychoanalysis and Language
Colin MacCabe (*editor*)

PSYCHOANALYSIS AND CINEMA: The Imaginary Signifier
Christian Metz

LANGUAGE, SEMANTICS AND IDEOLOGY
Michel Pêcheux

LANGUAGE, SEXUALITY AND IDEOLOGY IN EZRA POUND'S CANTOS
Jean–Michel Rabaté

THE CASE OF PETER PAN OR THE IMPOSSIBILITY OF CHILDREN'S FICTION
Jacqueline Rose

THE MAKING OF THE READER: Language and Subjectivity in Modern American, English and Irish Poetry
David Trotter

Forthcoming

STATE OF NATURE: Ethnography and Origins
Beverley Brown and Judith Ennew

TO REPRESENT WOMAN? The Representation of Sexual Differences in the Visual Media
Elizabeth Cowie

UNDERSTANDING BECKETT
Peter Gidal

THREE ESSAYS ON SUBJECTIVITY
Stephen Heath

EPOS: Word, Narrative and the Iliad
Michael Lynn–George

THE GENEALOGY OF MORAL FORMS: Foucault, Nietzsche, Donzelot
Jeffrey Minson

FEMINISMS: A Conceptual History
Denise Riley

POLITICAL CRITICISM
Michael Ryan

CONDITIONS OF MUSIC

Alan Durant

© Alan Durant 1984

All rights reserved. No part of this publication
may be reproduced or transmitted, in any form
or by any means, without permission.

First published 1984 by
THE MACMILLAN PRESS LTD
London and Basingstoke
Companies and representatives
throughout the world

British Library Cataloguing in Publication Data
Durant, Alan
Conditions of music–(Language, discourse, society)
1. Musical forms
I. Title   II. Series
781.5   MT58
ISBN 978-0-333-37277-7   ISBN 978-1-349-17591-8 (eBook)
DOI 10.1007/978-1-349-17591-8

Rebec, fifteenth century, an early model.
Photo by kind permission of the Horniman Museum, London.

Contents

Acknowledgements ix

Part I: Four Areas in Question

1 MUSIC AND ITS LANGUAGE 3
The unanswered question of music as a language–Musical 'languages' and musical change–The non-referentiality of music–'All art constantly aspires towards the condition of music'–Deryk Cooke's *The Language of Music*–Music and language: comparison or theory?–Historical change and musical terminology–Mousike–Continuity, change and purpose–The importance of transitions–Revaluations

2 CLASSICAL MUSIC 29
The 'classical' in 'classical music'–Canon of works or relations of address?–Beginnings of the concert–Balance and vision–The orchestra, format and history–Orchestra and orchestration–Composer and conductor: specialisation–Forms and their origins–Forms, listening and formal analysis: the symphony–'Classical' music and modernism–Serialism–Recording and the 'classical' composer–Collaborative music and listening

3 TUNING AND DISSONANCE 58
Music, dissonance and noise–Music, sounds and acoustics–Formalism or musak–Historical reference I: The Greeks–Historical reference II: The Middle Ages–The Middle Ages: sounds and symbols–The Middle Ages: polyphony–Historical reference III: tonality–The contemporary argument: three views–The contemporary argument: directions–Dissonance and today's ear

4 PERFORMANCE: SOUND AND VISION 86
Musical performance and spectacle–Locating sounds–The

significance of sound and vision—Barthes and the body: 'The Grain of the Voice'—Three points of position in sound and vision—Performance in transition—Musical reproduction and its technology—Reproduction and performance—Forms in transition—'Musica Practica' or musical image?

Part II: Two Case Studies

5 FALSE RELATIONS AND THE MADRIGAL: AN ALCHEMY OF ENGLAND'S GOLDEN AGE IN MUSIC   119
Golden Age or period of transition—Madrigal and madrigalist: employment and publication—The madrigal and religious controversy—Music by metaphor and rhetoric—Imitation and ornament—Madrigal, ballett and ayre—The ayre and the singing voice—The period and its prospect—Performance and contemporary cultural argument

6 ROCK TODAY: FACING THE MUSIC   167
Diversity of forms and its implications—Regional comparison: disco music in Jamaica, India and the USA—Meanings and options in one place—Identification and revolt—The Who, 'My Generation', and David Bowie, 'Fashion'—Groups—'Real' experience or conventional genre?—The rock song I: radio—The rock song II: 'shifters' and the term of address—The rock song III: position, polysemy and innovation—Albums I: *Sergeant Pepper* and *Dark Side of the Moon*—Albums II: new form or sell-out?—Albums III: implications for the contemporary scene—The current prospect: synthesisers and video

Notes and References   234

Select Bibliography and Record List   239

Index   249

Acknowledgements

A number of people have talked through with me many of the arguments laid out in this book, and some have worked over stages of the manuscript. I would like to thank them, especially: Rebecca Thomas, Andrew Blake, Simon Adams, Derek Attridge, Simon Emmerson, Graham Huntingdon, Eddie Prévost.

All photographs by (and with permission from): Jill Furmanovsky, unless otherwise credited. Jill Furmanovsky is a studio photographer who contributes regularly to rock music papers and magazines in Britain and elsewhere.

The author and publishers wish to thank the following, who have kindly given permission for the use of copyright material:

© Cambridge University Library, for photograph of 1617 edition of Thomas Campion's 'Fire! Fire!'.
© Chappell Music Ltd, London, for lyrics from 'Breathe' and 'Time', by Pink Floyd. Copyright 1973 Pink Floyd Music Publishers Ltd.
© Dwarf Music, New York, for lyrics from 'Rainy Day Women # 12 and 35', by Bob Dylan. Copyright 1966 Dwarf Music. Used by permission. All rights reserved.
© Faber and Faber Ltd, for words and music of Thomas Campion's 'Fire! Fire!', reprinted from *The Works of Thomas Campion: Complete Songs, Masques and Treatises*, edited by Walter R. Davis.
© Fabulous Music Ltd, for lyrics from 'My Generation', words and music by Pete Townshend (1966).
© Horniman Museum, London, for photographs of rebec and African kora.
© Island Music, for photograph of Bob Marley.
© Keith Rowe, for photograph of Keith Rowe.
© Northern Songs Ltd, for lyrics from 'A Day in the Life' (1967), words and music by John Lennon and Paul McCartney;

Acknowledgements

'Ob-la-di, Ob-la-da' (1968), words and music by John Lennon and Paul McCartney; 'Glass Onion' (1968), words and music by John Lennon and Paul McCartney; 'Maybe I'm Amazed' (1970), words and music by Paul McCartney.

© Oxford University Press, for words and music of Thomas Tomkins's 'Music Divine', reprinted from *The Oxford Book of English Madrigals*, edited by Philip Ledger.

© J. Walter Thompson Co, Ltd, and Elida Gibbs, for photographic still from 'Vivas' television advertisement. All rights reserved.

© Warner Bros Music Ltd, for lyrics from 'You're So Vain', by Carly Simon (1972); 'Pretty Vacant', by the Sex Pistols (1977); 'We are Family', by Sister Sledge (1979).

Every effort has been made to trace all copyright holders, but if any have been inadvertently overlooked, the publishers will be pleased to make the necessary arrangement at the first opportunity.

Part I
Four Areas in Question

1 Music and its Language

The Unanswered Question of Music as a Language

Playing and listening to music remain especially resistant to description and commentary. The difficulty of finding a vocabulary to speak of musical forms within their social contexts, whilst at the same time accounting for their expressive or affective potential, makes extremely precarious any notion of response that makes claim to something more than personal impression. In addition, the range of relations involved in a musical performance or experience involve considerations far more complicated than can be handled within present boundaries of formal musical analysis. These fundamental problems are widely acknowledged by musicians, by listeners, and by commentators. And they perplex discussions or assessments of musical activities, as well as participation in them. Indeed, they have contributed to the widely held view of music which attaches particular value to its assumed radical unknowability: in reverence for directly sensuous experience, music is often valued as a kind of immediate sensuality, seemingly something literally breathed into the body from the air.

Clearly, it is desirable to move beyond the evident problems of such an idealisation, to reconsider what is often referred to as a specific but unanalysable 'language' of music. In order to do this, it seems clear that attention will have to be given once again to fundamental questions of description and assessment: questions to do with ways in which the development of musical forms, related to larger social movements and processes of change, underlies a contemporary range of activities and responses. An urgent need for such consideration is clear. The circumstances of contemporary music are widely recognised to be ones of particularly major and rapid change, and of a crisis of understanding and confidence over a range of perspectives. So to trace elements of the history is to acknowledge and broach problems of musical practice and taste in the present: problems of choice, participation and support for musical forms and purposes.

Concern over present activity is especially important. The twentieth century has seen major technological innovations of production and reproduction of music, in manufacture and use of electric and electronic instruments, as well as in developments of tape recording, gramophone reproduction and broadcasting. These innovations have altered the ways in which, as well as the extent to which, music is heard. An importantly new configuration of contexts for music has been established (supporting film and television narrative, in jukeboxes, in day-and-night radio transmission, etc.); and this has led to suggestions of a fundamental divergence of musical 'languages', as well as, frequently, of proclaimed inequalities between them.

Musical 'Languages' and Musical Change

The divisions between the 'languages' have roots in social as well as aesthetic transition. New circumstances of musical performance and reproduction have had important effects on conventions of listening. Recording and broadcasting have created new conditions and relations of listening arguably as decisively as the advent of concert performance and opera in the seventeenth century changed the then socially dominant characteristics of performance and their related musical expectations. This earlier revolution of listening involved a shift of emphasis from a dominant mode of music-making in which performance was appended to courtly, religious or military ritual, towards a largely secular manner of performance governed by patronage, and by market relations and forces. One effect of this was the development, throughout Europe and later in the United States, of a new conception of music—music no longer as an accessory to various forms of social ritual, justified by its relevance to these, but as more a form of individual and collaborative achievement or art, justified by the pleasures and knowledges it can itself precipitate. It was one effect of the early concert-hall, with its widening base of subscribers and sponsors, to diffuse many old and some new musical forms and tastes through broader social groupings, themselves undergoing major change and realignment. But in this ascendancy of opera and concert-hall, a disjunction was established between the continuing musical forms, and the conditions of their earlier social performance and ritual. These were displaced by new cultural forms emphasising on the one hand composition, performance and notated publication of works, and on the other an organisation of listening increasingly linked to the position of being privy to the act of performance as itself a spectacle for entertainment. Before this major transformation, listening to music was largely the prerogative of classes whose positions in the prevailing social order were at least in part defined according to rituals, spectacles and performances, many of which incorporated music. But the new music and institutions of the sixteenth and seventeenth centuries came increasingly to be considered in terms of a personally expressive and individually consumable art-form.

The continuing, contemporary revolution in production of music, and in listening to it, may be decisive on a similar scale. A range of forms of music from earlier epochs, often composed with regard to specific ceremonies, listening conditions and social occasions, has now become available for frequent or continuous listening and for domestic ownership. These new circumstances involve almost no reference to original constraints on composition and performance, except in sleeve-note annotations and broadcast explanatory introductions. Even where such specificities are taken into account, in minutest detail (in qualities of recording such as period instrumentation or character of reverberation) what is gained is in no way the restoration of an original, fundamentally social experience of ritual or assembly. On the contrary, what is produced is an importantly new (in this sense 'original') phenomenon of representation, in the projection—frequently for private, domestic consumption—of scale, ambience of ceremony, or mass performance.

This reworking of earlier music appears all the more critical at present. Continuity of the same musical works being performed can obscure the importance and extent of changes in performance conditions. But continuing performance of musical works from earlier ages is also accompanied by innovation and original activity. It is mainly in these that exploratory extensions and modifications of the forms and means of making music—alterations to its 'language'—take place. Yet since such innovations have always to develop alongside, and often against, established conceptions of musical composition, performance and appreciation—conceptions often insulated against or resistant to new practices which meet fresh circumstances or conditions—it is crucial to acknowledge, and on the basis of understanding actively shape, the processes of change and adjustment through which music is defined and redefined.

Despite the clear importance of such questions, however, it remains difficult to clarify issues which surround maintaining existing works, whilst simultaneously engaging new initiatives. Frequently, reflection and exchange of views are restricted by evaluations in which the necessity of present activity taking one form or another—the actuality of music as continuous practice—is blocked by static judgements and preferences fixed somewhere in the past. This particular form of reverence for the past is especially perplexing in its most familiar form, a selective esteem for a 'classical' concert-music. For one thing which is especially striking about the history of European concert-music is its establishment of present conventions of listening or playing only through repeated novelty and disagreement; and this aspect of the history has to be stripped of evident implications for the present if the notion of a stable musical heritage linked to a canon of works is to be currently upheld. Against such fixed views, it might be said that contemporary revaluation of music is far less a question of regenerating cultural value around an established musical tradition (and so for an established and static 'language'), than of reassessing and reworking musical discourses of the past in relation to acknowledged contemporary concerns and requirements.

The Non-referentiality of Music

These difficulties of history, evaluation and direction are problematic enough. But it is often carefully argued that, irrespective of specific formations in which music is made, its non-referentiality precludes consideration in terms of analysable effects.

This view is familiar still (it was most energetically promoted during the nineteenth century with regard to traditions of 'pure' or instrumental music, and was then often supported by more general contemporaneous theories of art and expression). Broadly, the argument is that for music there are no clear means of conducting meaning such as appear to exist for language, whose properties of referring and defining can specify a context within which significant interpretations and responses will be made. The force of the distinction between language and music becomes that music is concerned primarily with aesthetic attractions of its own forms (and here the link with other nineteenth-century positions becomes clear). Or again, it can be supposed that the means whereby music embodies affective properties are at present scarcely understood: these means are then either characterisable as part of a mystery to be left to future discovery, or of a mystery to be valued precisely as such. Nor need the power of music be impugned in such views, being believed to be that of a preeminently effective, international 'language': one without any 'artificial' code or system for its production of meanings.

In such understandings, music is primarily an ineffable experience, rather than a set of created forms and relations. It is achieved by, but not reducible to, the material ways in which actual musical performances or acts of listening take place. Considered as quintessential experience of organised sound, music can be more than the score which prescribes it, and more than the particularities of any performance which renders it. This is the clear sense of distinctions between music and its orchestration, or (sometimes in combined formulation) between music and its notation on the one hand, and its performance on the other. Such idealising distinctions have also fed back on occasion into the analysis of language: it is interesting, for example, that in formulating the concept of *langue* (the range of distinctions available to a society in its language, and within which actual usages are made), Saussure postulates, at the beginning of modern linguistics, that the concept is 'comparable to a symphony in that what the symphony actually is stands completely apart from how it is performed'.[1] Difficulties continue to surround this kind of formulation, both in respect of language and as regards music: where these two are combined in comparison, opposition and alternation—in frequent definitions of music and its language—it is crucial to consider the particular distinctions and movements in play, if more general senses of music and its conditions are to be clarified.

'All Art Constantly Aspires towards the Condition of Music'

Formulated in the mid nineteenth century, Walter Pater's suggestion that 'all art constantly aspires towards the condition of music'[2] can provide a first bearing on much wider conceptions that musical effects are achieved, as Pater puts it, 'through ways not distinctly traceable by the understanding',[3] in a coincidence of form and content. It is this feature of music, the quality which makes it for Pater the 'typical or ideally consummate art' (he uses the example here of seeing a 'painting', or the image a 'painting' represents, to distinguish form from content) which makes music appear a medium of communication in which code and reference are coincidental, the same.

Several aspects of Pater's formulations can indicate nevertheless certain problems which perplex characterising a 'condition' of music, a characterisation with implications across a range of media in respect of their suggested aspiration to the same condition. Initially, in 'The School of Giorgione' in *The Renaissance*, where his speculations about music are most clearly laid out, Pater's attentions are directed against the notion that the various arts are simply transpositions of a single, common impulse. To this he counterposes the suggestion, important for his development of an 'aesthetic criticism' based on a refined level of artistic response, that all arts do in fact have specific and individual qualities. These, he argues, can occasionally be drifted across from one art-form to another. The quality which makes music preeminent is its indistinguishable union of form and content (a union most closely approached by that of lyrical poetry):

> It is the art of music which most completely realizes this artistic ideal, this perfect identification of matter and form. In its consummate moments, the end is not distinct from the means, the form from the matter, the subject from the expression; they inhere in and completely saturate each other; and to it, therefore, to the condition of its perfect moments, all the arts may be supposed constantly to tend to aspire.[4]

Such a condition of music becomes practically a level of perception. This can be seen in Pater's accent on 'temperament' for response rather than definition, argument and analysis. In this respect, the condition of music opposes any understanding of music as an interrelation of practices, techniques, conventions and skills. Indeed it only becomes clear what kinds of music Pater is writing about in occasional references to what are of course visual properties of Giorgione's paintings: depictions of instruments being tuned and touched (the 'momentary touch of an instrument in the twilight'), or of the spectacle of performance (as in the painting 'Concert at the Pitti Palace'[5]).

More important than this problem of abstraction and idealisation, however, is the difficulty of ascertaining from what position reference to music is being made: whether the writer is a practitioner or listener, and if a listener, then in what physical, spatial relation to the sound source or performance. Pater appeals in the paintings to a consummate or quintessential experience of life and suspension of time beyond specific relationships of physical or social position, a way the paintings retain an image in fine moments of extension into past and future. All the appropriate idealising and fetishistic accoutrements are present in the account, the 'embroidery and furs' and 'spotless white linen at wrist and throat'. Indeed for Pater in this passage experience itself is to be 'conceived as a sort of listening'.[6] In these terms, the aspiration of the arts is towards pleasure in a condition without conditions, a condition at all times and in all places identical, even as surrounding conditions shift and vary.

Yet such nineteenth-century emphases were not entirely new in this detail. Indeed, they appear to take up much earlier conceptions of music, often dramatised in techniques of concealing performers and sound source. In Italian pastoral, for example, and widely in Elizabethan stage drama (even allowing for the introduction of elevated music rooms in the private theatres), consider the role of musicians hidden above the stage, their sounds introduced as dramatic entries out of the encircling air. In such arrangements, sounds are furnished with new, dramatic contexts—as punctuations of stage narrative—for what are in effect much earlier ideas of a music of the spheres, unknowable vibrations and sounds in the world which whirl over the human mind. Equally, such emphases continue into more recent times. Consider Wagner's creation of the 'mystic gap' to conceal an orchestra at Bayreuth; or again, the popularity of the phrase 'the airwaves', in its sense of an immaterial passage of sounds for entertainment by way of broadcasting—the spontaneous arrival of sounds and voices which are absorbed and embodied in listening (though in fact these 'airwaves' are material exactly: waves and wave-forms, as witness the practical difficulties of reverberation or interference, or their controlled application in acoustic design and in the development of radio itself).

Deryk Cooke's *The Language of Music*

The kinds of argument of which Pater's remarks provide an exceptional illustration are faced with possible criticisms as regards the social value of music, too. It has often been remonstrated against them that music cannot be in this way simply a matter of arrangements of form which are simultaneously meaning and significance—not merely an impalpable, decorative art to be regarded with appreciation—if it is to be capable of expression or communication of deep human feeling and experience.

Perhaps most influential among these critical revisions has been Deryk Cooke's attempt, in *The Language of Music* in the late 1950s, to counter such formalistic traditions with an account of musical meanings and the forms which express them that would show how music can reveal 'the naked feeling direct'.[7] For it is only on the strength of some such 'language' of music, what in another framework might be called music's semiological codes, that musical works can be claimed to be more than arrangements of appreciable beauty alone: to be, as they are within an established humanist tradition, central documents of human experience and expression.

The project of *The Language of Music*, then, was not to establish an opposition between language's referential meanings, and the exceptional coincidence of form and (non-referential) effect in music, as Pater's was. Rather, the attempt was to show how musical works can be analysed in terms of a 'vocabulary' and a 'syntax'. These are explanatory terms derived for application from forms of analysis of language, though with a deference to literary criticism in general (and to the works of Wilson Knight in particular) obscuring the important fact that questions of the production of meanings in language themselves remain a site of contestation, and of difference.

Within the framework, nevertheless, a language of music is postulated to exist in 'various procedures in the dimensions of pitch, time, and volume'. These are procedures which present themselves for consideration by way of their repetition in a wide range of tonal works. An example might be a certain series of ascending pitch intervals traced, in selected contexts, through such diverse works as pieces by Byrd, Beethoven and Berlioz. Combinations of these minimal units, or signs (there is a distinction early on between iconic signs in programmatic works, and others in non-representational pieces) produce extended spans of expression. And techniques of development and transformation (in classic terms, the 'argument' which develops out of thematic material or motifs in a piece of music) are the syntax of the language, its movement or articulation. What makes the syntax of Cooke's chosen musical 'language' work, on this scale, is the development of harmonic tensions, anticipating and later supplying resolution. It is in turn the closure provided by resolution which produces an attending satisfaction in the restoration of consonance, and so the completion of a musical excursion or narrative (Cooke stresses in this respect the 'natural' acoustical properties, though changing cultural significances, of closing consonances: octave, fifth, fourth).

But there remain problems, despite the important polemical purpose and innovation. The first of these concerns the procedures by which the expressive units—the harmonic intervals, the characteristics of pace, and so on—can be taken to signify precise emotional qualities. For apart from contextual indications in titles and words, the meanings of this musical 'language' are inferred largely from intention, by way of evidence mainly from composers' writings. These testimonies, the various letters of Mozart, of Schubert, or others, endorse particular conceptions of music, important intentions and aspirations. And for the composer, these intentions develop with regard to realisable techniques and forms. Relatedly, also, it is by reason of unknown intention that folk music is considered unaccountable documentation of the 'language', since so many different aspirations have evidently contributed to its making.

But intentions alone, and parallels of context within a corpus, no matter how wide, cannot constitute a 'language'. Meanings, and their realisation through forms, rely upon far broader social relationships and shared conventions to make possible their circulation or exchange. They also rely on specific positions in and from which enunciations and interpretations are made. Something of this element of positioning *does* figure in *The Language of Music*, when personal attributions of meaning and value intervene. In discussion of duple and triple times, for example, there is the suggestion that duple time represents the 'regular, rigid, masculine rhythm of the two feet marching or running', and triple time the 'looser, swinging or lilting, feminine rhythm of the dance'.[8] Or again, concerning the overture to Wagner's opera *Rienzi*, 'the tone-colour of the trumpet evokes military and heroic associations'.[9] It is not simply that women also run and men dance, nor even that the history of dance-music composition shows a virtually consistent designation of these 'feminine' rhythms of the dance by men. What is important is that a language of music, with a proclaimed structure of intentions and associations across five centuries or more of usage, cannot be defined in this way. Even less can the codes of music be implied to be naturally ordained (which is the constant edge of taking as a 'natural' effect in listening certain acoustic properties of what have been characterised as consonances, and then deriving from these the differing removes of the various expressive dissonances). Indeed, what it seems safe to see in these perceptions of the masculine march and the feminine dance, or of the military heroism, is on the contrary that assigning meaning depends on positions of perceiving and interpreting which are as crucial as whatever intentions guided composition.

Music and Language: Comparison or Theory?

Significances and meanings exist only within social relationships, are defined in relations between positions. Composition seeks to express and address by coupling intention with practical techniques and resources; but for meaning, positions of address have to be practically, critically and institutionally achieved. It is this indispensable element of position, and of the historical construction of positions available, which is never acknowledged in *The Language of Music*. Codes are formulated without reference to the effective history of the musical practices under consideration. There is virtually no recognition, for example, of important differences of position between composer, conductor, performer and listener, or of these positions themselves changing radically across the historical periods in question.

To admit these factors into analysis of the semiological codes is to throw them back upon far wider processes in which conventions of meanings or expression are produced. These wider processes include institutions in which musical works come to be performed (the concert-hall, the church, the nightspot . . .), as well as those, often educational, means through which familiarity with intentions, with techniques and with antecedents is established and maintained, supplying music with socially specific frameworks of intelligibility.

The need for attention to these elements is clear, even within Deryk Cooke's own descriptions. Consider allusions to the 'composer', extended back as far as the social relationships which surrounded the composition of plainchant; or illustration of dissonances as expressions of pain taken from madrigals—exactly an important transformation, from sensitivities to sounds previously interpreted as notes of the devil into a resource of humanistic expression, to be passed through on the way to a new coherence of expression and identity in resolution and cadence.

Across important discrepancies of analysis and evaluation, two conflicting emphases made in appeals to a musical 'language' meet here; and between them lies an important point of divergence. On the one hand, there is 'language' as an assumed range of properties and associated affects, determined less by *social* factors (which vary) than by founding psychological or acoustic resources. These supply continuity for the 'language', and an overall framework for activity. Music made outside the framework is simply part of another 'language'. What would be most interesting about this 'language' would be the precise nature of the acoustic and psychological resources, even if these—failing some way of determining correspondences between forms and affects—will not explain very much about actual, particular pieces of music. In the other emphasis, there is 'language' as a set of properties and associated affects (still conditioned by psychological and acoustic resources), whose most significant features are those of social, regional and historical variation around those resources. Consider Mozart and Beethoven. They are important in the first emphasis on the 'language' because they were good composers *within* its conventions, because of their exceptional expertise in displaying (and so providing illustration of) that language's psychologically or acoustically endowed properties. In the other emphasis, what is more interesting is that they were massively influential in shaping and extending, in particular directions and for specific ends, a range of socially and historically available materials. In this latter emphasis, musical works do not simply exist within, or *use*, the musical 'language': they *make* and remake it, in particular realisations and directions of a potential importantly conditioned by social and historical definitions of technique, aesthetic and opportunity.

This latter framework for music and its language is seldom contemplated, despite all the interest in a 'language' of music which has developed in a number of theoretical frameworks: literary critical, semiological and transformational-generative. Frequently, the comparisons between music and language take the form of analogy and licence only—even in good introductory accounts, such as Otto Karyoli's *Introducing Music*: 'As in language words must follow a logical order within a sentence, so in music chords are linked together according to "rules" based on acoustic, aesthetic, and psychological experience'; then, 'the "rules" of musical "grammar" are very much like those of language. In the same way as it takes a true stylist to know just when to split an infinitive, so it takes a true musician to know when to use a parallel fifth.' Or, 'It is by means of the motive and its ingenious development . . . that a composer states, and subsequently explains, his idea. But in order to explain, in music as well as in speech, it is necessary to make intelligible phrases and sentences . . .'[10]

Such remarks clearly confuse bases for tonal music in acoustics and psychology with a presumed agreement over music's communicative efficacy and precision. But even in more careful and rigorous formulation, understandings which emphasise music's continual recreation and transformation of meanings, rather than its ability to express general, 'human' apprehensions in sound by exploiting established codes and effects, are at the very limit of familiar conceptions of a 'language': at the very limit, in being concerned far less with properties of the abstractions of *langue* or 'competence', than with conditions under which these might be conceived or contemplated, and in context of which they are remade and altered.

For these reasons, it is interesting to note with regard to the continuing debate over music as a language that when powerful techniques of linguistic description did come to be applied to the traditional problems (largely following suggestions made by Leonard Bernstein in *The Unanswered Question*, during the mid 1970s) the whole focus of investigation and speculation altered.[11] Within generative approaches (concerned so far mainly either with formalising rules governing text-setting within a chosen corpus, or with more general problems of how musical structures are perceived), hardly any interest at all has been shown in the earlier questions, or in possibilities for generating 'rules' for composing. Quite distinct from these problems, current interest has centred on employing techniques developed in transformational grammar in order to explore, in perception of musical forms, regularities that might indicate more general, innate cognitive capabilities. As such, the unanswered questions are no longer those of music as a language in any of the earlier senses. Indeed, concern with musical meanings and a definable musical semantics has even since Bernstein been displaced virtually altogether as an objective. Replacing it has been the more limited objective of assigning structural descriptions to intuitions of listeners. In these, the various inevitable idealisations (disregarding variation between those intuitions; problems of genre and periodisation; disregard of specific institutions, etc.) are explicitly acknowledged, but are no longer so damaging.

The new investigations are not simply in retreat from the earlier quandary, nevertheless. The reorientation of theory they are producing has both a concessive and an affirmative dimension: concessive, in that arguments over music's non-referentiality are accepted (though often less as an essential aesthetic attribute than as a limitation of present techniques of description); affirmative at the same time, in that an exclusive concern with musical 'syntax' is thought to lead in the direction of important musical 'universals' (human cognitive capabilities which determine aspects of listening to music, such as the parameters within which musical phrases will be recognised as restatements or variations of one another, and when they will not).

Historical Change and Musical Terminology

Consideration of linkages made between music and language in Walter Pater's criticism, in Deryk Cooke's theory of expression, and in contemporary psychological (and linguistic) theory appear to offer an initial, if limited, clarification of important questions concerning music. Yet the relations at issue are more complicated still than this characterisation would suggest. For the terminology in which musical experiences are conceived and organised itself designates meanings and understandings which differ importantly between times, regions and circumstances.

The terms through which music can be described and discussed offer no stable or reliable source of definition and authority. Rather, they have to be seen in the more troubling complexity of successive and frequently contradictory definitions and redefinitions. These are made at various historical moments, then adapted and applied to new configurations of musical institutions and practice. Clearly, it is necessary to acknowledge and explore changing senses of this kind, since they intervene repeatedly in any attempt to describe playing or listening to music, and introduce an element of fundamental confusion into discussion, when selectively cited as boundary and authority.

As illustration simply, a number of significantly varying histories are worth considering,[12] in words central to virtually all talk of traditions of European music:

Instrumental. The word 'instrument', describing a musical device, comes into usage in English at roughly the same time as more general senses of the term signifying 'tool' or 'implement', that is to say, in the course of the thirteenth century. Usually these early usages concerning music in particular carried an added specification of means, such as 'of strings' or 'of wind'. These were qualifications of means, rather than of purpose, aesthetic or occasion, because the latter would have been already provided by relevance to social or religious ritual, and taken for granted. As a consequence of fundamental changes in understanding of the social purposes of music which occurred in the sixteenth, seventeenth and eighteenth centuries, 'instrument' and 'instrumental' took on added complexities. 'Instrumental' came to refer intentions or purposes of music-making no longer to these conventions of occasion, but, ambiguously, onto both the performer (who takes up and employs the 'instrument'), and onto the properties or resources of the 'instrument' itself. This division and ambiguity in respect of the purposes and the means of making music has existed ever since. It has become especially problematic in the phrase 'instrumental music'. In certain emphases in the nineteenth and twentieth centuries, this phrase seems to refer questions of purpose directly to the *means* for realising those purposes, a music extensively addressing itself to, as well as drawing upon, the resources of its selected groupings of instruments. In such usages, agency and intentions are diminished as concerns, and it is prevailing ideas of intention, and existing models of 'instruments' which come most often to be assumed and accepted.

Technique. This originally French word (the substantive adaptation of an existing adjectival form—and with connections back to discussions of 'techne' already in Aristotle) comes into musical usage in the early part of the nineteenth century, when it displaced the older word 'technic'. This latter word had been a general term of skill, as well as being employed, if less and less commonly, in a specialised, artistic sense. The new usage of 'technique', in part necessitated by fresh attentions to the development of 'instrumental' skills, seems almost certain to have been one effect of the extension, in response to cultural changes during the Industrial Revolution, of already established and widening distinctions between artistic and other activities. 'Technique' (now the usual general term in place of 'technic') has continued in use, describing already existing solutions to practical problems ('technical' problems) in the making of music, especially with regard to known design features of 'instruments', and the kinds of execution they appear to dictate. But the question always remains, closed off in familiar senses of 'technique', to what extent personal or individual elements of coordination and articulation of the body and voice should be retained, within and even against the standardising influence of 'technique'. For technique can properly only be seen in changing interrelationship with means, and, more importantly, with purposes. The questions appear relatively straightforward in respect of the music of Haydn or Mozart, where a certain kind and level of technique are evidently necessary. But they become much more aggravated in considering the development of new music and musical improvisation within a prevailing influence of instruction, and of subordination to particular, already existing, requirements of 'composition'.

Composition. Coming into usage along with, if possibly slightly later than, its root form 'compose', 'composition' appears to date from the late fifteenth century when used of literary activity, and the late sixteenth century when referring to music. In the course of the seventeenth century, the term comes into far wider currency. This aspect of the terminological history coincides very closely with the emergence of new creative relationships in musical activity during these centuries. In particular the link is with new social positions occupied by musicians devising work for performance–positions linked to the new means of scored notation and developments in commercial music-publishing addressing that work, in more lasting form, to a wider public. But the word has continued to contain a significant ambiguity. 'Composition' can represent either an action and process or a completed product; and in this respect it has important parallels, as well as important contrasts, with the term 'improvisation', to which it is often opposed. The ambiguity is an important one, concerning temporally distinct elements of the musical process, since the activity of composition generates, finally, the resulting entity of composition which is heard. In some twentieth-century concert-music, the distinction has become crucial. Following the development of certain serial techniques, the process of deriving the end composition from germinal material, or from a set of procedural rules or 'laws', has taken on an especial, practical importance. But perceptions of composition, in creative response to performance, continue to work over the resulting product 'composition' alone, and produce across the ordered procedures of 'composition' a much more extensive range of possible apprehensions of symmetry and organisation.

Concert. Introduced from France in the sixteenth century, and at that time a much more general term, including senses of the present words 'concerto' and 'consort', 'concert' gradually lost its meaning of a collaborative group of performers ('consort') in the course of confused usage before the Restoration. Its present sense of an institution for musical performance dates from the middle seventeenth century, when such occasions begin to develop, slightly earlier in England than generally on the European continent. 'Concerto' is an adoption of the Italian source word for 'concert', and was employed, from the early eighteenth century onwards, to indicate a performance or work with an accent on display of individual accomplishment, precisely an inversion of the earlier emphasis on community of action served by 'concert', and still existing in one sense of the phrase 'in concert'. With the growth in the late seventeenth and eighteenth centuries of opera and concert 'orchestras', many previously isolated musical activities, such as singing or horn-playing, became more widely practised as specialisms within a more extensively divided and remotely organised process. The new organisation precipitates the roles of orchestra leader, conductor, soloist and virtuoso—and comes to represent as an enlarged and unified whole what had previously been a range of small, local musical undertakings. Its massing of performers necessitates, too, a more developed notation, with parts serving increasingly minor roles in the total conception, or composition.

Orchestra. In ancient Greece, 'orchestra' referred to the semi-circular area in front of a stage where the chorus sang and danced. In Roman theatre, this space took on a new function, and was gradually reserved for the seats of senators. The word then appears to have become rare, except for occasional usage in this first, spatial sense in the early seventeenth century, until revived under a new classicist influence of the later seventeenth century. In this reappearance, it overlaps with existing words such as 'chapel', 'musick' and the obsolescent 'concert' in designating a variable group of musicians. 'Orchestral' follows soon after, in the early eighteenth century, and 'orchestrate' slightly after that, as this compositional extension begins to emerge more clearly, in the mid eighteenth century. The term has now come to be most widely used of the symphony orchestra, as a standard performing format, although there continue to exist chamber orchestras and theatre orchestras, etc., with differing constitutions (or, in another sense again, 'compositions'). The earliest effective distinction concerning 'orchestra' appears to have been simply that of an ensemble organised around stringed instruments multiplied for a single musical part. ('Philharmonic', as used of orchestras, remains seemingly a title rather than any kind of more specific description.) In view of possibly extensive variety in composition, 'orchestral music' remains a difficult formulation, except in the extremely general usage which refers to conventions of instrumental combination made important by popularity and influence throughout the early period of European concert-music.

Mousike

These changing definitions may seem to offer only local difficulty to description, significant though these difficulties are in terms of the clear indication they provide of interrelations between developments in musical history and in the apparatus through which that history may be conceptualised or criticised. It might seem that in these cases extended definition, restricting and specifying the particular senses being drawn upon in any usage, might—at the cost of greatly increased length—clear away the local confusions.

Yet what these various terms indicate collectively is a much more substantial difficulty, one which enters centrally into designating 'music' itself as the overall activity or object of consideration of which the terms above are constituent parts. For the word 'music' cannot itself be used in any unproblematic way to indicate an entity or activity, certainly not one against which current practices can be compared and defined, or if desired, measured and excluded as not 'music' but 'noise'. It is only an accustomed ease and generality of reference to 'music' which obscures the important way in which its range of meanings has been constructed in these many changing senses of other terms, shaped and reshaped often through contradiction and conflict. Indeed, what is perhaps most striking about appeals to origin or to definition for a perspective on the present is the extent to which the practices described and defined by early, classic usages differ quite fundamentally from those which current adoptions of the same term are used to identify, and very often defend.

'Music' has its etymological origins in the Greek term 'Mousike', a grouping of arts and sciences established by common dedication to the Muses. This was a definition by sacramental and devotional purpose rather than according to specific procedures, forms or content. Initially, the Muses sponsored accompanied declamation or song as well as dancing, with generic distinctions between these following as the product of later separations, redefinitions and initiatives. But gradually the patronage of the Muses in Greece extended to cover unaccompanied and non-theatrical poetry, and indeed inspiration in general, and it is this last sense which has had most enduring influence.

To grasp early senses of 'music', however, it is necessary to see the term of dedication in its interdependences with the kinds of practice, institution and supportive knowledges or technology to which it then referred. 'Mousike' appears to have been largely practical rather than speculative in emphasis, encompassing various rituals of religious festival, and spanning what would now be considered to be a number of media: poetry, dance, song, etc. This practical emphasis has to be seen in turn in the broader relations by which Greek rituals were linked up with ethical speculations—themselves mediated through new and developing attentions to number, proportion and pitch relationships now most associated with Pythagoras and Euclid. These ethical conceptions of activity worked into contemporaneous metaphysics through the notion of an inherent, numerically based harmony of the universe, and in this way specific practices of music were linked up with a culture's most general apprehensions about the operation of the universe. Even if there was considerable lack of agreement between thinkers about the ethical properties of particular modes and scales, it is none the less necessary to remember that there was no position at all according to which pitch relationships, or the contexts in which they were deployed, could be considered ethically neutral.

There appears to have been a tradition of hymns, choral and work songs, and dancing in Greece, as well as some instrumental music, at least from Terpander's appeasement of the Spartan troubles and modification of the lyre in the seventh century B.C. onwards. But the main developments which distinguish Mousike occur with the rise of Athens in the sixth and fifth centuries (Pericles himself, for example, is thought to have been responsible for combining competitions in singing, flute-playing and lyre-playing with the athletic contests and processions to the Acropolis). These developments are in turn related to the growth of the theatre, with its chorus of monodic chant, sometimes accompanied on the aulos. The Muses themselves each supported a specialised activity with its own dedicated instrument: Clio for history with the cithara, Euterpe for the lyric with the aulos, and so on—with all the Muses presided over by Apollo, who held special responsibility for the lyre and for the voice. Yet Mousike referred also to other currents, opposed in many ways to the soothing and controlling emphasis of the Apollonian (and Orphean) traditions, currents more usually associated with Dionysus and the syrinx, and often energetically directed towards celebrations in ecstasy and abandonment. These two strands in the affective purpose of music, with their related notions of the place of the body in participation and in response, were both covered by Mousike, and appear not to have been specifically distinguished within it. Indeed, they have continued to coexist, frequently in tension, throughout the history of Western music.

Little remains of Greek music (in what forms could it remain?) to indicate quite how this Mousike may have sounded. Nevertheless, at least three crucial areas of difference from traditions of post-Renaissance music, and from broad assumptions consonant with it, should be distinguished and stressed. First, great attention was given to the activity of improvising around the basic *Nomoi*, or groups of notes, and no record remains of achievements of individual composers or precise compositions, the elements of the music (beyond local excellence of performance) being common, social property. Second, this element of improvisation owed its formal organisation either to qualities of the words to which it was accompaniment–the singing being syllabic rather than melismatic, and the rhythms quantitative, if with some element of stress–or to variation and repetition with little thematic development or cadential closure. Third, this activity of performance, calling for a sporting virtuosity encouraged in instrumental, especially cithara, competitions, occupied a social place quite different from later reverential attitudes towards displays of individual expression and composition. These three distinctions, and others, suggest that quite radical transformations of understanding of the place of the body and its social definitions as source of artistry and expression have been involved, along with more widely recognised formal and institutional changes, in subsequent directions of what we now refer to as 'music'.

Continuity, Change and Purpose

Clearly, then, the originary senses of Mousike (though of historical interest and importance) can in themselves offer little assistance with practical definitions for and perspectives on the present. Yet emphasis on continuity with a musical past has nevertheless been especially important for music, owing to the property of musicianship that skills required to perform works or in styles already available need to be developed over long periods of training. It is only from the close of the nineteenth century, with the advent of recorded music, that works could be retained from earlier times in anything more than a set of complicated prescriptions, could be stored without need of constant replenishment or regeneration. Before this time, and certainly throughout the main phase of development of the traditions of European concert-music from which are derived many of the controversies of the present, the techniques of performance necessary to play an existing repertoire of works had to be learned in variously institutionalised forms of a personal handing-on of techniques, in academies, in apprenticeships or in home lessons.

Several important distinctions should be made around this requirement by music of constant regeneration through the training of new practitioners. By way of these, it will be possible to begin to illuminate versions of the musical present which are conceived in understandings and judgements about a musical past.

1. Despite an emphasis in the concert-hall on a notion of occasion focused, except for social rituals such as clapping, around an aggregation of individuals (successive individual admissions, payments and consumptions), this institution of performance remains dependent upon a complex social form of production and reproduction. It is worth making this seemingly obvious observation, since frequently the concert form is offered in contrast with other, explicitly social, arrangements of performance, such as that of the Balinese gammelan, in which new practitioners may be taught in and during the process of performing. The seeming homogeneity and autonomy of what has increasingly come to be considered the European concert-music tradition conceal a complicated set of social relationships, continually changing and unevenly responsive to a variety of direct and indirect pressures. Traditions of notated composition need accordingly to be seen in a revised and much wider frame, that of

an array of ancillary activities and relations, including among other processes selected techniques and knowledges for producing instruments, and a pedagogy for producing capable performers. These ancillary processes are themselves substantially defined and redefined by directions within wider economic and social relations, upon which they in turn rely.

2. The constant need to remake musical traditions indicates an inevitability of new practices. Conservation for music cannot be simply passive: in order to preserve elements of existing music and musical traditions, practitioners and practices are required–practitioners coming to works and forms in new ways and with different experiences. With notated concert-music, the stability of the score and of an accumulated knowledge of traditions and techniques tends to slow down change and innovation. But despite this, the passing of time and generations alters effect and significance, inserting works in new circumstances where they function differently. This is one clear lesson of pieces of famous disruption, such as the works of Beethoven or (perhaps more familiarly for recent generations) Stravinsky's *The Rite of Spring*, becoming equally famous markers of older initiatives and customs, valued for qualities they appear to have sought to challenge. On this account, it seems necessary to value existing works not simply on the basis of their longevity or stability, but in terms of specific purposes and development or alteration of the forms or relationships of music-making. To acknowledge musical practices in this way as important constituents of wider processes of social continuity and reform is to recognise a muted history of music. From understandings of this history, or in neglect of it, contemporary musical designs derive combinations of influence, comparison, protest and divergence.

3. This making and remaking of music signals a fundamental difference between music and a number of other media, from which, on occasion, musical commentary and criticism have derived arguments and positions. Music differs in being emphatically a combination of intersecting practices and relations whose frequent perception as spectacle and consumption is one effect of particular historical developments in Europe during the seventeenth, eighteenth and nineteenth centuries. Until the advent of recorded sound, music did not have, except in prescriptive and

mnemonic functions of notation, any temporal separation between its creative activity and the experience of its products, in the way that much of what is now referred to as literature and painting had. Indifference to this important contrast of means and techniques can obscure and diminish at least two areas of contemporary musical transition and argument: first, the extent of the revolution of creative relationships in music and in conditions of listening brought about by technological developments in the early years of the twentieth century; second, the ways in which, during the eighteenth and nineteenth centuries, the appearance of concert-music as consumption of an abstract, unmediated inspiration of the composer and soloist resulted from direction of attentions away from significant contributions, in knowledge and experience, made by a wide range of other players and technicians. Representations of musical history as achievements of individual composers, giant men (nearly always men)–a Machaut, a Mozart, a Beethoven, a Schubert or a Richard Strauss–are the very beginning of an ideal pantheon, and of the abstracted condition of music which isolates from surrounding practitioners, impresarios and conventions a series of perceptions and actions of exceptional individuals.

The Importance of Transitions

Continuity provided by music's requirement of practice and performance should itself, however, only be considered in the context of important changes. Alterations in forms and techniques of performance have been of such a scale (even between the Greek antecedents selected above and the present) that any application to the history of ideas of direct inheritance or evolutionary refinement is inappropriate. As applied to music, versions of evolution are constructed only by reading an extremely varied history in the restricted terms of ideals such as that of composition or composer, and by casting back beyond historically substantiable limits Renaissance definitions of music as beauty of proportion and artistic expression.

Faced with such reduction and simplification of the past, it is useful to remember that as late as the end of the fifteenth century, Caxton could still use 'musical' in the sense of devotion to the Muses, and that in the late sixteenth century 'musick' could refer to a group of players, a group of instruments, or, as now, to the sounds the two in combination were producing. Indeed, the distinction between music and non-music, between what can count as music within a society and what is excluded, has itself been extremely variable. Some sounds and arrangements of sound are for a given period and a given place music, others not. This is the sense, frequently appealed to for authority, when it is said that something is music or is simply noise, in an evaluative, usually polemical distinction.

As demonstration of fundamental alterations in what has counted as music in this way, several important changes, actually obscured because of their sheer scale, might be recalled:

1. Present forms of interrelationship between instrumental and vocal music are largely an effect of major changes of the fifteenth, sixteenth and seventeenth centuries, even if the widest currency of instrumental or 'pure music' traditions (at least as regards concert-music) come arguably much later, during the nineteenth century. From the mythical invention of instruments by Jubal in Genesis onwards (Genesis 4:21), from Terpander, or from other origins in a range of musical traditions, interrelations between vocal and instrumental music have been the subject of conflict and dispute; and vocal music has repeatedly been considered preeminent, on a range of different grounds: theological, anthropological or aesthetic. Nor is the point simply the minor one of alternatives in genre, since the kinds of interest and enjoyment musical works precipitate are importantly modified by existence or lack of accompanying descriptive text.
2. Even the apparently complementary relationship of 'performing' and 'listening' has to be disentangled through its history. Considered closely, this complementarity appears an asymmetrical combination of relations: expression and consumption between performer and audience (though only on condition that consumption is understood in the widest implications of active response, work on material heard); mutual expression, or dialogue, between collaborative performers (though with the whole question of execution as against improvisation requiring still further definition and division— prescription and interpretation between composer and conductor/executants, more active collaboration in forms of

extemporisation and improvisation).
3. Sponsorship of music according to religious or ethical theories of sound has undergone radical shifts of emphasis. Greek and Roman music was indissolubly linked to social and religious rituals, as were the socially dominant forms of music-making (apart from broadside ballads, carols, etc.) throughout the medieval period. The advent of secular patronage and market forces which accompanied the opera and concert-hall in the course of the seventeenth century marks a decisive shift in this respect: a shift not simply from religious to secular and from church to the new institution of the concert-hall (new arrangements of admission, payment, seating), but of a much broader musical aesthetic, with effects on musical forms as well as upon the ways those forms were interpreted (with changes in treatments of dissonance as perhaps the clearest and most important example of major revision).
4. Investment, development and commercial application of the gramophone, radio broadcasting and, later, tape recording have radically altered ways of listening. A focus of attention has moved from an active presence in performance into controlled, mechanical reproduction—with implications from supporting institutions and finance of these processes. Many of the early forms which were drawn upon to support and encourage the sale of machines and musical products of the new technology were derived from an existing repertory of concert and opera works and popular songs (and it is now a part of the mythology how Caruso and others hastened to the studios to preserve their talents for posterity); but subsequently the new listening arrangements have created and are continuing to create major directions for further investment, research, innovation and exploitation—with important repercussions on what will in future constitute relations of music-making, as well as what will be thought of as musical form.

Revaluations

The sheer scale of changes such as these can make them difficult to recognise, when faced only with contemporary musical forms and institutions, and with versions of the history which frequently seek to minimise contradiction and fundamental divergences of interest or direction. But it is with regard to currents within continuing processes such as these that concern for music in the present needs most importantly to be articulated. To take bearings on the present, thinking through its alternatives, initiatives and directions, or to participate in contemporary music as performer, listener, advocate or enthusiast, it is necessary to reflect on ways in which contemporary musical forms have been historically shaped. Little is to be gained in such attentions simply by evaluation and revaluation of proven resources and genres, or by acceptance and repetition of inherited practical conditions. What follows from changing conditions of music—within which music's 'language' or 'languages' will develop—is an urgency for broader, if more difficult, arguments than exist at present: reflections on groups of works and conventions of practice; considerations of technology and the interests of capital and leisure in relation to which it is directed and against which other kinds of activity must take place; attention to issues of pleasure in playing and listening to music.

2 Classical Music

The 'Classical' in 'Classical Music'

The word 'classical' has far wider currency when used of music than of other cultural forms. Within complex and varied usages, it constitutes different grouping of pieces and practices, and makes importantly different distinctions of emphasis and value.

At least three kinds of usage can immediately be distinguished:

1. Describing Greek and Roman music. This usage conforms to a much broader historical distinction employed across a range of cultural activities. It causes difficulty usually only when applied to music, where it conflicts with other less precise (though equally specific) senses. Rarer than those other senses, it is often substituted and explained by 'Greek', 'Roman' or 'Ancient'. For the sake of clarity, such music might be termed 'Classical' rather than 'classical'.
2. Describing music thought to be subscribing to or organised by aesthetic tenets of classicism, such as formal rigour or general humanity. These tenets, of course, are not necessarily 'classical' in the first sense. Indeed, most of them come into currency largely in cultural ordinations of the sixteenth and seventeenth centuries, in some instances on the strength of flimsy evidence of actual 'Classical' practice. In this sense, the aspiration to what is 'classical' involves a commitment to new practices, and to innovation. It seems almost certain, for example, that there was already in earliest formulations of a new 'classical' music, a neoclassical music, a substitution of admiring retrospect as well as notions of a standard linked to what was actually formal innovation, for imitation of or adherence to specific doctrines of music production. In many cases, this was despite scholastic endeavour to find out and decide even smallest elements of Classical practice in the first sense. This usage, often in contradistinction with 'Baroque', 'Romantic or

'Modern', determines a corpus by comparison with theoretical precept, or with regard to one particular and accepted version of music history.
3. Describing a general position or representation of music associated, individually or in combination, with the orchestra and/or concert-hall. This sense–frequently in effect an opposition between an old music and a new, between products of a completed tradition and processes of contemporary activity–makes distinctions (in addition to those of matters of form) of economic, practical and ideological relations within which music is made. What separates 'classical' music in this sense from jazz, rock or country, is not so much particular features of its realisation, such as instrumentation or use of certain harmonies, as an overall conception of esteemed artistic expression, or of work continuous with established compositional traditions. In its most general application, this sense can indicate a corpus of works or pantheon of composers; concert or orchestral music in general; or even simply an attitude, usually contextually clear, for or against.

Canon of Works or Relations of Address?

More is involved here than contradictions in usage and changes of emphasis surrounding a simple term of description, significant though these would be in any case. What is of particular significance in the word 'classical' is that the two most frequent usages, for all their possible range of attitudinal difference, have in common the characterisation of what has been a continual transformation of materials, activities and relations as a stable corpus–a corpus possibly to be valued for precisely its image of longevity and imperviousness to further upheavals on the scale of those which produced it.

Reference to 'classical' music in this general way is often no more than an allusion to a contemporary repertoire of the concert-hall. Yet to think of concert-music in this way is instantly to indicate not simply a category of works, but to refer to purposefully constructed relations of address. It is to refer, moreover, to conceptions of musical creation and performance served by institutional and economic forms, as well as by theoretical, didactic and critical discourses. To survey the eminent tradition of European concert-music invoked in such a usage, from the birth of opera and concert in the early seventeenth century onwards, is to see clear evidence of changes within these material, economic and social pressures and limits:

1. In factors affecting development of instrument technologies directed towards certain acoustic properties (e.g. suitability for making pitched sounds, for equal temperament, or design for increased volume); in cost and availability of instruments.
2. In pressures for theoretical and practical continuity, generated by musical treatises, by textbooks of harmony and orchestration, and by polemics, as well as in personal teaching in academies and conservatories.
3. In institutional forms, such as the arrangement of seating to accentuate attention to performance as spectacle, admissions to performance by subscription and later by ticket, the mid nineteenth-century darkening of the lights as dramatic focus associated with Wagner, etc.
4. In social and political factors affecting exchange of ideas, experiences and innovations between musicians; travels, engagements and reputations of performers and impresarios.

Even the simple ranging of audiences in attendance upon performers, or the introduction of rituals such as applause, ceremonial bouquets and encores to surround performance, involve a significant inversion of earlier arrangements in which musicians were themselves 'attendants', waiting upon patrons and monarchs with their entertaining diversion of musical performance. Changes in relations of performance and listening such as these led to a gradual objectification of music as composition, and of bodily coordinations of performance as images of artists, stars and virtuosi. In such processes can be seen, too, a more general movement for music, from a dominant function as a decorative accompaniment, towards a dramatisation of what can be heard, in the embodied form of spectacle. It is this movement, its consequences, and changing reactions to it, which the history of concert-music can most importantly reveal, but which the familiar representations and currencies of 'classical' tend to conceal.

Beginnings of the Concert

Beginnings of concert-music in Europe occur almost simultaneously with a phase of separation between musical performance and the rituals of prayer, festival and civil occasion to which music had been attached throughout the medieval period. The phase is accompanied, too, by developments of specialist musicianship, invention of synoptic scores, and expansion in the industry of commercial music-publishing. Drawing on and reflecting these changes, secularisation of music can be seen to have created conditions for new arrangements of listening in which musical activities themselves became, as compositions and works, an object of attention and concentration, rather than, as previously, an accessory to other activities within which musical performance occupied a subordinate place.

The arrangements of listening which were gradually established in this way as concert-room and auditorium are now so accepted as to appear a 'natural' or 'neutral' way of hearing music. Indeed, they are frequently cited as the measure of proper attention, when compared with gramophone listenings or radio broadcast continuity. Yet they have their own controversial development, in varying interrelation with opportunities for leisure, in significantly changing social formations.

Early forms of concert in England can be seen in exploratory initiatives of the late sixteenth and early seventeenth centuries: Nick Yonge's evenings of madrigal performance for friends in the 1580s leading to his commercial publication of *Musica Transalpina*; John Bull's celebrated recital for King James in 1607 at a dinner at Merchant Taylor's Hall, London. There is, too, the later parallel in Germany (England was relatively early in its development of concert performances), Buxtehude's *Abendmusiken* in the 1670s: occasions of diminishing religious relevance focused rather in the music they provided, and highly praised on that account by J. S. Bach. Developing from these disparate forms of social gathering (commercial venture, patronised municipal occasion and religious ceremony), what would now be considered as more properly forms of concert begin in England in the later seventeenth century, in part as a minor specialisation within operatic performances already existing in Italy in regionally varied forms from the early 1600s, and in England almost immediately following the Restoration. These early interrelations with opera—as well as with drama, masque, court-ballet and pastoral—make clear an interdependence of the concert from the outset with an important visual element, a pleasure in seeing which, viewing at source, confirms that the sounds heard by the ear are not just sounds overheard, but are sounds purposefully addressed to an audience. It is the knowledge this viewing produces, that the sounds being made are offered in communication, which initially creates for concert-music its distinctive mode of address and expression.

Looking simply at the situation in England, then, concerts proper can be seen to date from the immediate post-Restoration period. They are influenced both by new fashions witnessed abroad by expatriates during the Commonwealth and period of closure of theatres in England (the famous new French tastes, for example, of Charles II upon his return), as well as by existing if declined traditions of masque and pastoral. Beginning with John Banister's advertisement in the *London Gazette* of 30 December 1672, which leads to a series of afternoon recitals, or with Ben Wallington's early proto-recitals of 1664, arguably earlier than Banister, a variety of related innovations can be seen, including those of Thomas Britton, William Davenant and Robert King. Specialised venues for recitals appear slightly later, following complications of finance and licence surrounding these early initiatives. With delays and problems surrounding Thomas Mace's plans of 1676 for a popular concert-hall, it is John Hickford who takes his room off the Haymarket for the public presentation of concerts, the first specialist concert-house in London in 1713.

Balance and Vision

From these first establishments, traditions of the concert proceed in parallel with developments in operatic performance. Both adopt the format of performance delivered for vision and hearing in arrangements such that all the instruments may be heard in an appropriate balance from a chosen audience position. Later, this position is itself gradually refined, by arranging the audience at a certain distance and in a certain manner relative to the orchestra or ensemble, focusing sounds for perception as the unity of a single, corporate source; waves of sound are channelled and focused, to produce the idealised balance of total audibility. To move from this position of listening is to overemphasise certain sounds–they become too loud and others disappear; correct positioning within the music is lost, it becomes simply a disordered cacophony, out of true.

Auditorium design follows, towards elimination of a partiality or variability in listening. New designs optimise musical performance as a singularity of perception, even if the music has to sound different from various positions *within* the performing group–the instruments not being all equally audible in these practically essential but aesthetically marginal balances. Balance and vision: dual qualities of the concert-hall which serve as a framework within which music-making becomes presentation and consumption of an expression of ideas and feelings realised in front, but conveyed from beyond, from the composer's unseen place of direction. Throughout the eighteenth and nineteenth centuries, it is arguably this accentuation of the forum or arena of performance (as object of admiration and concentrated attention) which is the most consistent trajectory of concert development, drawing a heterogeneity of musical practices into one centralised means of expression.

Certain tensions are evident in the process nevertheless. Consider the movements of admiration and fashion which accompany the conductor or soloist, or arguments which surround increasing payments made to visiting, especially Italian, soloists during the vogue for Italian opera in the eighteenth century: the criticisms of John Dennis among others, and the finally rejected proposal by Defoe in 1729 that an English Academy of Musicians might more usefully deploy equivalent resources to develop indigenous performing skills.[1] But if there was still this discussion and controversy during the eighteenth century, attention to outstanding individual skills is consolidated in the course of the nineteenth century, in combined virtuosities of performance and composition–in Liszt, among others (indeed, beginnings of the solo recital might be marked by Liszt's famous concert of 21 April 1844). Such effective and lasting resolution of the earlier arguments is a decisive moment for relationships of music-making. Conventions of employing minstrels within households and institutions are overturned by a property of attracting audiences gained by the performer. In turn, this new eminence of the performer is secured and promoted in the successive new concert arrangements: the rows of chairs and the rostra, the musicians arranged and facing their audience, the lighting of the performance arena, and the changing styles of dress.

Nor is this strand in the history isolated from certain consequences of the concert origin in forms of social occasion and assembly. From beginnings in ceremony and ritual, the concert-hall reforms festive association in its secular mode of art-appreciation, in ceremonies with revised codes of obeisance and reverence. This dimension of social meeting exists from the earliest, socially exclusive concert occasions, and is gradually codified in provision of intervals; of corridors, bars and salons; of elevated boxes at the opera. Later, it links up also with other social traditions of musical entertainment, the pleasure gardens (such as Marylebone Gardens) and the spas of the eighteenth century. Together, these feed into the promenade concerts of the nineteenth century, which appear most clearly as a kind of intersection between the popular forms of association and the traditions of the subscription concert.

This new popularity of the concert as an entertainment in the late eighteenth and nineteenth centuries is surrounded, too, by increased capital speculation and interest in musical forms. The famous cheap editions of musical scores in the mid nineteenth century (such as James Harrison's *Messiah*, or the various publications from Novello and the other expanding trade publishers) were new, relatively mass forms of circulation for music and music criticism, and are exemplified in Harrison's *New Musical Magazine* of the 1780s. And no longer accompanying particular social occasions, works come increasingly to be subject to different pressures of direction and relevance to occasion. In particular, they come to be performed under sponsorship from publishers and promoters in order to advertise their product, the published score (today it is generally the record companies who sponsor and timetable tours to coincide with record releases). The creation of the musical work, then, as an object and an art, in balance, vision and in conditions of circulation, intersects in a series of contradictions throughout these phases of development—well before the now familiar arguments over commercial versus state funding—with demands of advertising and of sales.

The Orchestra, Format and History

Classical music in this most general sense has the orchestra as perhaps its primary agent. It is concert programmes for orchestra, more than string quartets and chamber music recitals, which have become the dominant constituent of the concert repertoire and tradition. The orchestra embodies this uniform instrumentality, in its black suits and dresses (pullovers only for the avant-garde), as well as in its fixed layout and known ceremony: the conductor's anticipations, introduction of the first violin and soloists, intermediary coughing, conventions of applause and encores.

But if the format is standard, the history is varied. Beginning in the sixteenth and seventeenth centuries, groups of instruments emerge to play the new forms of secular, instrumental music—their context the opera and music drama, then only slightly later actual concert performance. The new instruments organise around a string group, doubled for parts, and a keyboard (occasionally a lute, harp or theorbo). In combination, these provide the main harmonic structures of the new tonal music. It is not groups of related instruments such as wind consorts, popular in the late Middle Ages, which materialise into the orchestra. These are merely appended gradually as individual instruments to the crystallised unit of the string group.

First orchestral definitions consistently isolate the strings and especially the violin, itself going through complicated technical changes and revaluations. And here aspects of alteration and refinement within the orchestra can be followed particularly clearly: the violin, emerging from disrepute as folk fiddle in the sixteenth century and becoming accepted gradually by the 1640s in England, earlier in Italy; dominant by the 1650s (though it is worthwhile to recall that the baroque violin differs from today's instruments in having gut strings at lower tension, a different shaped bow, still changing in the late eighteenth century, and being rarely played with vibrato). Gradually the whole viol group is displaced, bass viol resisting longest against the cello; double bass, related to viol more than to violin, coming later and standardised in orchestras only after 1700, though before that coopted for dramatic effect in storms and fights.

Outside the string section, too, corresponding revisions are taking place. Instruments appear and enlarge the group: oboes replace shawms; there are new transverse flutes. Indeed, there is a widespread and sustained new instrument technology, though the acquisitions involve almost simultaneous disappearances (whistle and transverse flutes coexist in the seventeenth century, but the whistle types disappear during the eighteenth century; there are several types of clarinet, standardised later as the 'A' clarinet; trumpets and drums are annexed from the army, horns from hunting, trombones from the church, but simultaneously decline there . . .).

The Orchestra and Orchestration

This development of new instruments alongside and for use in the new concert-music is significant in itself. But it is also necessary to see the extension of means available for making music as part of more important processes of redirection as regards uses the instruments serve. Whilst instrumental contrasts can be seen as far back as antiphonal effects in works of sixteenth-century polyphony, as in Gabrieli, controlled variation in tone-colour appears to have been of little interest at that time. First real orchestration appears with opera and drama, in Peri, and in Monteverdi's doubled string and chorus lines evidently for dramatic effect in *Orfeo* in the early 1600s. These particular contrasts of texture are for whole sections or movements only. But what they indicate is an important beginning of instrumental writing, as opposed to transference of vocal writing onto instruments, or simple exploitation of technical, instrumental resources such as runs, trills and arpeggios.

From such usages follow new requirements: of extended string techniques, further specification in notation, and new delineations of pace and dynamics. But the early explorations are intermittent, and varied in scope. Well into the late eighteenth century, instrumentation remains variable–though with increased use of instrumental skill and variety, as instruments are more elaborately manufactured. Yet despite all the major extensions and reform, it remains inscribed in the social relations of concert-music at this time that variation relies as much on circumstance, finance and skills available, as on compositional intention. It is only in the changed social relations of the period following that instrumental variation is adapted to particular skills of an orchestra or of a virtuoso, in concerti.

There is a flurry of changes across Europe around the end of the eighteenth century, all tending towards a kind of standardisation. Communications during periods of peace between regions extend the circulation of scores, and this encourages a known orchestral format. Composers travel. And with relatively stabilised instrumentation, calculable resources are exploited in new ways. Orchestration develops as both a specialist understanding of technical requirements of instruments (what they can play, what they cannot), and as exploration of expressive textural possibilities. Tone-colours become integral resources of composition. A gradual shift from polyphonic and contrapuntal music towards homophony, well established in the course of the seventeenth century, accentuates the importance of accompanying melodies, and with the new styles of accompaniment, tonal contrasts become increasingly important in recapitulation of stated themes, which are decorated with orchestral variations as well as with counterpoint and embellishment.

The rise of song-like forms in cantabile phrasing and accompaniment can also be seen as further reform of a far earlier primacy of the voice, now returning indirectly in conventions of instrumental writing linked to other surrounding extensions of orchestration. Early dynamics in the Mannheim orchestras of Stamitz and Cannabich introduce crescendo and diminuendo, influencing Mozart; dynamics are increasingly and more precisely specified. And new inventions expand the orchestra: valves for horns and trumpets, adding a new section of potential contrast (though Brahms prefers valveless horns until his death in the late 1890s); the clarinet, invented in the 1690s, is accepted as a standard appurtenance of the orchestra only after a century.

Extended in these ways, the orchestra is transformed from an ensemble of musicians into a huge instrument or machine which the composer plays by notation; and embellishments by performers are increasingly taken to disturb the overall artistic intention. Adaptations of the orchestra cease to be made primarily according to practical necessity, and are used for artistic purpose. Wagner, Strauss, Schoenberg in turn extend its instrumental resources. Hence, then, at least part of an explanation of the contemporary image of formality and standardisation: spatial arrangement as of a great musical machine, uniform black of corporate anonymity, so as not to distract from the work itself, or from the conductor's rendering and interpretation.

Composer and Conductor: Specialisation

This extending ideal of composition and expression is reflected in changes in organisational relationships within the enlarged instrumental group. There are, for example, changing relations between players and their notation: from variably available talents to be written for, through unequal talents to be allowed to embellish a work in cadenzas and variation, becoming specialised executants of the detail of the score. And carried forward as standard format, as orchestra, these relationships have a continuing importance. Playing and listening to music take place within definitions of purpose, participation and organisation, and it is orchestral music—the paradoxically massed incarnation of individual inspiration and expression—which provides still one of the most influential contemporary models, against which the changed creative relationships of jazz, rock and other musical forms are often compared and evaluated.

Yet elements frequently assumed to be standard arrangements of the orchestra (and so, implicitly, exemplary relations of music-making), are in many instances comparatively recent innovations. The conductor, currently an interpreter and eminent personality in concert billings, box-set collections and interviews, only appears in a series of initially practical reforms in the course of the eighteenth and nineteenth centuries. As first a time-beater to keep together performances with large groups of musicians (especially operatic works and oratorios), the conductor has origins in the Roman 'scabellum' or shoe used to beat time in 'Classical' music. Seldom listed in early programmes, through being considered insufficiently important, early conductors were expected to keep time by beating very loudly, with little of the present gestural rhetorics of interpretation and control. Indeed, until the late eighteenth century, most conducting was managed from the basso continuo, or from the violin stall. Beethoven and Spohr conducting with batons in the 1820s displaced the earlier traditions of waving from the piano (as Haydn did during his visit to London in the 1790s). But such refinement and specialisation has to be seen as simply one part in a larger simultaneous extension in range of instrumental forces and orchestration, an extension coupled with a major phase of transition from a music centred on the basso continuo to forms of harmonically less centrally directed composition.

For the composer, too, there is a shift from domestic servant to isolated genius, dramatised in the respective lives of Haydn, Mozart and Beethoven. Yet this again occurs within wider revisions in musical employment and in forms. It is only a later phase of developments, with a continuing influence of Beethoven throughout Europe into the 1840s, which sees the growth of conservatories for specialist training of composers rather than, as previously, their being trained largely as practitioners on individual instruments. In this stabilisation of a compositional ideal, alongside related changes in literature and in painting, emerges the new and later very important aspiration of works to be judged, if not against the social relations of a given occasion or the tastes of a paying audience, then in discernments of an always hypothetical posterity. Many of the concerns which perplex contemporary music's divisions between 'classical' and 'popular' forms gather around such imaginary constructions of an audience, and the version and role of an idealised 'culture' which these can uphold and promote.

Forms and their Origins

Contrary to such accents on a stable and unified 'culture' and 'classical' music, it is only in terms of complex social relations that what has become the current classical canon can begin to be grasped. Contemporary representations of the 'classical' collide repeatedly with these various determinations; but so much disappears under the impact of the orchestral rostrum, the uniform dress, the rituals and the expectations of the concert as occasion, that, when the sponsorship of 'culture' is removed, it is frequently only an unexplainable enjoyment and some rudiments of formal analysis which remain. Countering this sense of an uncontrollable passage of sounds through time, sophisticated techniques for analysing the forms of 'classical' music have been devised, and have been linked even from earliest formulations to practical, musical training. Yet such terms of formal analysis and

Classical Music

criticism are themselves scarcely free from the kinds of historical reconstruction which surround the orchestra and the concert-hall.

Orchestral forms can be seen to have been created in conflicts of opinion, influence and change. To conceive them as isolated, ideal or abstract forms with successive, partial realisations—rather than as specific historical formations and transformations—is exactly a 'formalism': a process of isolating and abstracting forms from wider social conditions in which they are realised, and from effects they can induce. Abstraction and idealisation are present, whether the overall position adopted reveres genius and excellence, or simply acknowleges in the musical forms a set of material constraints to be learnt and recognised, if the music is to be appreciated.

In order to approach contemporary significances of the orchestral forms, it is useful to recall at least three of the early contexts in which many of them developed:

1. From various social occasions for dancing, dance-forms were transferred to the concert-hall, and incorporated as units within larger cyclical patterns: allemande, sarabande, anglaise, minuet, polonaise, gavotte, galliard, etc. Removed from actual dancing, it is the exploration of symmetries and movements (in an organisational rather than physical sense) which is carried over in composition and performance.
2. Dramatic contexts of action, spectacle and narrative, in pastoral, masques, madrigal cycle and opera. Early opera crystallised a contrast between recitative and chorus parts, developing later into sinfonie, overture, etc. Out of these early alternations for dramatic purposes develop concert forms of overture, symphony, intermezzo and sonata, in a process of separation and adaptation. Isolated from dramatic situation, as organisations of purely musical elements, such forms also assume new significance as primarily investigations of formal relations.
3. Religious contexts, including mass, hymns, conductus; works and forms developed for liturgical or devotional purposes, often with ritually functional antiphon. These are frequently performed in secular contexts, as indications of human achievement and art.

What is common to these three extractions is that, displaced from original ceremonial contexts, it is repetitions, contrasts and permutation of materials which become of focal interest, rather than surrounding relations of occasion, patronage and commerce, or means of distribution.

New forms develop in addition to these early extensions and borrowings. The emerging music of the early seventeenth century, predominantly tonal, is quickly followed by a movement of emphasis from polyphonic to homophonic interest–from many interlocking lines to the supported centrality of a single, dominant line. In many earlier European polyphonic forms (roughly until Bach and Handel), notes might be thought to have significance almost equally in two dimensions, vertical and horizontal; they are given a place as part of melodic interest in contrapuntal phrasing, and yet simultaneously create intervals or successive harmonies. The established forms of this music, such as the fugue or the passacaglia, had related kinds of internal organisation (e.g. counterexposition, and the stretto or overlapped entry of subjects, as in canon); they involved more or less continuous transformation of material, but with little dynamic or textural variation. Contrastingly, the new music of themes and tunes (especially 'cantabile' tunes) which, extending tendencies of the later seventeenth century, interested the new aristocratic audiences of the eighteenth century, developed different organisations of material. Progression in tonal music between tensions and resolutions produced a consequent emphasis upon 'movements' as units of form, harmonically enclosed or self-sufficient sections within larger cyclic pieces such as the suite or symphony. From the continuum of earlier music, thematic and tonal interests established a new dimension of development and expression. The continuous kaleidoscope of polyphonic interest was gradually displaced by structures of formal and psychological drama.

Forms, Listening and Formal Analysis: the Symphony

Generated in complex accumulations of repeat, contrast and permutation, forms are discerned in various attentions, overlapped and embedded. Between them are points of resolution, intersection, repercussion and echoed recognition. In some relation to beat or pulse appear thematic figures, moulded and developed in phrasing within (frequently binary) patterns of resolution, and across interrupted and full cadences. Larger structural patterns emerge between the phrasal groups (binary, ternary: a,b,a, etc.); then, larger still, compound forms: A (a,b,a,), B (a*,b*,c*), A (a,b,a), etc. The celebrated forms of the concert-hall (the sonata, trio, rondo...) consist, through changing constituencies, in such patternings of material.

Listening takes these up in processes of arrangement and rearrangement—like and similar, contrast and inversion—but with compositional order of preconstruction ('primary' statement, development, etc.) unavailable except with the score or selective technical analyses. Heard across various figurations, music precipitates its associations and knowledges: the rondo, developing out of the rondeau or strophic ballad of the trouvères, retaining alternating variation and repetition; the suite, a sequence of dance forms originating in dances made continuous by tonal consistency, with the order of the movements (here exactly movements, the dances) alterable according to changing fashions in the eighteenth century; variation and ostinato forms, popular in recitative and returned in jazz, but without the tonal, thematic development of eighteenth-century tastes; sonata, with its statement of first theme, modulation and statement of second theme in related key, argument or development of material, then recapitulation and resolution. Discernible forms, then, but always a history too: the early sonata is often a binary form, becomes later as often ternary; it is harmonically rather than thematically organised in early versions, then there are a succession of changes; in later versions, it becomes frequently an integral part of larger compositions, such as the symphony.

Forms, it is clear, run across wider processes than the kinds of organisation of material indicated here. Wherever there is a phenomenology of appreciation, there is also the history of these further relations. Consider in this respect the symphony itself. This form can be traced through varied formal, instrumental and institutional conditions, but despite that protracted formation and variation can come to appear the definitive concert discourse, with composers often linked to the number they wrote—even, with Beethoven, Bruckner, Mahler and others, to a mythology surrounding that number.

Early usages of the term 'symphony' overlap extensively, until the mid eighteenth century with 'overture' and 'sonata' (a sounded piece, as opposed to 'cantata' or sung piece, or 'toccata', a played or touched piece). Gradually transposed from operatic beginnings to the concert-hall, the symphony crystallises as three separate movements, fast, slow, fast, with the transition to the four-movement standard occurring in late works of Haydn, and early works of Mozart. The standard is varied subsequently in Beethoven, in Mahler, ever since. So, too, the internal organisation of the movements alters: sonata form appears around the time of Haydn, with variation and rondo forms gradually emerging around the same time for the last movement (though never becoming 'standard', always in competition with the minuet). Following influential innovations of the court orchestra at Mannheim, sonata form becomes crucial for Mozart, with its complex permutation and integration of two tonally-related themes and domains. The scherzo is adopted at roughly the same time (symphonic form incorporating in this way already existing forms within its larger cyclical relations).

Yet no sooner are definitions of the 'classical' symphony established than they are altered. In transitions between Bach and Handel, and between Haydn and Mozart, there is a shift from qualities of symmetry towards more dramatic techniques of what is now considered Romantic interest. Tonal permutations are increasingly displaced as the central organising element by thematic material drawing more extensively on techniques of contrapuntal elaboration associated with earlier fugal writing. There are also increases in performance time, and more remote intervals between the tonal centres around which movements are constructed; the coda itself is extended and includes development; there is elaboration of the scherzo from its germination in Haydn; there are more movements than four, with no necessary break between them. And from Beethoven onwards, the new scale, dynamics and range of the symphony make this form the declarative document. Yet even following so defining a moment there is Mahler's inclusion of cantata, solo song and chromaticism; programmaticism in Berlioz's *Symphonie Fantastique*, 1830, and in Richard Strauss's *Alpine Symphony*, 1913 (arguably the high point of that particular tradition); in the early 1890s Carl Nielsen's first symphony starts in one key and ends in another.

'Classical' Music and Modernism

Even these brief glances at certain developments within European concert-music indicate a degree of change seemingly incompatible with the assumed stability of influence and tradition that underlies many contemporary usages of 'classical'. Music to which the description is frequently applied indeed appears on the contrary a complicated series of 'modernisms' and their gradual assimilation—or their gradual neglect, as avenues without continuing relevance or interest. The problems of value and selection which are precipitated by such continuing inflection of musical forms lead exactly towards a need for critical reflection on present currencies, priorities and direction, rather than towards immobile dependence upon tradition and definition of the 'classical'.

But whilst that urgency may be clear, simply to dislodge conceptions of an idealised stability of tradition with description of continuous change is still to give insufficient attention to certain important moments of transition. From these, implications for playing and listening in the present can be drawn more particularly. Changes in forms need to be considered not simply in terms of their novelty, but in respect of ways in which they address and respond to existing understandings and relations of music-making at points where these are faced with altering social circumstances and pressures.

Many questions which perplex contemporary concert-music can be focused in one well-known period of transformation, the development of atonal and serial music during the first decades of this century. With this in mind, it is useful to consider changes in concert-music before Schoenberg's first atonal compositions around 1908, and between these and the second, serial phase of what is now generally thought of as the distinct musical 'modernism' of the early 1920s.

During the later nineteenth century, extended chromaticism in orchestral and operatic writing appears to have made increasingly indistinct the symmetrical blocks or units of composition which were juxtaposed and synthesised in the tonal musical forms described above. Relatedly, frequent modulation through an increasing number of complex changes before returning to a cadential closure extended to listening limits conventions of suspension and resolution around which much of the pleasure of functional harmonic music had traditionally been built. Overrun by tonal ambivalences and displacements, the closure of cadence and completion which made much concert-music structurally intelligible became obscured and of relatively less aesthetic importance in works of Mahler, early Richard Strauss and Wagner. Moreover, the largely continental-European discourse of concert-music (if with important elements of national variation and competition at the end of the nineteenth and beginning of the twentieth centuries) faced new critical questioning and comparison in three distinguishable areas: in exploration of regionally specific forms, often drawing upon folk material and in some instances on modal harmonic organisation; in usages of poly-rhythms and textures, including percussion and timbres deployed beyond purposes of harmonically functional pitch; in absorption of elements from non-European music, and in cross-currents with literary and pictorial modernisms.

These are conventional 'musical' pressures for change, pressures which are often taken to account for fundamental divergences of composition in the early years of the twentieth century. They need to be seen also, of course, in larger perspectives: that of continuing political and ideological crisis across Europe prior to the First World War; that of an importantly changing audience, reduced both by declining metropolitan entertainments following increased rail communications, and by interest in contemporaneous new, mechanical means of music reproduction.

Broader, social influences such as these are important for assessments of the forms of twentieth-century concert-music, particularly in understandings of their frequently alleged 'dissonance'. Yet it has become usual, despite this, to understand Schoenberg's early music—from the turn of the century until works produced near the end of its first decade such as the *Three Pieces for Piano*, op. 11, *Erwartung* (1909, with words by Marie Pappenheim), or the *Book of the Hanging Garden* (1908–9, with words by Stefan George)—in the simply aesthetic terms of an 'emancipation of dissonance', that is, as a radically libertarian enlargement of intervallic potentialities employed in composition.

In order to see larger implications of this phase, however, it is necessary to consider the major disturbances of prevailing conventions of pleasure and of musical entertainment which these works introduced. As is well known from his simultaneous production of a theoretical work on harmony alongside compositional excursions into atonality, Schoenberg took the view that tonality is an overall musical system, which cannot be observed merely by peripheral allusion in a concluding cadence. To compose within a tonal framework was for Schoenberg accordingly not simply to conceive musical passages which end with a cadence, but to construct interwoven elements to which the cadence is only the culminating and systematically derivable conclusion.

What is important about this understanding is that the structures of tonal music are created entirely according to conventions of permutation within the tonal framework. Correspondingly, important questions of overall organisation of material arise from music outside these definitions: questions not only concerning how, when and why a piece will end, but concerning the conventions of coherence according to which any individual element of material may be articulated *within* a work. For listening, 'free' atonal composition precludes the previously assumed precipitation of pleasure in resolutions of tension which tonality consistently promised and then provided. Tonal music might be understood as a kind of narrative musical drama. But what displaces resolution as the foretokened end of composition in Schoenberg's early works is an arrangement of material through devices adopted mainly from pre-tonal, polyphonic music: in ostinati, canons and continuous variation.

For such pieces, the concert-hall becomes an arena in which what is addressed to an audience is no longer a formal object unified by convention throughout its duration. Musical composition involves, relatively, a more heterogeneous set of elements and materials. Indeed it appears largely a continuing observance of earlier aesthetic and institutional conventions of concert-music (particularly notions of the expressive artistry and calculating judgement of the composer, and the arrangements of seating, lighting and acoustic balance) which impose effective limits on the spread and scale of polyphonic atonality, containing its otherwise unreturnable departures. Conversely, the disruption or 'modernism' of this music was most importantly that it questions the earlier conventions of performance and composition, by introducing possibilities of formal relations which overspill constraints of a consumable symmetry of 'expressive' arrangement realised within the overarching frame of balance and vision.

In this sense, Schoenberg's early works might now be thought to have introduced into concert-music an element of disturbance far broader than that of relative harmonic dissonance alone. Polyphonic or 'free' atonality undermines an important passage in tonality through loss and dissonance on the way to a coherence of conclusion and unity. But this broader disturbance is only glimpsed in these early works of Schoenberg. Even within them, material can be noticed to be significantly organised in ways which maintain and consolidate earlier aesthetic conventions of the concert. As in Wagner's chromatic antecedent *Tristan and Isolde*, Schoenberg's explorations of new formal properties of atonal polyphony take place, in these early pieces, mostly within a dramatic framework. In *Erwartung*, for example, and in *Pierrot Lunaire* (1912), a new technique of *Sprechstimme*, or speech-singing, evokes a scene or state implied by Marie Pappenheim's words. Qualities of the music may then be taken to interpret this lyrical scenario. Indeed, it is the dramatic contexts which have often provided the terms of analysis and explanation for the musical techniques of these early pieces: dream-states and the unconscious; Expressionist anguish. Yet what remains challenging in such frameworks for interpretation, given much of what has been said subsequently about atonal music and about serialism, is that these first instances of the new atonality are scarcely taken in such definitions as a fundamentally new potentiality (as might have been expected, pursuing the grand emphasis of an 'emancipation' of the dissonance). Instead, the properties of atonality are made merely a kind of expressive negation or inversion of tonality, which is itself assumed to evoke opposites of dream-states and anguish, being conscious, systematic and rational.

One thing which is made clear by contemporary forms of interpretation of such atonal pieces is an urgency, in order to gain bearings on twentieth-century concert composition, for some clarification of notions of 'dissonance' (and recently 'distortion'). That clarification has to be made with regard to a far more extended reference than concern only with which notes may be used, when and where. Particularly, it is necessary to consider in detail what kinds of affective property (and so what kinds of rhetorical function) are being assigned to dissonance within any notion of an address, or 'language', of modern music.

Serialism

These larger questions of an atonal mode of address in music are provoked in early works of Schoenberg, and continue to surround innovations within, and evaluations of, contemporary music for the concert. Yet Schoenberg's own later works cannot be said to have explored such problems or directions very far. Later serialist compositional techniques build a new order of systems and structures, rather than of a wider mode of address which would take up and reform disturbed patterns of cohesion of the concert as institution. Significantly, it is this order of forms, more than the earlier explorations of polyphonic atonality, which has provided the terms of what has come frequently to be called the new musical 'language'.[2]

In Schoenberg's development of serialism, then, problematic questions evidently provoked by atonal modernisms, and by the situation of concert-music in the early years of the century, are reconstituted as more restricted questions about a logic of composition with twelve tones, arranged according to particular intervallic, textural and rhythmic constraints. Based on the principle of a series which utilises in turn each of the twelve tones and then undergoes permutation in forms of retrograde, inversion and transposition, early serial techniques appear in Schoenberg's works of the early 1920s, and figure in such exploratory pieces as the *Suite for Piano*, op. 25. Complicated by minor historical ambiguity (Josef Hauer, for example, was simultaneously working upon a loosely similar system to that devised by, and now credited to, Schoenberg), these techniques have had varied and uneven effects on subsequent traditions of composition.

Two important conceptual strands within the innovations and arguments might be distinguished:

1. Serialism conceived as a set of procedures for composing within already existing aesthetic definitions, as practical rules for use in accordance with overall conceptions of expression and occasion not themselves accounted for in the techniques. In this sense, it is not necessary that the series should be heard

for its own virtues at all; it is used primarily as a means available to the composer for organising materials according to notions of artistic purpose carried over from conceptions of art and expressions which surrounded tonal music. Such new codes of practical ordering are required in composition in order to be able to produce new sequences and arrangements of sounds pleasing to the modern ear.
2. Serialism conceived as again techniques, but as techniques which, in using all the notes of the scale as the material for larger musical forms, direct attention from artistic expression onto supposedly intrinsic properties of the acoustic structures themselves. It is this strand in the thinking which appears to have promoted the possibility of valuing works directly for the coherence generated in their compositional structure, on the basis of extrapolation from nodal elements or rules. This kind of structural justification, proposed as being independent of acknowledged human or social definitions of music to a degree without precedent in music at least since the Renaissance, seems implicit already, for example, in Webern's suggestion that when the full series has been heard, then a piece of music is complete (although this interest combines in Webern's works with other continuing aesthetic emphases). Developments of *total serialism* in the 1950s in works of the early Darmstadt school, however, made far clearer an aspiration towards proclaimed autonomous structures in sound, by increasingly appealing to mathematics and geometry for formalisation of acoustic parameters, whilst holding the position on questions of perception and general intelligibility that audiences will finally learn what is a distinct, new musical 'language'. In effect, these developments of theory and practice were a new and major phase of changes already taking place in the course of the nineteenth century. What can be seen in them is a move from compositions addressed to given social positions (actual players, occasions and techniques, music offered to play as well as to hear) towards composition for idealised or imaginary positions (the 'uncompromising', notorious difficulty of the music to play; associations to be left behind for perceiving symmetries and movements of composition; economic provision neither from existing audiences or practitioners, but from governments, arts councils, radio stations and universities).

Recording and the 'Classical' Composer

These disturbances and reformations of musical traditions of the eighteenth and nineteenth centuries explore, mainly, new musical structures and forms. But in order to pose what seem currently central problems surrounding 'classical' music, it is necessary to consider such developments alongside certain other innovations and experiments. It is necessary, for example, to consider areas of activity which have engaged, in different ways, problems posed to composition and artistic expression by changing conditions of musical performance, distribution and consumption: problems posed, more particularly, by declining concert audiences, by significant expansions of other, 'popular' musical traditions, and by development of mechanical means of music reproduction and conventions of extended, even continuous, listening.

Perhaps most critical among these contemporary difficulties has been a new uncertainty, as regards contemporary relations of music, surrounding notions of the primacy of an original artistic expression to be consumed. Reverence, above all, for the intentions of a composer, and in consequence for interpretations of works commensurate with such intentions, has come to seem incompatible with ways in which properties and associations of pieces of music change, not only according to familiarity and taste, but according to institutionalised aspects of the occasion for listening. Such variety in interpretation becomes especially clear concerning contemporary forms of musical distribution outside the concert-hall (such as by broadcasting or circulation of records). Where significantly new contexts for, and combinations in, listening are established. Mechanical reproductions of music challenge longstanding assumptions of abstract, 'disengaged' expression—assumptions on which many present valuations of 'classical' music depend. In doing so, they force on educationally and institutionally protected imaginary constructions of an audience and a culture a pressure of music's changing conditions.

The full extent of this transformation has been obscured, however, by a process of adjustment and assimilation. In the nineteenth century, a composer's musical vision took the initial form of notation. In order to be realised as music in performance, this notation then required large numbers of executants.

Assemblies of instruments and musicians could accordingly be explained as a practical necessity for realising a single, original perception. As the composer's inspiration or overall vision, this perception could be thought to be of a different order from any of the constituent musical parts; and the primary aim of performance would be to reconstruct that unitary position for an ideal listener in the auditorium. For this listener, the various musical parts were assembled, and to him or her they were, as a unity, addressed. It is subsequently this emphasis, rather than an increased variation in listening which mechanical reproductions of music introduced, which has been reconstituted in assessing 'classical' music records largely according to accuracy or appropriateness of the conductor's interpretation.

It is clear, however, that the appearance of composition as a singular and defined object of attention was the carefully prepared result of specific relations of the concert-hall as institution, achieved through seating, lighting, rostrum, etc. And the circumscribing effect of those arrangements is not directly reproducible within the altered relations of hearing music when broadcast, or on disc. When compositions were of necessity devised in the form of notation, only later to be realised in performance by assembled musicians, it is the composer as author of the score to whom the musical 'text' or composition is referrable. In recordings of music, on the other hand, it is largely the recording itself which has become the musical 'text'. So it is no longer necessarily referrable to an authority of the score individually composed, but to details of performance involving all the musicians, and subject to whatever forms of organisation (including partial or even complete improvisation) are employed for the sake of recording.

It is this changing reference which is tacitly in question in assessing recordings of the classical composers. And in such a context, it appears historically significant that the development of the gramophone, roughly contemporaneous in its first commercial phase with the first serialist compositions, was widely seen in early comments by 'serious' musicians and composers as almost without exception merely an outlet for existing musical forms, rather than a means through which new forms, as well as new sounds and new ways of making music, might be explored. But contrary to any such simple assimilation of the new technology to existing critical canons, new conditions of listening outside the concert-hall might more appropriately be thought to emphasise the complex, relational character of music-making and appreciation. Alterations in relations of performing and listening challenge constructions of 'classical' music's idealised position of expression as the 'natural' mode of music-making. In addition, they belie the possibility of address from composer to audience through some virtually invisible medium of performance, to be praised or not praised according to its 'authenticity' or discretion of interpretation, rather than for its own material mediations.

Collaborative Music and Listening

Given these changing relations of participation, circulation and consumption of music, two kinds of reflection and comment should be made: first, some consideration of relations of music-making alternative to those traditionally supposed by notions of 'classical' and working historically into concert-music from dance-forms and from jazz; second, some consideration of contemporary listening to concert-music or 'classical' forms.

1. As regards 'classical' music's relations between composer, performers and audience, consider other music composed for particular performers, occasions and commissions rather than inspired by abstract artistic conscience or inner compulsion. Suggested, for example, in Hindemith's theories of *Gebrauchsmusik*, as well as in opera and music theatre, this emphasis encourages shifts for musical composition away from ideals of musical evolution on the basis of an imposed new musical 'language', towards activities which recognise, as more than practical or technical restrictions simply, existing conditions of expertise, technology and familiarity. Through acknowledgement of an active role of practice in developing aesthetic conventions emerges an importance of music performed in fundamentally different relationships of participation and collaboration from those traditional within 'classical' music.

In certain twentieth-century concert works can be seen an incorporation of elements from jazz, especially in celebrated works of the 1920s, such as Ernst Krenek's *Johnny Strikes Up* (1926), Stravinsky's *Ragtime For 11 Instruments* (1919) and

Piano Rag Music (1920), or Darius Milhaud's *The Creation of the World* (1923). Alluding to fundamentally different creative relationships from those of 'classical' composition, such usages—analogous in this respect to 'folk' quotations and references—involve a reorientation of initiatives in jazz concerning movement and shared creativity in performance and in response (often in dancing). These are reworked as local details of arrangement such as certain scales, tone-colours and syncopation, and an overall ambience or cultural connotation. Much of the significance of the jazz forms can be seen to be lost in this borrowing. Often lasting a number of bars recycled for embellishment (according to historically varying conventions governing combinations between programmed performance and improvisation), minimal thematic composition in jazz introduced an element of individual creativity distributed fully across the larger group format. Whilst such creativity in participation existed in much 'classical' music-making before the mid nineteenth century, it has become contrary to dominant concentrations within twentieth-century concert-music upon precise notation and realisation of rhythms, tempi and dynamics in the service of the composer's overall statement.

In incorporations of jazz along lines of quotation and allusion, then, major redirections of music-making are reduced to marginal thematic references, and absorbed within existing frameworks of concert-music traditions. In many recent compositions, however, performance options are indeed presented to executants. Yet even for these, appreciations continue to divide between established critical terms of extended techniques of expression devised by the composer, and new relations of participation between performers. Whilst the latter framework might enjoin major revision in the ways music is heard and valued, a possibility for continuing containment of such issues remains, in reducing them simply to questions of formal innovation. That musicians can participate in arranging as well as playing music can come to appear—within present currencies of the 'classical'—an important gesture by the composer. Indeed, on occasion interest in performance choices has been addressed (in irrationalist opposition to total serialism) less to the practical and economic problems of participation than to a mythology for the composer of chance and changes, in influences on composition such as that of the *I Ching*.

2. Two concluding considerations of listening:

(i) In respect of structures of 'serialist' composition and the new musical 'language', frequent claims are made for a logical and systematic derivation of compositional forms. But in listening, even accepting such claims as regards composition, there remain always subjective, educational and cultural constraints.

This can be illustrated by way of the familiar analogy between music and 'language' itself. For composition, rules of 'well-formedness' within a system can be generated (though it is worth remembering that prescriptive rules or grammar devised by a composer for creating a piece of music differ fundamentally from the descriptive grammar of a natural language). In addition to these rules, however, there will also exist constraints of 'acceptability', or limits in workable usage (or 'performance'). These are limits on apprehending, in practice, certain constructs which are nevertheless 'well formed' within the system. In natural languages, such limits of intelligibility can be reached by recursive embedding of clauses. In music, correspondingly, at some point of extension or elaboration, a composition's structures will be confounded by perceptual and memory limitations, beyond which 'well-formed' orderings of the musical material will not be discerned as such. In this sense, there is nothing guaranteed simply by rule-orderings for composition worked out irrespective of audience or performance, even under authority of a proclaimed new musical 'language'. What is called 'octave equivalence' in serial composition provides a further interesting anomaly in this respect. 'Octave equivalence' is a rule according to which elements of the series may be used in any octave position, the octave functioning as an identity of the first position. It seems likely, nevertheless, that although such usages conform to the rules of the system and so are 'well formed', the usages they legitimise are not generally recognisable as such—the octave more often than not failing to be recognised as duplication of the first position.[3] Taking conditions of audience and conventions of genre into account, indeed, it might seem rather that for contemporary practice, it is points of limit and breakdown of structure (directions suggested more in Schoenberg's earlier atonality than in later procedures of serialism) which are the prime resource for a new musical concert-discourse.

(ii) Evidently contrasting with this concern for abstract musical forms are suggestions that much pleasure and interest in listening derives from immediate, pure sonorities of sounds, rather than from patterns of their combination. Suppressed in techniques of tonal functional harmony (where sounds serve primary harmonic and structural functions), such sonorities and textures, it can be said, should now be the focus of exploration.

This emphasis arguably has its origins, within European traditions of composition, in impressionistic attentions to sound-colour in Debussy. Currently, it is perhaps most associated with the writings, compositions and liberal anarchist politics of John Cage. For Cage, affirmations that sounds might exist in and for themselves have been frequently linked to a view that decisions as to their order should be handled by aleatory compositional methods. This amalgam in Cage has lifted claims for 'natural' qualities of sounds from ones of simple enjoyment of sonority to a more elaborate political direction. But for all the evident contrast, this emphasis has something of a likeness with the serialist and total serialist positions to which it is generally opposed. For sounds to have their own identity as 'pure' sonority, it is necessary to imagine them without intervening physiological processes of hearing, and without cultural processes, conventions and limits of perception and interpretation.

In both these currently dominant positions of 'modernist', 'classical' music, abstractions of sound are preferred to acknowledgement and direction of material conditions of music-making. Despite the neglect, nevertheless, such conditions and processes ensure that listening to sounds, and so to music, will involve relations between sound sources and particular constructed relations of listening–in distance, volume and vision–as well as of developed positions of interpretation. To isolate 'sounds' themselves as intrinsic, spontaneous or autonomous–imagining them outside some determinate relation of hearing–is an idealisation which has its counterpart in the would-be invisible social relations of Cage's politics. But despite present polemical virtues in Cage's activities, it is futile to link pressures for musical forms to develop and change to a bid to be liberated from all expectations and connotations–from cultural determinations in general. Such a vision merely wills to vanish the social and historical creations of sound as music and noises around which any initiative of composition, performance or agitation can be made. And it is clear, in any case, that elements of position within listening cannot be so easily expunged. If it is doubted, in the West, that organ music will often have ecclesiastical resonances even outside a church acoustic, it is less often denied that a classical sitar concert will have, beyond its renderings of particular ragas, a dimension of exotic connotation, an Eastern voicing. Or again, consider performances of Baroque music with early or replica instruments. In these, an aspiration towards historical accuracy or specificity is compounded with variable, moving resonances of antiquity.

'Classical' technical analyses marginalise such associative slippages, as they do synaesthetic response, or acknowledgement in general of the creative, participatory character of listening of which these processes are part. In contrast with such confessedly mobile and ephemeral responses, accounts of music frequently assume a position of knowledge, at which connotation and evaluation reappear as analysis and criticism. But where this is the case, the accounts remain composed of specific knowledges, tastes and familiarities only: of things heard and remembered. In neither instance do associations of music merit being dismissed as insignificant or ignorant. On the contrary, they emphasise importantly that the enjoyments of playing and listening to music take place in practices shaped always by preparation and by positioning; and these are open to changing conditions, education and experience.

3 Tuning and Dissonance

Music, Dissonance and Noise

There is an important sense in which to think of music, either directly or in metaphor and analogy, is to conceive mellifluous arrangements of sounds which offer pleasures of harmony and agreement. A whole range of literary and pictorial representations testify to this broad conception. Indeed to trace the sounds of music in their apparently widening development in Europe and the United States (in monophonic, polyphonic, dodecaphonic and polytonal musics, and in sounds of the emerging new instrument technologies) can be to imagine a kind of continuous extension or evolution, as an ever greater range of sounds and means of sound generation are employed to create enjoyable aural effects.

Yet to consider euphony, harmony and pleasure in this way is to presume a distinction between these attributes of sound and others, the disagreeable and the intolerable. Beyond all social conventions of what makes music enjoyable there remain biological strictures of hearing, the ear having its ascertainable thresholds of pain. Ways of making the distinction frequently seem themselves of little importance, simply excluding from attention what is not of interest, and focusing by way of that exclusion on significant, changing areas of concern or investigation. But since it is the shifting terms of this legitimation and exclusion which identify music as agreeable registers of sound, it is also in the terms according to which the oppositions are made that much important history, and a number of continuing controversies concerning the 'tunefulness' or dissonance of contemporary music, can begin to be worked through.

Often to be heard in judgements of music sounding 'in tune' or 'out of tune', distinctions between agreeable sound and what is not to be counted as music continue to underlie and justify a wide range of tastes and preferences; and to these are frequently attached much partisan feeling and on occasion prejudice. If there is an evident ease with which terms such as 'in tune', 'out of tune' or 'dissonance' feature in discussion of music, the complexities of understanding and of history which they engage are much more formidable. Even simply considering senses of 'tune' and 'in tune', for example, reveals surprising variation and change. The phonetic mutation which produces the word 'tune' out of the existing form 'tone' in fourteenth and fifteenth-century English introduces a number of simultaneously available senses: that of 'tone' carried over and indicating any generated sound; that of alternatives in selection of pitch between these sounds or 'tones', as scales or modes (the eight 'tunes' of the Middle Ages are the eight modes out of which the various kinds of music might be made); that relatedly of a succession of 'tones', as melody (by the late sixteenth century, the eight 'tunes' of Archbishop Parker's psalter are no longer its harmonic modes, but its melodies); that of standardised intonation according to conventions of pitch correlation (the currently dominant sense, as in the phrases 'in' and 'out' of tune).

Of the four senses of 'tune', it is only the last two which have passed into contemporary usage. But even where it is possible to distinguish between them by context, what is nevertheless signalled by their history of overlap and contradiction is the importance of change and conflict surrounding parameters according to which selection and combination of sounds for music have been made. Occurring both what might be called paradigmatically, in scales and as harmonies (in a more conventional musical terminology, what would be called 'vertically') and syntagmatically, in constraints on melodic or thematic construction ('horizontally'), judgements of the agreeable and the unacceptable contribute importantly to wider perspectives on what makes music pleasurable or interesting.

Deliberations between music and 'noise' evidently operate across a variety of formal considerations, such as those of pitch, texture or timbre, and intervallic relationships, as well as across changing social contexts and institutions of performance. But it is largely only in respect of pitch intervals in particular, in relations between simultaneously sounded tones, that detailed attention has been given to questions raised by dissonance or its effects in listening.

Music, Sounds and Acoustics

Within conceptions of sounds and their combinations in acoustics, it has become usual to conceive dissonance as predominantly a function of intervals, irrespective of the framework in which the effects of particular dissonances, or of dissonance in general, are to be explained. There are thought to exist specific properties of simultaneously sounded notes, or of notes sounded in immediate succession, questions which can be examined in operations and experiments largely distinct from any given musical context.

Two things at least need to be remarked about this mode of formulation:

1. There is a specific history and outstanding problems which cannot be overlooked. Within the framework of acoustics, dissonance has been subject to two quite distinct criteria of classification, and it is only in forms of correlation between these that arguments about its operation are made. On the one hand, experimental evidence is collected from subjective affect, across such oppositions as mellifluous/cacophonous, or pleasant/disagreeable; on the other, classifications are made according to experimentally analysable properties of tones (often pure tones, with extrapolation made to accommodate more usually encountered complex tones). These latter classifications are regularly made in terms of proportions between frequencies: the ratio 2:1 produces the octave, 3:2 the fifth, and so on. Yet various problems perplex the twofold taxonomy. There is, for example, a circularity of the affective being explained by the physical, but the physical only being isolated for consideration in such terms by way of the affective; or again, there are questions of the role of aural harmonics and distortion in the ear itself. Despite these difficulties, nevertheless, the distinctions have been employed to investigate dissonance conceived outside social determinations of context, as an isolable and autonomous phenomenon.

Both constituents of the compound definition have individually long histories. For the 'affective', that history includes compositional strategies and tastes as well as cultural stipulations of the admissible and inadmissible in music; as regards the 'physical', there are the various musical theories of sound, from Pythagoras onwards. In Helmholtz (1862), by way of example, consonance and dissonance are determined by coincidental harmonics and the beats they produce, 'roughnesses' produced as overtones intersect; and dissonance in these terms is a physical property of sounds, an interference brought about by cross-currents in wave modulation involving waves of differing amplitudes. With concessions to outstanding problems (of mistuned consonances or of equal temperament, which disrupt the simple proportions of 'natural' sounds, but are still heard as 'in tune'; or of binaural tone generation producing 'beats in the brain', suggesting a less clearly external, physical explanation), this general perspective has retained a broad and practical currency.

It is only after proving certain exceptions to the theorisation of dissonance as beats that new conceptions bring to these physical properties an important physiological emphasis. In 1885, Lipps proposes the idea of unconscious frequency-counting, in which particular combinations of frequency-ratings produce pleasurable effects, others not. And thirteen years later, Stumpf suggests 'fusion' as the property which synthesises consonances, making the fact of combined, simultaneous notes inaudible and unifying the notes as harmonies. Reducing the accent on predominantly physical, acoustic properties more recently, the developing theory of critical bandwidth has attributed a central importance to the placing of sounds as stimuli, when the basilar membrane which runs the length of the cochlea is activated, producing consonances only when distinct, different parts of the membrane are affected. It is when parts close together or overlapping are stimulated that interference of response is taken to produce the effect of distortion or dissonance, dissonances—in the theory, at least—appearing to decrease as intervals between the simultaneously sounded notes are increased.

2. Almost whatever the present state of developments within this kind of conception, the terms themselves can obscure significant difficulties which only emerge when the intervallic characteristics are returned to the contextual and social situations in which they feature as particular kinds of music, or as what cannot count as music. In these larger terms, dissonance is not simply a property of sounding notes, whether their particular effect is induced by physical qualities of the transmission of waves in air, or of perception and categorisation through the faculty of

hearing. Returned to context in the affective and the social, dissonances figure as relations between sounds, certainly, but sounds formulated as a limit or transgression of what it is agreed is enjoyable to hear.

This enlarged context suggests at least two immediate and substantial qualifications to the experimental approaches. First, the designations of affect which distinguish consonance from dissonance within analysis and experiment are already shaped by social and historical factors. It is not that intervals do not have specific and different properties, but that the correlations with pleasure and discomfort (which provide the empirical material for attention in the acoustics or psychoacoustics) are distinctions already made within and carried over from understandings of sounds articulated and addressed as music, or, as regards isolated tones, against a background that sounds require certain kinds of discrimination or judgement. Second, and following from this, dissonances have varying functions in music. They are deployed relative to cadence in tonality, for example, but feature very often elsewhere as what has to be excluded, what is not authorised for agreeable arrangements of sound. These differing functions engender a range of effects and sensations which cannot be suggested within confines of isolated experiment. More than this, too, in acquiring their intelligibility in relation to particular musical forms, dissonances have a further active function, preserving or challenging the conventions of these forms, and the kinds of affect with which they are associated. So there are never simply static contexts of usage that can form a backcloth to judgement; dissonances enjoin a complex process of interaction between acoustic forms and listeners, across social and historical divisions, as well as across the biological determinations of the hearing apparatus.

Formalism or Musak

For its contemporary forms and effects to be understood and directed, then, dissonance needs to be seen in an enlarged context. For such purposes, it is clear, concerns broader than simply those of intervals between simultaneously or immediately sequentially sounded notes need to be engaged. As an embedded history which runs across formal, technical and institutional distinctions, dissonance emerges as a point of limit or dysfunction, represented—in a number of different ways—as a borderline area of what is able to constitute music for a given society.

Questions of dissonance have, too, their contemporary importance. A history of ethical, religious and aesthetic constructions around what has been deemed acoustically unacceptable for music underlies many still popular and revered musical forms. The theories of tuning and dissonance which initially gave rise to the conventions of many of those forms have lost much of their impact. As a result, the significance and effect of certain textural or harmonic properties of those kinds of music have been repeatedly altered and revalued. And for music produced in the present also, dissonance remains a practical problem. There is an intractable locking of opinion and practice, within a number of scenarios (in classical music, in jazz, in rock), between forms of music-making which, in seeking accessible, popular address, or 'communication', restrict the sounds they employ to existing conventions of tuning and tunefulness, and others, more concerned to experiment with untried ranges and combinations of sounds, and so for many listeners, more dissonant.

In view of this spread of continuing concerns, which cut across most other ways of considering music, it is useful to consider more closely at least some of the linkages that have been made between sounds and their anticipated effects, in order to approach larger questions of the positions and purposes for music they address or to which they appeal.

Historical Reference I: The Greeks

In the music of the Greeks (as in most music in Europe before the Renaissance) the sounds to be used were decided largely by religious authority and by philosophical speculation. Arrangements of sound not conforming to properties associated with particular scales or sequences of notes—the culture's dissonances—were proscribed not simply because of aesthetic judgements, but because of more important ethical or philosophical ones.

In the famous passages of Book III of *The Republic*, Plato alludes, in order to comment on the social and philosophical implications, to an accepted range of affects of the scales, scales which in turn gain further expressive character by their interrelation with rhythms, singing and combination with dancing and dramatic gesture. For the Greeks, the properties of sounds corresponded to the character of a particular scale being drawn upon: Lydian is intimate and lascivious; Mixolydian is piercing, lamenting; Dorian is manly and strong; Phrygian is ecstatic (outraging many, for whom it indicated moderate behaviour or well-being).

These conventions are disputed even within extant theorisations, and have been subject to fundamental alteration subsequently. The Lydian, for example, then lascivious or sorrowful, takes on in tonal music—as close to what is now the major scale—conventional effects earlier ascribed to the Dorian. But disagreement over properties of the respective scales seems not to have interfered with the overall development of correspondences regarding their differing attractions or dangers. Plato discusses a need for prohibiting music based around certain scales, accepting the kinds of influence on character its enjoyment might induce. He argues that it is because music has the capacity for powerful effect that its resources need strict control, in order to direct musical activity towards creating good citizens by way of musical education. In these terms it is certain social consequences of music, rather than what might now seem the questionable local properties or associations, which Plato emphatically challenges.

In Aristotle, too, an emphasis is placed, in the abruptly terminating discussion of musical education at the end of the *Politics*, on music's capability, in addition to providing entertainment during leisure, to mould and produce good character by representing or imitating desirable qualities. Hence, in Aristotle, there is a reservation about teaching young people to play the aulos, since this instrument appears to have been associated, at least until a later phase of use for military exhortation, with frenzied celebration of Dionysiac rites, and so with excitation and catharsis, rather than with contemplation.

These suggestions that arrangements of pitch and melody can convey definite settings of emotion and character, virtually irrespective of pace, texture or inflection, are themselves embedded in philosophically important theories of harmony derived from a presiding music of the spheres. To refer once more to Plato, there is in 'The Vision of Er' at the very close of *The Republic* (Book X) the famous and subsequently very influential description of eight tones which are generated by the revolution of the spheres, each one producing its own distinct sound. From these eight tones of the universe, it was thought, practical musical scales and forms should be derived, to imitate the celestial order.

What is common to these formulations, and to the far wider social currencies to which they evidently allude and which follow from them, is a link between practical materials of music-making and notions of morality and order. That link is produced in practice by correlations between particular scales and their assumed emotional affects. Accordingly, to make music in Greek society was, in musical form as well as in ritual, to take up position within socially defined ideals of activity and behaviour. Sounds of music were coded for the society not simply aesthetically, but also in terms of the moral consequences they would have for a listener. What lies outside the endorsed music is not to be heard, is not conducive to character or sound education. Indeed, elements of philosophical proscription in Plato appear to have become practical policies for Solon, Lycurgus and Minos, despite a suggestion already in Plato's *Laws* that misappropriations and amalgamations of the various affects of the scales were already occuring, by neglect and on occasion simply by ignorance. To transgress the allowances of prepared music, or related constraints on improvisation, would be not simply to introduce a dissonance of sound, but a dissonance of character and of humanity. The sounds of music are described by the Greeks not as a range of practically transformable materials to be explored in practice, and assimilated in listening; rather, they are considered to be already religiously and philosophically replete with meaning, and so taken actively to define experience and social standing.

What seems clear about these general accents of Greek music—amid all the difficulties the extant formulations present—is a way in which sounds admissible and those not admissible (the complex tonoi, nomoi, and so on) are more than simply results of particular aesthetic directives linked to available material resources. Instrument design, particularly in respect of open strings, does appear to have been closely connected with questions of the scales and their performability. But concerned also with a level of effect beyond such practicalities, the definitions of music and what is not music are intertwined with more general positions, and losses of position, with regard to broader social relationships. Dissonances here—as more than misplaced notes or the passing devices accentuating a later consonance they become in tonal music—transgress a conception of musical practice indissolubly linked to an image of human character. As such, dissonances were exactly what for one particular society could not tolerably be stated. Excluded by cosmological proportion, by religious ordination and by philosophical argument, the Greek dissonances were forbidden in the very composition of the world.

Historical Reference II: The Middle Ages

Traditions of the medieval church inherit and preserve some of these accents, if combined and inflected by argument, revision and criticism. Centrally, however, spirituality remains linked with avoidance of dissonances that come to be associated with the Fall or with unacceptable lasciviousness. Most familiarly, the tritone (that is to say, the augmented fourth, or interval between, for example, the notes F and B) came to be known as the 'devil's note', or the 'devil in music'.

For the Christian Church, the form of the mass was largely settled by the fourth century, although still regionally varied under direction of a bishop and shaped by local oral traditions. And in liberal and ascetic strands, early church music embodied both an influence of, and a hostility towards, the earlier Greek and Roman ideas. Even as Cassiodorus is advocating study of the liberal arts as a foothill of the central undertakings of theology, there is a countervailing current of devotional monasticism within which Gregory the Great promotes the act of chanting as a path to God—the chants being referred to God both by origin of the scales they used, and by way of the religious texts to be sung.

But it is the advent of the medieval curriculum around the fifth century which most decisively introduces into the medieval church classical ideas about music, ideas ultimately from Plato, Pythagoras and Aristotle, if more usually mediated through later teachings of Chalcidius, Plotinus and Augustine. In a preserved and extended version of Plato's 'music of the spheres' in the influential *Somnium Scipionis*, as well as in Christian notions of God as the author of everything in the world, the understanding continues of music as a reflection of divine proportion and purpose. In Boethius, for example, from whose *De Musica* most contemporary knowledge of early medieval musical theories comes, music is to be understood as number made audible, a matter of universal proportions and simple, perfect ratios revealing God's harmony by vocal and instrumental reflection and imitation: 'At the beginning of a discussion of music we should consider how many types of music have been discovered by those who have already studied the subject. There are three. The first relates to the universe, the second to human beings, and the third, to instruments, either the cithara or tibiae or other instruments on which a melody may be played.[1]

It is the implication of formulations such as these that admissible arrangements of sounds in music will reflect and serve God. The numerically simple ratios and the intervals they produce are deemed consonances; all other ratios and intervals, by contrast, are dissonances; and these, not speaking of God, are condemned as speech of the devil. Deliberation between which sounds can occur in music and which cannot is referred through the questions of ratio to God's composition of the world, and this precludes interest in sounds lacking His authority. Conceived as the mirror of God, the early church music marks out divine proportions in its forms, and proscribes everything else. Yet in order to understand the larger questions of the universe through theology, early medieval doctrines encourage investigation of the numerical relations of musical sounds as a way towards divine enlightenment. It is from this primarily theological interest that the distinction arises, important for ten centuries, between *musicus* (the theological scholar interested in what sounds can say about God), and *cantor* (the practitioner working in accordance with those findings, practising God's music in religious ceremony).

The Middle Ages: Sounds and Symbols

If in the beginning the new Christian modes differ only locally from classical antecedents, the music develops and incorporates new elements. Leading and final notes become more important; increasing decoration of the liturgy attracts skills of embellishment; the sequence appears, embellishment again, only without explicit correspondence between liturgy and added text; the conductus, music for processions, accentuates the element of ritual, and is an important antecedent of the later medieval church drama. And the practical elements constantly threaten to overspill the ways in which doctrines of *musica speculativa* reconcile actual arrangements of sounds with requirements of service to God.

There is, too, a continuing and developing concern with symbolism across nearly all aspects of music-making, and visible still in 'perfect' time, the triple time of the Trinity, and 'imperfect' or duple time. There are the varied symbolisms: that of St Augustine, likening the stretched skin of the tympanum to the body of Christ; that of St Basil, comparing the ten strings of the psaltery to the ten commandments in the tenth century; or much later, at the founding of the St Sulpice seminary in the seventeenth century, there are proposed links between the organ and the Trinity–the organist is God the father, the blower the son, and the wind the Holy Ghost, with a multitude of angels all around in the form of the numerous pipes. The symbolism persists, too, within composition, even to the descending musical figures for the Fall and curling figures of the serpent's temptation in J. S. Bach, as late as the eighteenth century.

These are aspects of religious symbolism familiar from many other cultures (e.g. the eight drums of the Dogons in Sudan corresponding to the eight stages of the creation of the world, etc.). What particularly relates this iconography with proscriptions of unholy dissonance is the way not only sounds and relationships between sounds, but the instruments which make sounds and indeed all aspects of music-making, are provided with a religious significance which is to exhaust potential for meanings with a given interpretation–and which designates other understandings or practises heresy.

In earliest moments of these medieval musical traditions, as in their final contortions of theory and theology, it is possible to see proscriptions and curtailments, to restrict practical elements from overspilling the religious understandings. There are, for example, edicts banning heresy, such as that of the Council of Laodicea in 361, which excludes hymns from religious rites, though as heuristic and polemical forms they continue, and are later regularised by St Ambrose. And centuries after the liturgy is extended from its early forms by troping (adding words as melismata bound in meaning to the text), this extension is condemned—in one of the last church pronouncements to define musical practice in terms of a superordinate theological system—by the Council of Trent in its resolutions on music in 1562. And despite social marginalisation of the debate in the course of the sixteenth and seventeenth centuries by a new secular impetus, a certain emphasis remains, in the differing religious conceptions of Thomas Browne, Martin Luther, Samuel Sebastian Wesley and others.

The Middle Ages: Polyphony

The practice of ascribing meanings to musical sounds is mainly concerned, in these early formulations, with notes to be sung in succession. Music of the early Middle Ages appears to have paid little attention to the possibilities and problems of notes sounded simultaneously. It is only later, with the development of polyphonic music, that the full scale of conflict between sounds charged with religious meanings, and dissonances which interrupt them, becomes critical for the church.

From early beginnings in monophony (only one note sung or played at a time) rudimentary polyphony develops, throughout Europe, between the seventh and ninth centuries. Evidently beginning in decoration of liturgical melody for important occasions (in context of devotional decoration it is mentioned, for example, in a seventh-century treatise on Latin poetry in Britain by Bishop Aldhelm, and referred to there as *Organum*), the simultaneous sounding of notes comes gradually to dominate over other formal decorations or embellishments. Influenced extensively during this development by speculations of Guido D'Arezzo in *Micrologus*, organum develops as part-writing in parallel intervals, where pitch differences between the sounded notes remain constant throughout the music. Variation of the intervals appears only later again, in what comes to be called Free Organum. Whilst like tropes or hymns polyphony moves from origins in the monasteries and ritual of the hours into more general service, it remains nevertheless restricted by definitions of the modes, and by limitations on allowable intervals and improvisation accompanying the invariant and sacred liturgical texts used for plainchant. It is the line of word and melody which remains the primary authorised statement around which any musical embellishment can be made.

Possibly as early as the ninth century, polyphony was appended to the quadrivium, and, along with related theological speculation, was thought to be exploring music's manifestation of inherent proportions of the universe. As a result, it was increasingly valued for the guidance towards spirituality it might offer. Distinctions begin to be made between a simple, physical or sensory pleasure of sound, and a higher, rational pleasure of polyphony, the latter focusing on the resonant harmony of the spirit and of the universe. Yet for that beatitude of contemplation to be saved, in some instances notes have to be flattened, in order to avoid the occasional dissonance of the tritone, since without correction this interval can appear in the parallel harmonies of strict organum.

These developments of polyphony—often retrospectively seen as welcome innovation and liberalisation—produced almost continual crisis for medieval understandings of the position of music in the world. They emphasised conflicts between legitimate notes and the dissonances, as well as between theologically explicable music on the one hand, and uncontrolled innovations of performance on the other. When in the eleventh and twelfth centuries polyphonic and organum passages are combined in a single piece of music or ceremony, and when musical decoration, taking on an increasing prominence, extends into simultaneous variation of musical parts, the theological accountability of medieval church music is further fundamentally disrupted.

A range of other new, practical developments are introduced during this period, too. Under influence of Notre Dame in the twelfth century, both within and outside France, there is a phase of major innovation, producing the new notational and rhythmic systems of Léonin (use of shorter pulse units—the term *minim* comes from 'minima', the smallest unit). Through lack of manuscript space for vertical representation, musical parts begin to be written out alongside one another, with different, non-systematised spacings. New variations are made to the *duplum* or added line, with the result that it is no longer so reliant upon the original chant for its shape; and the *triplum*, or third line, is introduced (giving the still current word 'treble'). Around the same time, the conductus becomes isolable as a distinct, separate form. And again, further division between *musica speculativa* and *musica practica* follows in the early fourteenth century with the Ars Nova (so-called after the title of a treatise by Philippe de Vitry), and with the introduction, alongside the theoretically explicable 'perfect' or 'triple' time, of the less easily explicable 'duple' times. There is, too, new and extended variation within metres, and a use of isorhythm or uneven overlap of melodic and rhythmic modes so that they circulate unevenly, cross-overlapped. If the tritone posed from the outset a problem for the theological sponsorship of music in proportion and acoustics, it is clear that these practical complexities of the extending polyphonic techniques called for more fundamental reconsideration and revision.

Theological argument and authority, however, appear to have lagged behind, and are felt only later, in the form of a renewed urgency of prohibition and restriction. Whereas the earlier Cluniac deliberations might be thought, in general, to have sought to reduce theological sponsorship of music and to encourage practical developments, the bull of Pope John XXII in the 1320s, by contrast, anathematises polyphonic experimentation, forbids use of the vernacular or rapid note decoration in coloratura, and advocates the older acceptances of organum. But the successive alterations and innovations by this time have already diffused across habits of practice. The modern roles of 'composition' and 'composer', for example, seem to date in earliest forms from required avoidance of the tritone, and from a corresponding need to dictate to philosophically untrained cantors, as well as, later, from organisational problems of incorporating a sacred text within more elaborate, polyphonic musical forms.

Repeatedly, these various changes are concerned with dissonance. New practices displace, and throw into question, in their extension and variation, existing and explained strictures on sounds in the world charged with God-given meanings which it is only necessary to incant. Emphasised instead are processes of musical development between dissonance and consonance, and a need to make meanings for sounds in alternation and movement. Meanings and proscriptions in the world were gradually replaced by techniques of development in composition and human achievements of art.

Historical Reference III: Tonality

In Greek music, music of the medieval church and a wide range of other kinds of music, dissonances are classified as sounds outside a set of specified musical codes. From such classification follow the constraints on composition and improvisation: modes, scales, harmonies, all with associations and conventions of usage appropriate to a social condition of music thought out in terms of ethics or religion. Against these, there is the range of sounds and intervals to be avoided, on pain of loss of character or of heresy.

In these terms, it is not primarily the new harmonic arrangements of European tonal music which is most striking: the triads and relationships between triads, or the way in which, apparently in Britain in the fourteenth century before elsewhere, thirds and sixths, previously dissonances, become consonances, whilst the fourth, previously a consonance in organum, becomes a dissonance. Far more distinctive is the way in which movements of harmony and effects created between emerging strong and weak beats in musical rhythm rely upon a planned exploitation of dissonance.

Tonal music is created in exactly an alternation between what is agreeable, tolerable and stable (the resolutions), and the tensions, suspensions and displacements of dissonance. Such music does not simply proclaim by authority an area of response for listeners. Rather, it seeks to produce that area of response and interpretation by experience, in dramas of feeling and perception which are conducted through dissonant suspensions, leading finally into a coherence of resolution and identity. Dramatising creations of individual and social identity in the experience of art, tonal musics have been occupied with innovation, extension and changes in style, but always in relation to precipitating pleasure through techniques of excitation in suspensions and modulations, later relieved by resolution and cadence.

This new place and function for dissonance marks a fundamental transformation of later medieval polyphony, and occurs through a succession of developments in the late fourteenth, fifteenth and sixteenth centuries. These in turn channel finally into music of the opera and concert-hall. Concert-hall and opera are the accompanying institutions of the new dramatic, expressive music, a music no longer of a prescribed continuum, but made up of an internally developing dramatic coherence.

Tuning and Dissonance

The transition, of course, has its phases. There appears to have been first an inclusion of dissonant intervals on short or unstressed notes in the course of melody, as accidents (a term still used to define notes out of immediate harmonic context). Even the proscribed tritone intervenes occasionally as harmony, a possibility seemingly already countenanced in the early fifteenth century, as by Prosdocimus:

> The first rule is this: what we call discords, namely, the second, fourth, seventh, and diminished fifth, diminished and augmented octaves and their equivalents, are intervals never used in counterpoint, because they are averse to agreeability in harmony by nature of their dissonance. They are used, however, in shorter note values, because in the latter they are not considered dissonant on account of the speed of the notes.[2]

Subsequently, too, there is an incorporation of these dissonances as suspensions, as movements against consonance, in auxiliary or passing notes within ornaments, as in varieties of portamento. And gradually these conventions of usage acquire local, expressive associations, especially of pathetic feeling and pain. It is in this last phase that the expressive dissonances of the madrigal appear, in Palestrina as elsewhere, a symbolism of intervals supporting the words, with the madrigal itself also important in other ways, as a preliminary to the opera, pastoral and later concert.

In subsequent movements, this new mobility between dissonance and consonance itself develops, in further shifts of centre of the harmonic relations of key, in modulations. Modulation might be thought of as an exchange of one key centre for another, and an incorporation or embedding of new, contingent relations of suspension and resolution. However, the increased use of, and aspiration towards, harmonic modulation creates new problems and possibilities for the musical forms, and for the design of instruments. Modulation accentuates a usefulness to the new tonal music of regularity in the intervals of the octave, such that a cycle of notes returning to exactly the same pitch might be an available instrumental resource. In the existing pitch systems of the period, the divisions of the Pythagorean scale led to a series of perfect, simple ratios which then, however, subdivided slightly unevenly for the chromatic intervals. This means of division was workable for an harmonic cycle beginning on one particular note, but the cycle would not then be transferable for other leading notes, since the intervals would be noticeably uneven and misplaced.

In varied response to this complexity of the scales, and to the impetus of the new musical forms, approximations of the intervals follow, calculated to attain a cyclical property of equitable scales from any leading note. There are the deliberations of Ramis in the fifteenth century and of Gioseffo Zarlino in the sixteenth century; the development of mean-tone scales by Schlick in Germany around 1510, and by Francis Salinas in Italy in the 1570s; then 'equal' or 'even' temperament, put forward in theory by Mersenne in France in the 1630s and first in use in North Germany in the late seventeenth century, employed in some newly-built organs of the 1690s and advocated by J. S. Bach in *The Well-tempered Klavier* in the early eighteenth century, but evidently only assimilated in commercial British piano-manufacturing as late as the mid nineteenth century.

What is significant about this planning and design for modulation, as regards dissonance, is the purposeful extension which can be seen in dramatic usages of dialectic between suspension and resolution, between dissonance and consonance. Paradoxically, the extended harmonic variation exerts a pressure to make the previously distinctive individual scales conform more closely to one another, so that the compositional possibility of repeated modulation and harmonic returns by novel, indirect routes might be increased. In traditions of Greek music and to a lesser extent in medieval religious music, modes and scales had specific characteristics and associations. But the new tonal music required instead as far as possible an equivalence between scales, to accentuate a compatibility which alone, particularly on keyboard instruments, might achieve repeated modulation, and make a continuity of thematic material in different keys a compositional possibility.

Inevitably repercussions of this standardisation can be seen across the existing symbolisms. Previously attached to individual scales, and to physical properties of instruments, ascribed symbolic qualities transfer extensively around this time to textures and to orchestration instead. Increasingly it is individual resources of compositional technique, rather than socially ordained character, which are taken to generate music's emotional, ethical or religious effect. And the associations which remain today, for keys and key signatures (in for example the melancholy of the minor or the march of the major), have a marginalised, archaic importance, much diminished even from that of Marc-Antoine Charpentier's catalogue of keys in *Règles de Composition*, in the early 1690s.

Incorporation of expressive dissonance, and delineation of a developmental experience of listening, define in terms of musical form an accentuated individualism of tonal music. For what might be thought particularly to distinguish dissonance in tonality is the way in which it displaces kinds of prescriptive harmonic convention with processes of listening open to experience and judgement. Aesthetic effects of tonal music are created in deferral or annulment of elements purposefully introduced and developed, dissonances intervening largely in order to lead, frequently by way of modulation, to their own resolution in cadence. Knowledges and pleasures of listening are achieved in perceptions of structure, of developing musical 'argument'. But the temperament and the harmonies establish their new musical individualism of 'argument' only within wider patterns of change: it is only in wider social relationships of manufacture and sale of appropriate instruments, in demands of the new opera and concert audiences, and in conceptions of the composer as esteemed entertainer and artist, that the formal devices of suspension and resolution acquire their force and influence.

The Contemporary Argument: Three Views

If dissonance in tonal music differed in these ways from its functions in medieval, Greek, and many other kinds of music, there is an equally fundamental transformation in certain forms of concert-music of the early twentieth century. In tonal music, dissonances had a function both formally, projecting the music harmonically forward towards cadence, and subjectively, establishing a dialectic of desires and expectations which are subsequently gratified in pleasures of resolution. Across this developmental arrangement there is a play of associations and perceptions, but that play is contained, finally, by an overall harmonic organisation. In new atonal concert-music of the twentieth century (from Schoenberg onwards), however, experiment is made with radically new ways of conceiving and experiencing dissonance. Formal exploration is no longer linked to notions of expectation and gratification, is so far as outside the harmonic bounds of tonality there appears to exist no equivalent of final harmonic restitution. In a variety of conceptions, dissonance becomes in these shifts of emphasis once again less an element within a dynamic process of thematic development or argument, than an assumed property of sounds in the world.

At least three general strands in the contemporary argument surrounding tunefulness and dissonance might be separated in relation to these developments.

1. Dissonance within a terminology of polemic, as formless and continuous noise, particularly in arguments that there can be no pleasure in music from which the subjective drama of excitation and resolution is removed. Concerted attempts to develop atonal music can come to appear in such terms a counterpart to a larger cultural decline into a meaninglessness for the individual of the modern world. Familiar over a range of positions, the view can be glimpsed, for example, in the following terms of exultation in Hindemith:

> Anyone to whom a tone is more than a note on paper or a key pressed down, anyone who has ever experienced the intervals in singing, especially with others, as manifestations of bodily tension, of the conquest of space, and of the consumption of energy, anyone who has ever tasted the delights of pure intonation by the continual displacement of the comma in string-quartet playing; must come to the conclusion that there can be no such thing as atonal music, in which the existence of tone-relationships is denied.[3]

Hindemith's enthusiasm over tonality is closely linked to the developmental affect in a listener this kind of music can produce. And generally, in the argumentative framework of which Hindemith here provides an exceptional instance, contemporary music should continue to develop within the conventions of tonality.

In its many variants and degrees of sophistication, this is a view of atonal dissonances as merely negation of the values of tonality. Where tonality indicates humanistic rationality and control over forms and expression, dissonances can signal only meaninglessness and anguish. So it is interesting that even in certain formulations which are not explicitly critical of atonality, the sense of lost meaning and need for restoration still appears. Despite enthusiasm for Schoenberg's work, for example, this is the general sense of Charles Rosen's suggestion that resolution is indeed available for atonal music: in closing, plenitudinous glissandi of pitch which saturate the full harmonic span of the octave.[4] In views of this sort, the specific effect of dissonance in tonal music is displaced, but the larger, corresponding understanding of music's dynamic function as argument or exposition linked to an enrichment of experience remains intact. Musical means are taken to vary, but the broader structure of a production of knowledge in experience for the listener achieved by resolving musical conclusion is taken to persist.

2. Dissonance in a kind of musical egalitarianism or libertarianism, where it is often combined with a view of temporary public ignorance to be overcome either simply by familiarity with experimental music, or by a reformed musical education. Conceived along these lines, dissonant relations between the twelve tones of the scale are the product merely of restrictive attributions of value and function made in tonal music; and in order to replace the categorical oppositions between consonance and dissonance, what is required is acknowledgement that harmonic differences are relative, simply a matter of degree. Consider this emphasis in Webern's *The Path to the New Music*:

> But we must understand that consonance and dissonance are not essentially different—that there is no essential difference between them, only one of degree. Dissonance is only another step up the scale, which goes on developing further ... anyone who assumes that there's an essential difference between consonance and dissonance is wrong, because the entire realm of possible sounds is contained within the notes that nature provides—and that's how things have happened.[5]

Atonal music in these terms appears to involve effects and kinds of interest quite fundamentally different from those of functional tonal harmony, the implication being that accentuated structural opposition between dissonant and consonant intervals in tonal music is merely a limiting technique. What might usefully displace such procedures would be a parity of function and importance extended to all notes and sounds: an 'emancipation of the dissonance', whereby all notes share equal possibilities of interrelation with others. Such understandings appear to lead quite directly towards 'modernist' atonal, dodecaphonic and microtonal music, on the basis that since the distinction between consonance and dissonance is simply relative, the structures of contemporary music should not be confined by restrictions on usage conditioned merely by social expectations which are themselves only restricted and relative.

3. Dissonance as a means of reflection in music of social relations—as a figurative representation of social life. This conception can be found in Adorno, for example: 'The dissonances which horrify them testify to their own conditions; for that reason alone do they find them unbearable.'[6] It can also be seen in aspects of the work of Hanns Eisler:

> To the uninitiated listener Schoenberg's music does not sound beautiful because it mirrors the capitalist world as it is without embellishment and because out of his work the face of capitalism stares directly at us. Due to his genius and complete mastery of technique, this face, revealed so starkly, frightens many. Schoenberg, however, has performed a tremendous historical service. When his music is heard in the concert halls of the bourgeoisie they are no longer charming and agreeable centers of pleasure where one is moved by one's own beauty but places where one is forced to think about the chaos and ugliness of the world or else turn one's face away.[7]

Atonal music in this sense presents a new musical 'realism', in which arrangements of sound once again speak truths of relationships in the composition of the world. In this case, the truths are not ones of God's creation, but of contemporary social relations under capitalism. The virtue of music would be its ability to alert listeners to present social conditions, and imply alternatives to them.

The Contemporary Argument: Directions

Each of these understandings seems to modify quite fundamentally the conventions of dissonance at work in composed tonal music. Each attributes character and value to dissonance prior to its specific articulation or perception as music. In the first conception, it is a property by virtue of the nature of sound which has to be controlled and aesthetically directed in music which is to be meaningful, since there is an ordering function in the 'purity' of intonation. In the second, it is a property by virtue of the nature of sound which should be sought out and explored, as liberation from currently restricted harmonic possibilities, since there are no categorical distinctions between pitch relations in nature. In the third, it is a property by virtue of the nature of sound which, being recognised as unpleasant and inequitable, can serve to represent a disagreeability of contemporary social relationships.

To grasp how these understandings can work into, and on occasion confuse, an opposed tunefulness and dissonance of contemporary music, it is necessary to consider larger arguments concerning musical forms and institutions within which they are frequently developed. Again, the three strands are useful:

1. Atonality as unmusical dissonance. In an emphasis carried over from tonal music, dissonances acquire their significance in relation to the consonances to which they are opposed. This conception seems to impose, as a general form of organisation of music, kinds of attention in composition and listening developed within a regionally and historically restricted, if influential, set of aesthetic and institutional conventions. Increased influence in the twentieth century of cultural forms originating outside Europe or the United States emphasise an insularity in this view, and impress a need for revision and comparison. Moreover, when upheld in the present, exclusively valuing tonal music no longer engages social conditions in which the early tonal forms gained popularity, displacing medieval precursors; rather, the view addresses circumstances in which the tonal forms have acquired a frequently retrospective, often avowedly 'classical' or 'neoclassical', connotation that importantly overspills workings of harmony simply.

Accentuating changes such as these which distinguish qualities of earlier tonal music from certain of their successors in the twentieth century, Adorno has put forward arguments in favour of formal innovation, dismissing static repetition of tonal musical forms as a retreat from changing social circumstances. Currently pressed in, he suggests, by atonal modernisms on the one hand, and by an expansion of mass distributed music on the other, the pleasures of experience and identity formerly achieved in tonal concert- and opera-music have moved extensively over into traditions of 'light' or 'popular' music, where—in reduced and often cynically exploitative forms—they have lost their earlier exploratory qualities.

Presenting twentieth-century music in an essay of the mid-1930s as involving an opposition between 'incomprehensibility' and 'inescapability', Adorno describes a tyranny of listening in which the tonal music of concert, ballet and opera have shrunk to being focused on merely spectacular elements: the cost of a concert ticket indicating worth and esteem; the extreme eminence of 'star' performers such as a Toscanini, or of instruments, a Stradivarius; voices evaluated according to their extremes of pitch or volume, rather than to discretion in their use. This kind of fascination Adorno terms a 'fetishism' of listening, stressing from Marx the consistently commodity character of the phenomenon within currently dominant institutions of music production anad distribution. In addition, he argues, such idolisation is complemented by a way of listening which is arrested or 'regressive', constructed around preference for individual instruments over forms of their interrelation; which prefers very short musical themes, or eight-bar tunes; which involves inverting passive consumption and subjection into active adulation, in fan-club activities, imitative fashions in clothing, etc.

Regression and fetishism are, for Adorno, responses not only to contemporary conditions of music itself, but to a broader crisis of social relations; they are devices, in leisure and entertainment, for forestalling any kind of active intervention. In this sense, atonal music radically threatens and challenges them. Adorno argues: 'The terror which Schoenberg and Webern spread, today as in the past, comes not from their incomprehensibility but from the fact that they are all too correctly understood. Their music gives form to that anxiety, that terror, that insight into the catastrophic situation which others merely evade by regressing.'[8] The changing impact of tonal music and the ways it is heard, then, implies a need for new forms, incorporating dimensions of dissonance beyond any conjectured stability of 'natural' harmonic relations, or of tonal music in general.

2. 'Emancipation of the dissonance', encouraging use of what are presently termed dissonances, on the basis that in principle pitch relations are equivalent. Even with specific expectations for pleasure associated with tonal music displaced, there remain questions concerning what will make atonal music enjoyable; and these include questions concerning which sounds will continue nevertheless to be considered unpleasantly dissonant (it would be utopian to imagine that a music will develop from which no sounds at all are excluded as being disagreeably dissonant).

But these immediate and practical questions remain obscured by two areas of confusion. First, the difficulties in practice confronting any anticipated end to dissonance cannot be adequately grasped, so long as atonal music is linked to belief in the luminary powers of the composer, and an imputed, corresponding endorsement for art by posterity. When qualities of aesthetic forms are projected primarily forwards in time towards an imaginary audience for assessment and value, contemporary judgements become simply temporary obstacles; and relevant, practical questions are exchanged for long-term professions of faith. Second, in the various arguments over dissonance there are two conflicting metaphorical senses at work. Again, Adorno's writings can be drawn upon to clarify the distinction: 'dissonance' as sounds empirically unliked, or experienced as being 'disquieting' (a sense taken over largely from tonal music, and visible in Adorno's suggestion, illustrated above, that radical music is capable of reflecting social relations); 'dissonance', by contrast, as sounds radically desirable and attractive, and so to be incorporated in 'emancipated', 'rational' musical forms. ('The predominance of dissonance seems to destroy the rationally, "logical" relationships. Dissonance is nevertheless still more rational than consonance, insofar as it articulates with great clarity the relationship of the sounds occurring within it—no matter how complex—instead of achieving a dubious unity through the destruction of those partial moments present in dissonance, through "homogenous" sound.'[9])

In Adorno's speculations on musical modernism and on a crisis of popular music (as in many wider arguments essentially constructed around them), these complexities are repeatedly circled. Schoenberg's music, for example, is both a representation of capitalism's cacophony, and yet also, heard properly, a satisfying totality of musical relations. But that 'unity' or 'totality' is not one of synthesis, and in this lies a further difficulty. The suggestion is rather of a 'clarification' of relations (of sounds as of society, as the metaphor would have it), a clarification which would occur only if the homogenising and fetishising effect of bourgeois music and society could be displaced. Dissonance is viewed here as at once a veil to, and a prefiguration of, a future musical and social accord. In these two—not necessarily compatible—conceptions (as musical emancipation, and as a reflection of contemporary society) dissonance remains ambiguous. In one version, a hypothetical condition of musical liberation is conceived, in comparison with which present actualities fade into insignificance beside a more important artistic evolution. In the other, an unpleasantness in present music acts out blockages which divide that hypothesised condition from the present.

Yet if the sense of grievance is common across the ambiguity, the implicit programme of musical and social reform differs. Within the 'egalitarian' conception, education and exposure to modernist music will render dissonances euphonious to the ear, liberating pleasure from existing restrictions imposed by tonal music. Within the 'reflective' argument, on the other hand, fundamental political change alone will remove the social conditions which the music serves to reflect. After social revolution only would dissonance become euphonious, then reflecting an actual social concord. But it remains less than clear what actual sounds would be able, in this latter perspective, to 'reflect' the newly-acquired social harmony. And in any case, there seems no reason at all to believe that the acoustic properties and social resonances of dissonance are so closely linked as Adorno and others have suggested.

3. Dissonance working to reflect social relations within musical arrangement. By considering certain currents in the writings of Hanns Eisler (or, about music for the Epic Theatre, in Brecht), it is possible to work through some of the difficulties surrounding the understandings of dissonance proposed by Adorno. For Eisler, as for Adorno, dissonance has to be perceived with regard

to social ramifications. But, distinct from Adorno's notion of musical 'reflection' linked to certain arrangements of sounds, Eisler treats dissonance as more a situationally specific relation of listening. The synthetic, homogenising function ascribed by Adorno to the forms of tonal music is for Eisler predominantly an aspect of the particular listening arrangements developed for this music, especially that of the concert-hall. It is primarily the positioning of this music as an object for spectacle and idealising fascination which according to Eisler is able to produce the effect of mystique and uncritical absorption.

Yet produced in the historically changing, and so changeable, material relations of the opera and concert, for Eisler the positioning of music and music-making as an object for consumption is consequently the site of important contradictions. Accordingly it is made—in definitions of a radical music and musical theatre—a focus for new practices of listening, transformed from consumption into active deliberation:

> Composers, irrespective of the purpose for which they believe they are producing music, must become aware of the social function for which their music is being used. If they free themselves of all prejudices they will discover that regardless of their intentions, their music plays a great part in what can be described as a trade in narcotics . . . In fact, music not only serves certain social functions, but allows of a change in these functions, so that it is then made to serve an aim different than that for which it was written . . . Instead of trying to bring about a state of psychic stupefaction or chaotic excitement in the listener, music must endeavour to clarify the consciousness . . .[10]

The clarification of consciousness proposed here is clearly different from that suggested by Adorno. It does not simply address relations between notes and intervals within musical forms, but also engages relations between musical forms and the musicians by whom, as well as the audiences for whom, these musical forms are created. The specific forms that clarification takes in Eisler's work cannot be separated from the particular conception of politics within which his Workers' Music Movement has played, and would continue to play, a part. Challenging an assumed positioning for listeners, Eisler proposes agitation over conditions for new musical practice: exhortation and political counter-identification (with here an accent on vocal music, especially in satirical and didactic songs); entertainment at events such as political meetings and demonstrations; participation and organisation outside existing conventions of, and limitations on, who makes music, when, for whom, and authorised by what kinds of training. Much of Eisler's politics remains extremely problematic. But what is of continuing significance in the arguments he puts forward is that dissonance is neither simply a property in the nature of sound (a constant property, only the implication of which alters with social change), nor a representation of society in the form of a musical reflection of discordant social relations. Rather, as a set of effects on audiences, varying between occasions and social groupings, dissonance is far more broadly relational, depending on surrounding conditions both of musical forms, and of the institutions through which these forms are represented, learnt and reproduced.

Dissonance and Today's Ear

Developing these terms, dissonance can be directed towards displacing idealisations of music as an engrossing, spectacular object; it can prepare reflection *on* social relationships rather than offer a reflection *of* them. And from such acknowledgement of altering properties of dissonance follow two general considerations for listening. First, as regards music of the past, listening involves moving conceptions of dissonance. Tensions of harmonic structure in Mozart, in Palestrina, or, more clearly still, in free organum, function differently in the present than at the time of their composition or early performance; and so continuing valuations of, and decisions to perform, such musical pieces demand some account being taken of this kind of changing effect. In this sense at least, the quest for ever greater authenticity in respect of early music (in instrumentation, manner of performance, location, etc.) recedes beyond quite fundamental difficulties of changed and changing aural expectations, which are embodied in intervals and instrumental textures, as well as in the more general connotation of antiquity.

Second, as regards contemporary musical activity, it might be said that arrangements of sounds for which there are no established conventions of association open up possibilities for new attachments of meaning and value. Over a range of musical practices organised according to radically differing understandings of dissonance, this potential for new positions and new meanings in music has been developed. Within concert traditions, it has frequently been associated with extended instrumental technique, and with violences of rhythm and texture; in rock and jazz, as often with forms of electronic distortion, sustain and synthesised white noise (to the extent that even diatonic rock music can sound dissonant to many ears).

Beyond questions of particular intervals, or of superordinate ethical or religious explanations, it is the capability of dissonance and distortion for altering and redirecting meaning and value in music which presently needs to be made clear. Despite the breadth of argument concerning tunefulness and dissonance, this property of sounds and of music-making is rarely explicitly distinguished. It is not simply–though this remains one constant edge of arguments made by composers of the 'classical' avant-garde–that existing instruments and the sounds they conventionally produce have become worn out and need to be updated. This characterisation of the situation leads only into a need for the composer's art to progress by drawing on new instruments and developing structures of an emancipated or enlarged world of sound. More important than this formalistic programme for musical art is the perception that newness of practice is also disturbance and reformation of positions of meaning of the old. In relation to presently available resources for generating sound, and across broader patterns of social connotation and reference, music in the present acquires its powers of reflection, commentary and redirection.

4 Performance: Sound and Vision

Musical Performance and Spectacle

It is a familiar and understandable usage to speak of 'listening' when describing acts of perceiving or consuming music. There are the attitudes of visual exclusion, the closed eyes or simultaneous engagement in conversation, dancing, working–various suggestions of a superfluousness of visual attention for pleasures of sound. And from oral traditions of poetry onwards, there is a recognisable mythology of blind music-makers: Homer, by tradition, and Milton; Maria Theresa Paradis, for whose playing Mozart composes his Piano Concerto No. 18 (K 456) in 1784; or again, singers and instrumentalists in blues, extending customs of accompanied begging in the Southern United States–Blind Lemon Jefferson, Gary Davis, Sonny Terry, Blind Willie Harris or Blind Willie McTell; currently, musicians in jazz, rock and soul–Roland Kirk or Ray Charles; José Feliciano or Stevie Wonder. There is more widely, too, the specialist skill of piano-tuners: a mythology of especial attentions to sound in the absence of sight.

But for all these exceptional instances, music is far more often produced and consumed in some purposeful relation to vision and spectacle. This is the case in concerts, opera or ballet; on the military bandstand, and in accompaniment to parades or firework displays; in jazz on the stand; as television and film music; recently, in rock films and record promotion videos. So the usage, and its category of an isolable property of hearing linked to a distinct aesthetic form, remains difficult and ambiguous. Music may be whatever is not included by the visual or the spectacular, may be whatever is exclusively heard. Or again, the music may be seen as occasion or practice incorporating integrally a visual dimension.

To take as music in all instances only what is heard is to

abstract, and in that process inevitably idealise, an acoustic dimension of practices always and only realisable within definitions and limits of a given scenario. But to acknowledge that music consists in interrelations between elements and media, especially between sound and vision, has major consequences; it is not only elements in combination, but also the nature of the relation between them, which must be taken to require attention, analysis and initiative. Concerts, for example, are sites of hearing, but always arranged around an element of sight and focus. In precursors of the concert form, by contrast–in the late medieval mysteries and miracles, and on occasion in pastoral, masque or court ballet–there is frequently an invisibility of the music-making; musicians were placed behind scenes or on one of the 'mansions' or platforms constructed to represent Heaven, their sounds diffusing magically, as of the spheres. Between these forms occurs a transition of performance conventions, in a transformation of relations of seeing and hearing (it is for *Orfeo*, for example, that Monteverdi, on classical precedent, moves the orchestra from backstage into the pit). Effectively in this transition the physical articulations of music in performance emerge as a new kind of attention, pleasure and interest.

Locating Sounds

In such forms of combination and interrelation, the sounds of music may be thought to be contextualised, or positioned. Currently, there are photographic images for record-sleeve designs of the performer or composer, as well as images of less precise suggestion (a picture of the Alps, a Kandinsky reproduction, instruments enhanced by lighting and complex reflections); there are filmic images which depict a source for the sound (of singers and performers, or, by metonymy, of parts of instruments: trombone slide, guitar neck or drum sticks)–images which place sounds according to the means by which they are made; there are images synchronised with sounds, engaged rhythmically (cars and trains, footsteps, light shows, stage effects and lasers)– sounds as programmatic representations of actions and processes; more distantly, there are images related to sounds by less direct association (in couplings with dynamics and connotations of known styles, as in Hollywood or television soundtracks)–

sounds whose programmatic element operates within wider rhetorics of composition. Such forms of connection are presently achieved by way of a number of technical processes, in addition to earlier, already elaborate, machineries of musical stage-drama: live sound, and studio recreations of 'live' sound, mimed and dubbed; sounds and reverberation sometimes changing with cuts and panning, sometimes placed across montage with no alteration that conveys distance or siting of sound source. Or on occasion, the superimposed relation of soundtrack on image is deliberately broken, with an unexpected crossing from the level of dubbed accompaniment to that of integral dramatic function, as when in film or television an overlaid music is stopped or modified by an actor in vision, turning off a radio or gramophone which was until that moment merely an inert, incidental prop of the set.

In all these interrelations of sounds and vision, sight and hearing are provided with positionings and contexts. Through these, music acquires much of its conventional intelligibility. The contextualisation is achieved largely in fixings of sound by perceptions of the eye, an organ—to follow at least psychoanalytic evidences—more directed than the ear towards an exhaustion and control of meanings and interpretation.[1] It is seemingly the challenge to the controlling property of vision which creates the jarring effect when a sound not initially seen in the image is discovered there, as when the radio or gramophone is switched off or adjusted in the kind of scene described above.

Such knowledge provided by the eye for experience of sound is clearly of great significance within the history of music. The advent of visual emphases in sixteenth- and seventeenth-century musical performance is also a decisive moment in progressive relegations of music's supposed magical and religious properties, an arrival of music as dominantly a secular entertainment divorced from earlier metaphysical significances, and incorporated in emerging conceptions of human achievement and art. What is in question in this process (obscured by the historical complication of music's varied interrelations with existing dramatic forms during the periods of transition) is a new kind of interest in looking at actions and attitudes of performance. In many cases, there is indeed a compounding of mannerisms with sounds in forms of spectacle, as public fixings of a display or bearing of the body.

The Significance of Sound and Vision

In drama, spectacle and ceremony, then, are created coordinations of sound and sight, and, in these, there is a pull of the visual in changing conventions of the body in performance. Historically first appear a wide range of forms of presence (performing and dancing, live orchestras, ensembles and bands). Then, in the course of the twentieth century, a major extension and transformation takes place, in developments of film, in recording and in sound reproduction. With these possibilities of fixing sound on disc or tape, in an exactly replicable acoustic image, there is a new accent on what is exclusively auditory, in radio and gramophone. But equally, there is a return of the image in film soundtrack, as later in television. And it might be argued that, subsequently, an ascendant interest in the image has produced a further important shift in the kind of pleasures generated by music–from pleasures of listening only, towards those of visualisation and identification, across (and in many instances overtly against) actual procedures and social relations of musical composition, performance and distribution. It was only in this century that forms of mechanical production and reproduction of music were developed in which seeing played so much a subordinate part; yet recent developments and commercial applications of video technology appear to be emphatically extending and amplifying an impact of the image, with its capture of sounds suggested or coordinated in front and in sight, rather than all around in the air, for hearing only.

It is possible to see in these interrelations a neglected strand in accounts of European music, a strand of particular importance for three reasons: first, because other than in the twentieth century on radio and disc, music has been most widely experienced in forms of relationship with a pleasure of seeing, and so radio and records were quite fundamental innovations as regards listening; second, because crucial redefinitions of music as an art-form took place in the sixteenth and seventeenth centuries in conjunction with the development of ballet, opera and concert, as exactly forms of seeing-in-listening; third, because questions of the body and voice have been historically crucial to successive major transitions of musical forms–madrigals, masques, opera; *Sprechstimme*; now contemporary lyricism and popular song.

As regards the present, an importance of this strand in the history is clear. In major expansions in the fields of television spectacular, film narrative and musical, and videotaped concerts or record promotions, new relations between existing traditions of performance, and changing conventions of visualised musical response are being worked out. It is almost certainly these new relations, and the forms in which they are produced and reproduced, which will most actively shape conditions of music and music-making in the foreseeable future.

Barthes and the Body: 'The Grain of the Voice'

To broach this fascination with seeing-in-listening in performance and reproduction, it is necessary to consider representations of the body in music-making across historical transitions and continuing pressures. But such visual orientation is importantly related also to ways in which acoustical properties of vocalisation become (in what can be seen as a distinct process within the forms of combination) interpretable discourse, in addition to providing simply a musicality of poetry and song. Even as regards vocal music heard with closed eyes, or on disc or radio, there exists a framing effect, by way of which a seeming freeplay of sounds as noises generated by the lungs and differentially modified in passage through the vocal tract, becomes also—through phonological organisation, inflectional contour and stylistic and paralinguistic convention—an expression of feeling and thought.

Because of this organising property of language, it is necessary, in order to develop reflections on voice and body, and body and image, to look at intersections between the physiological and articulatory properties of the voice on the one hand, and notions of sense and meaning on the other. Considering such a contrast effectively between the voice as bodily sound generator, and the voice as an assured mechanism of expression, Roland Barthes—in the essay 'The Grain of the Voice'—proposed a distinction between two as he thought different kinds of voicing. That distinction he formulated more specifically in terms of a taste for the singing of Panzera, and a lesser enthusiasm for that of Fischer-Dieskau. The point of aesthetic division is between an expressive or affective voicing (meaningful pauses and breathing, attention to stylistic or generic detail—what Barthes, acknowledging Julia Kristeva, calls 'phenotext'), and a kind of voicing with 'grain' (voicing of the body in language, beyond particular cultural meanings or intelligibility, the voice eroticised–for Barthes 'genotext').[2]

It was the proposed importance of this distinction that a certain kind of music-making, in which these latter processes of enunciation are displayed, has disappeared or is disappearing, under pressure from a music-making in which the body finds itself replete with cultural meanings, individually and socially represented. Barthes here and elsewhere tentatively links the historical transition with stages of a protracted decline in practical musical education and amateur performance. And the prevailing or saturating expressive mannerisms of vocal performance Barthes relates accordingly to a much wider contemporary condition of music. In this, music's extraordinary access to processes of desire and the body, through qualities of enunciation and articulation, is repeatedly captured and closed off in exhaustive attributions of meaning or value.

In view of a decline in perceiving these properties of music in practice and in theoretical and critical commentary, what Barthes implores is a fundamental revision of musical discussion and education. That revision would be in the direction of attentions less concerned with changes within music's forms (such as the development or supercession of tonality), than with music's capability, within and across these forms, to overflow conventionally attributable meanings in an access to traces of the body and of desire.

Linking questions of voice quality both with concerns of subjectivity as something organised in movements of language on the body, and with aesthetic forms and criticism, Barthes's essay has become more influential than other, primarily descriptive, phonational investigations conducted within linguistics. And to distinguish, as the essay does, contrastive pleasures in performance and listening has been important, because of the radical questioning of current critical approaches to sounds and music such distinctions imply. Barthes was able to exhibit dimensions of performing and listening continually suppressed in familiar assessments of musical forms and their anticipated affects.

But it remains nevertheless a weakness of these observations, when reworked as a more general critical orientation, that what is sought everywhere is a kind of musical modernism, emphatically removed from specifiable conventions of interpretation or association. To consider music and the body (as either a pull of the visual, the expressive and imaginary—or a play of desire in enunciation) is, in all instances, simultaneously to engage a complicated social history, in which any musical activity and its articulation of the body has been organised. Incidentally, it is this important qualification—that coordinations of the body operate within, across, or are excluded by, surrounding aesthetic conventions—which has to be kept clearly in mind and applied, in relation to the practice of categorising individuals as dispositionally either 'musical' or 'not musical'.

Whilst musical activities can indeed be divided between Barthes's respective categories in new attentions of listening, the condition of enunciation to which these might aspire is always also social. The 'genotext', and the bodily history it speaks, can only exist within wider circumstances. This is implicitly recognised in the movement of argument in 'The Grain of the Voice' away from tastes, and towards historical investigation and account. Correspondingly, the central problems which can be addressed by referring to Barthes's essay are less ones of disengaging the 'genotextual'—hearing everywhere new graduations of inflection or finenesses of performance—than looking over the ways in which the conjunctions and contradictions have been effected and managed in the past, in order to reflect on those processes in the present. What can be gained is seeing the 'genotextual' as a constituent of contemporary musical activity, but acknowledging such activity to be always also social both in its forms and in its changing and changeable limits.

Three Points of Position in Sound and Vision

For the voice and body in performance of music before major changes in the twentieth century, then, three aspects of this social positioning might be considered, as regards constructions of identity and meaning in sound and vision:

1. *Voicing*: song and drama. From resonant bodies (lungs, vocal tract, flaps, nostrils), and in conjunctions of physical attributes of voice with social properties of language as discourse, issue chants, songs and ballads. Repetition and phonological patterning in these divide interest between meanings and a level of

sounds as primarily acoustic material, when properties of vocal sonority interlock with points of social circulation and reference. Performance of operas in the original language or in translation remains, on account of this discrepancy, always a question for debate: whether the language of the libretto is made up mainly in dramatic meanings translatable between languages, or in a patterning of sounds, clausulae and inflections peculiar to a language of original conception. (This point of argument can be followed in detail through nationalist arguments of Purcell, Dryden and others in the late seventeenth century, and their extension, on this question, of demands for vernacular and for ready intelligibility already existing as an intellectual current from the Reformation onwards.)

Identification of the sounds of words as meanings is also involved in further compounded forms of dramatisation: historically, in movements from ceremony and spectacle to character, and from character to character in action and in narrative. In early opera, masque and court ballet, dramatic elements were frequently interwoven with existing procedures and interests of ceremony and dance, producing loose cohesion and development. That combination, and the kind of cohesion it produces, is discernible both in the constituent operatic forms (aria, chorus, etc.), and in more local techniques of musical composition, as in techniques of 'cantabile' writing during the early eighteenth century (melodic phrasings for instruments conforming to conventions and regularities of the speaking and meaning voice, in phrase length as if with breathing, pauses and pitch in vocal register). Throughout such experiments, the song continues as distinct unit, in the form of the aria, alternating with the chorus. Whilst representations of character and action develop in sophistication, they remain bound nevertheless to a table of entertainments, display and an overriding institution of social occasion.

It is only with the polemic and practice of Wagner (Mosel is often cited as a minor antecedent) that insistence on the loose cohesion of festivity, succession and repetition is displaced by an accent of integration. There follow a series of related disagreements and revisions: objections over *Tannhäuser*, concerning the timing of operatic ballet within the evening's entertainment, and the scandal which ensues; new emphasis on unity and development, reflected in the darkening of the auditorium, in use of the leitmotiv as the minimal and recurrent constituent of composition, and in the insistence on the audience being in place and silent throughout the opera. These innovations contribute to a more general unification in the way opera addresses its audience, with aesthetic significance coming to be considered as an overall effect of the music-drama, rather than, as previously, an aggregate of successive entertainments. Nor is the drama made up any longer simply of bodies in action as characters with things to sing; rather, a wide range of elements are combined and organised as a single dramatic and symbolic construct and expression.

As consequence of this synthesis, the new operatic techniques have as one of their effects a re-mystifying of music, displacing its earlier function as an isolable background to entertainment and association. Wagner devises a half-covered orchestra pit, or 'mystic gulf', in order to conceal visually the actual music-making at Bayreuth, and this contributes to a restoration of the formerly theological mystery of musical revelation, which becomes subsequently, however, exactly artistic vision. And for Wagner, these transformations in the technical procedures of opera are recognised to have major cultural implications. Considering Greek drama as the exemplary artistic form to contrast with a cultural decadence of the nineteenth century that needs reviving through artistic and wider cultural revolution, Wagner consistently emphasises the operative union of elements, and its creation of individual, cultural and national identity:

> With the Greeks the perfect work of art, the drama, was the abstract and epitome of all that was expressible in the Grecian nature. It was the nation itself—in intimate connection with its own history—that stood mirrored in its artwork, that communed with itself and, within the span of a few hours, feasted its eyes with its own noblest essence.[3]

Or again,

> With the subsequent downfall of tragedy, art became less and less the expression of the public conscience. The drama separated into its component parts—rhetoric, sculpture, painting, music, and so on, forsook the ranks in which they had moved in unison before; each one to take its own way, and in lonely self-sufficiency to pursue its own development.[4]

This aspect of Wagnerian influence has a complicated and troubled history. And something of a political character in the amalgamation of elements in music-drama can be glimpsed again in certain countering practices and emphases in the twentieth century—in particular in arguments that unacknowledged processes of cultural positioning should be broken down and distinguished, in order to dissolve any self-evident unity of meaning and identity into multiple, frequently contradictory, components, as a basis for questioning and reform. Recall this emphasis in Brecht, for example:

> When the epic theatre's methods begin to penetrate the opera the first result is a radical *separation of the elements*... So long as the expression 'Gesamtkunstwerk' (or 'integrated work of art') means that the integration is a muddle, so long as the arts are supposed to be 'fused' together, the various elements will all be equally degraded, and each will act as a mere 'feed' to the rest. The process of fusion extends to the spectator, who gets thrown into the melting pot too and becomes a passive (suffering) part of the total work of art... *words, music and setting must become more independent of one another.*[5]

Or, implying alternatives to prevailing film and television techniques of superimposing sound and vision (as well as, implicitly, to later commercial initiatives of videotape and videodisc as forms of homogenisation of sounds, body and voice in a primary power of the image), consider this concrete proposal in Eisler: 'A new way of using vocal and instrumental music is above all to set the music against the action in the film. That means that the music is not employed to "illustrate" the film, but to explain it and comment on it.'[6]

2. *Dancing*: music and movement. There is in the history of dancing an overlay of body and society emphatically contrary to conceptions of the body simply speaking itself in a natural expression which is prior to cultural constraints. As gesture and mobility, bodily movements are subject to socially and historically variant conventions and divisions, according to which terms of address and effect are established over and beyond physical resources and restrictions. There is quite fundamental division, for example, between participation and pleasure in action

and movement, or pleasures of performance seen—with corresponding institutionalised positions of participation and expression, or of more passive spectation.

Even restricting consideration to Western Europe alone, movement to music can be traced through a series of revisions: from religious rituals with codified roles and necessary accoutrements (as well as with successive prohibitions and restraints), through festivals, interludes, Moresques and tournaments, into the elaborate displays of court ballet of the sixteenth and seventeenth centuries, accompanied by new systems of choreography and dance notation. Subsequently, with the emergence of opera, masque and concert, there is stage ballet. In Italy in the sixteenth century Cesare Negri emerges as an eminent dancer, and begins to formulate the movements, exercises and routines of what is now thought of as 'classical' dance; and John Playford stands out in the overlapping English histories of concert and dancing as both impresario and theoretician. Later, too, this transition of the sixteenth and seventeenth centuries is consolidated: further formalisation of steps follows in the eighteenth and nineteenth centuries (pirouette, cabriole, pas de deux, entrechat, pointing), as the ballet refines its properties of representation and expression in postures and motions, with famous choreographers and ballerinas, and costume, scenario and machinery designers.

These refinements are accompanied by corresponding changes in understanding of the gesturing body. From religious rhetorics of gesture, there is a shift for the new, secular artistic institutions into versions of expression (more naturalistic scenarios; new interest in mime and narrative forms of dancing, associated in France with Jean-Georges Noverre). Much later, in the twentieth century, the modernist, expressive aesthetic of Isadora Duncan and others in the United States overspills these conventions of naturalism, but on the strength of what was by then an assumed assurance of the expressive capability. There are intersections throughout this history, too, with other traditions of the spectacular: with pantomime, with virtuosity of acrobatic dancing, and with the visual dimension of musical performance itself, in displays which engender admiration and identification. (Consider Barthes again, on identifications which take place while listening: 'does not musical fantasy consist in giving oneself a place, as subject, in the scenario of the performance?'[7])

Yet dance as this kind of ceremonial or dramatic spectacle is only one among a number of concurrent forms of music and movement. Within differing conventions of occasion, other forms of dancing have involved less this exhibition of motion for passive spectators, than displays which are more directly coupled with interaction through reciprocal gesture and motion: various social, often disingenuously called 'folk', occasions (morris dancing, country dances, reels); pair or duo dances, especially in Europe in the nineteenth and early twentieth centuries, in closed, contact positions (tango, waltz, foxtrot, Latin-American forms such as the bossa nova or rhumba); non-contact pair partnerings (bunny hug, rock'n'roll, contemporary disco dancing); solo (sword-dancing, forms of dancing to rock music, such as pogo).

In these styles of display and interaction, the body is figured in radically differing relations of address: identification, exhibition and sexual initiative; projection and sublimation of sexuality and the body as entertainments and leisure in a history of dance-forms (basse dance, galliard, chaconne; minuet; waltz; charleston, quickstep, black bottom, lindy hop, turkey trot, twist . . .). Indeed, a contemporary element of sexual activity has been widely acknowledged, and often condemned, in respect of musical forms—from the sexual innuendoes of jazz and blues onwards—into rock and roll, soul and disco music. Yet against the flow of these criticisms, this sexual dimension can be traced equally in a number of more traditionally revered forms also, to instances of a posturing or fixing of the sexual as property or commodity. Consider, in this light, Roman temple prostitution of tibicinae and ambubaiae, or linked images of sexual propensity and artistry in reputations of eighteenth-century ballerinas, Barbarina or Marie-Madeleine Guimard; or again, changing fetishes of the female body that are interwoven across fashion and pursuit of extended physical mobility, as in the innovative crepe skirts and tights of Maria Medina in the 1790s, or the advent of the tutu in the late nineteenth century; or consider enhancements of the displayed leg as well as of balance in ballet pointing, taken up later and extended in Hollywood precision leg-kicking, and in further shows of the body under differing conditions and interests, in go-go or striptease. In movement and gesture, then, are figured important pleasures of the body in music, to be felt and to be viewed. But these are always addressed across specific conditions and aesthetic purposes, in rhetorics of deportment, clothing and mannerism through which are represented the mobile, the muscular and the physical.

3. *Notation* marks an ordering of bodily movements of musical performance in addition to immediate verbal directives, and provided historically the possibility for pieces of music of a specialised, if restricted, kind of permanence. In this sense, notation was one necessary condition for music to take on, as composition, a temporal and aesthetic independence from particular versions and collaborations of its realisation.

Developing first in Egypt and Sumer alongside early forms of notation of language, in writing, musical notation offered both a record or mnemonic of performance, and a means of prescription for it–a prescription nevertheless requiring subsequent reincarnation in voices and sounding bodies. Following these beginnings, a number of significant moments of redirection within European music can be distinguished. There are developments in formalisation, such as those surrounding the Gregorian Neumes and Modal notations of the twelfth century; the advent of the Franconian system in the late thirteenth century; or innovations in the early fourteenth century associated with the Ars Nova in France and Italy. In the twelfth century again, there is the important adoption of paper as the means of preservation, with its later links to developments in printing (music-printing, from Petrucci around 1500 onwards, lagging behind that of words, and with the amount of detail to be notated or left to be embellished by way of tropes and melismata appearing to rely on paper available, as well as on the power of notational techniques).

For monodic and early polyphonic music, notation appears to have recorded general lineaments of successful improvisations, more than prospective, compositional intentions. And whilst music-printing later stabilised the process, the extensively copied manuscripts of the Middle Ages themselves contain great variety of transcription, embellishment and alteration. So whilst notation, and printing in particular, assisted the coming to prominence of the composer in the course of the fifteenth and sixteenth centuries (it is then that musicians who compose begin to become identifiable, and in the sixteenth century at least, that specialised education for composition is implemented in the curriculum of various universities), little respect appears to have been shown in the early notations for precise details of performance, or for intentions of that initial composer.

Alongside these early interests in composition, there are also further major refinements of notational techniques during the sixteenth and seventeenth centuries. There is the introduction of synoptic scores with part-books, as well as a stabilisation and expansion of the commercial music-publishing industry. But despite these major changes, there remain in scores of the late seventeenth and eighteenth centuries substantial freedoms of instrumentation, as well as for improvisation and embellishment (especially in figured bass parts, in irregular performance of sequences of notes marked as being of equal duration, and in variable graces, such as the appogiatura, fermata or mordent). But for all that continuing latitude of performance and interpretation, a crucial phase of transition is enacted in adoptions of synoptic scoring and the developed notations of the sixteenth and seventeenth centuries. A far broader range of effects to be consistently realised in performance is defined, in an accentuation of notation's prescriptive, rather than commemorative, aspect.

Increasingly linked to functional harmonic relations of tonality, and to an interest in dramatic properties of orchestral texture, the gradually acquired capability of notation for stipulating complex harmonic developments, recapitulations and contrasts make it in the course of the eighteenth century indispensable to the preconstruction of large-scale musical works. In successive revisions, more detailed directions are incorporated as elements of composition, rather than being left to performance or improvisation (revisions exemplified in Haydn's songs being printed on three staves to specify accompaniment, rather than leaving this to initiatives of continuo playing). There are also, in the period immediately following, more exact rhythmic instructions, dynamic markings and expressive prescriptions, and new markings for legato, staccato, bowing and breathing. Some freedom of interpretation remains to nineteenth-century orchestral players, in respect of rhythm, in rubato; but it has been one subsequent direction of twentieth-century concert-music that, across a range of otherwise significantly different musical styles, creative participation of musicians has been further curtailed—curtailed by instructions from composer and conductor; by difficult and elaborate scores; and by a frequent requirement to develop specific techniques for reading notationally idiosyncratic scores in order to achieve precise execution.

Notation, then, begins as signs which are to represent agreed arrangements, and so as something–subject to appropriate educational provision–that promised extended access to and participation in music-making. It becomes increasingly, in reforms of several centuries (Lully, Gluck, Verdi, for example, were all vociferous in restraining embellishment in performance), a set of definitions of aesthetic intention in accordance with which precise execution can be attained. Notation in this way often confines rather than enhances a creativity of performance; and in view of massive notational illiteracy among those wishing to play, much interest in collaboration in music has moved, since the late 1940s and early 1950s, into forms less reliant upon graphic prescription, into learnable variations ('changes') and improvisation: into jazz and rock music, as before and still within 'folk' music.

Performance in Transition

These three strands of history and argument surrounding the voice and body in music (song and drama, bodily gesture, notation) need to be understood as more than simply historical conventions or styles, removed from and secondary to what was characterised by Barthes as the 'genotextual'. They need to be understood as more than this, in that it is through such rhetorics and techniques that the 'genotextual' properties of the voice and body are perceived and directed, both by performers themselves and by listeners and viewers.

The movements of desire and body aspired to by Barthes and others have existed and continue to exist in and through forms of representation; and it is largely in interlocking histories of spectacle, movement and notation that the performing body acquires its positions, as well as its contemporary resources, limits and stresses. So to speculate on possible future dispositions of musical activity not only involves the familiar questions of altering preference or taste, but must also address these further practical difficulties of the conventions and institutions within which new forms might be developed.

Here the comparatively recent instruments and technology for mechanical reproduction and broadcasting of music are particularly significant, because of the way in which they have extended and redirected certain of these conventions. In its nineteenth-century developments, notation led to an increasing emphasis on reproduction, as against creative, collaborative performance. Indeed, the term 'reproduction', when used of music, seems to have itself encroached, during this period, upon senses previously attached to the word 'performance'. But it has been perhaps most importantly in mechanical reproduction and broadcasting that present conditions of music have been and continue to be shaped. In a large-scale shift from notation and performance into production and distribution of music in recorded forms, a major change in musical activity has occurred. What is reproduced repeatedly on disc or tape is no longer one single realisation of a score–a music continuous and recognisable by way of notated properties of its composition, despite residually variable executions–but exact articulations of one particular performance.

The transformations through which this mechanised reproduction of music developed are complex and varied. There is, to take simply one example at the very beginning of the process, an ambiguous musical instrument, suspended between assisted performance or instruction, and reproduction for more passive listening. As such, this ambiguous position of the pianola in the late nineteenth century can be taken as one point of connection between the traditions of active, domestic performance, and what is now accepted as reproduced music.

The customs of domestic performance into which the pianola was introduced have a development throughout the eighteenth and nineteenth centuries, alongside the more social gatherings of concert and opera. Longstanding demands for domestic music-making can be seen to have been met during this period by a range of forms: piano transcription of concert or operatic works and songs, as well as, later, royalty ballads flourishing on the strength of publishing sales (even if the songs in question were mainly advertised through professional, public performance). And a variety of instruments are used to make music in the household: the guitar, popular in the 1750s, the harpsichord, the piano, becoming dominant among domestic instruments during the nineteenth century. Following John Isaac Hawkins's prototype 'Portable Grand Piano', the familiar upright in Britain dates from the early nineteenth century, contemporaneous with a phase of developments in tooling of springs and keys; and with repeated modification and refinements (such as the sostenuto pedal of the mid 1870s), new instruments are supplanted commercially in quick succession, by improved capability and changing fashion.

Patented in 1897, however, the pianola announces an importantly new kind of instrument within these traditions of home performance. A piano-type machine driven by bellows, and producing sounds from a punched roll depressing the keys, it could duplicate a pre-programmed performance. As such, it could be used for almost completely passive entertainment, as well as for practising. Popular if relatively expensive in Britain, and appearing alongside other machines such as the orchestrina (again a piano-like instrument, but capable of imitating qualities of orchestral tone colour), the pianola occupies a position both in practical music-making, and in passive consumption, by being an apparatus manufactured and sold for admiring consumption, as well as for practical instruction and assistance.

Musical Reproduction and its Technology

Following what might be thought of as these intermediary developments of pianola and orchestrina, invention and manufacture of means of sound reproduction lead more into centralised production and general consumption of music, than into new instruments for participation and practice. The gramophone is produced, and then, later, radio broadcasting, magnetic tape recording, stereo and quadrophonic sound, and recently multitrack and digital recording technology.

These are initiatives of a scale of research, investment and development far larger than those of the more specialised new electric and electronic instrument manufacturing, though there are periods of significant expansion in these areas, too: early electric guitars in the 1930s, becoming known in the United States through the playing of Floyd Smith and, more widely still, of Charlie Christian; Fender Telecaster and Gibson Les Paul guitars, commercially available and widespread from the 1950s, and extending access to music-making to large numbers of untrained performers in rock music during the 1960s and 1970s; or Laurens Hammond's electronic organ from 1933 and (following this and the subsequent 'Novachord') the continuing synthesising keyboard sales boom, spreading from the electronic sound studios in the later 1960s, and further dramatically expanded by recent microchip technology.

These developments of instrument manufacture and reproduction technology have significantly altered the circumstances in which music is made, and affected currently popular musical sounds and forms. Several lines of development can be isolated and catalogued, with a view to considering some of their continuing effects and implications.[8]

1. The history of gramophone technology itself, in relation to its supporting interests and researches, is complicated. Edison's celebrated 'Mary had a little lamb' in 1877 takes over from Edouard-Léon Scott's non-reproductive phonautograph of the 1850s, and appears around the same time as a method for decoding sounds devised in France by Charles Cros, shortly before Berliner's adoption of flat disc, as opposed to cylinder, signal storage.

These developments were evidently grasped early on as a major commercial opportunity as regards domestic musical consumption—itself expanding in Britain, for example, at this time alongside a decline of the metropolitan concert audience. In a speculation on increased leisure and consumption, the early machinery was accordingly often made relatively inexpensive, with revenue deriving from the subsequent sale of discs. And the interests in production channel directly into existing forms and expectations of music, with the early systems reproducing 'light' music, such as the royalty ballad, better than orchestral music, owing to the latter's increased dynamic range and usual size of ensemble.

So in the first phase, the new recording industry gives a commercial lead to the contemporary songs and dance tunes. And, significantly for the later history, it links a fresh prestige of possession of the equipment to what had previously been less culturally elevated musical forms. For technical reasons, then, as well as for reasons to do with the sudden fashion for dancing in the United States around this time, there is a redefinition of the cultural currencies of musical forms accompanying first distributions of the new equipment; and these redefined relations hold, fairly consistently, until another change in audience constituency during the 1940s, brought about by competing price reductions between manufacturers, by disruptions in leisure-time during war, and, in Britain at least, as an effect of extensive importation of American recordings and equipment.

Further competition in research and marketing between manufacturers follows the early discoveries, leading always to new, replacement equipment and capabilities. There are the electrical recording systems of the mid 1920s, with amplifier and speaker replacing tone arm and amplifying horn, though (as with radio) only after delays while the necessary and foreseen condenser microphone and valve-amplified stages were developed into the Audion triode, vacuum tube amplifier–following exploratory work by Edison that was consolidated by Marconi designers Fleming and Lee De Forest.

A range of initiatives then follow this fundamental reorientation. There is a gradually-acquired capability for reproduction of extended dynamic ranges, and increased time per record side, overcoming certain problems of sound deterioration (problems negotiated by optimising on conflicting variables of recording duration and reproduction speed). Arguments over revenue from playing records, as itself a kind of performance, arise; and Phonographic Performance Limited becomes the agent for collecting and distributing money levied on use of recordings, from 1934 onwards. Microgroove recordings date from 1948; and jukeboxes, occupying a position somewhere between private domestic consumption and social occasions for listening or dancing, are tried out in the 1930s, but only become widespread after 1945. From then on, there is far more widespread licensing of shops, aircraft, ships, etc., for the reproduction of music.

In the late 1940s, too, Columbia Recording Company introduce long-playing discs, following intensive research begun in 1944 for an already envisaged market; and Victor Recording Company's 45 rpm discs appear around the same time, displacing 78s commercially by the early 1950s. Stereo becomes commercially practicable in terms of disc-cutting less than a decade later, and is introduced, with technical standards agreed between manufacturers prior to marketing, so avoiding conflict between systems. (Stereo had been workable on tape at least from A. D. Blumlein's experiments in Britain in the early 1930s, and in that form provided the basis for the much later multichannel recorders.) Shellac is replaced by plastic for disc production, and there is gradual automation of moulding and pressing stages of manufacture. Marketing experiments are made with quadrophonic sound (seemingly a commercial miscalculation–extended 'naturalism', but of a radically non-specular kind, sounds all around and the field for consumption and judgement dispersed); later, there are explorations with audio time-delay systems, also using four speakers, but primarily in this case to simulate auditorium acoustics; research is made towards the video-disc, and forms of combination between sound and vision are pursued (with many continuing developments in all these areas, such as laser-read discs and extended videotape response limits, resolving some of the existing problems of quality deterioration in audio reproduction induced by bandwidth and stylus-wear).

2. Later in development than the gramophone, broadcasting lags not simply in technical development. Through early years of coexistence, the gramophone is said to lead in fidelity of reproduction, with broadcasting overcrowded in the 9000-cycle bandwidth limitation of medium and long wavebands, resulting in restricted upper frequency limits. It is only in the 1950s, with frequency modulation and so a broadened bandwidth, that radio competes in music reproduction–so extending, by way of the technical development, the possibilities for reproduction of concert music (previously difficult for broadcasting, as for the gramophone, because of its relatively large dynamic variation). FM is made stereo, subject to problems of distance and signal direction.

The technical questions are continually overlapped, however, with those of social policy. There are competing conceptions of centralised cultural direction and commercial enterprise in Britain, but the latter more or less exclusively in the United States. The BBC charter of 1927 takes over from the powers of an association of wireless manufacturers of 1922, and so there is a complex link up, here as elsewhere, between initial interests of research and manufacture, and prospective returns from consumption. Composers and performers themselves are at first reluctant to accept broadcasting, fearing lost revenue. But this initial rejection is later translated into pressure for 'needle time' restriction, in order to encourage the broadcasting of 'live' musical performance and limit the proportion of airtime given over to reproducing gramophone records.

'Pirate' radio stations outside the centralised control appear later, during the early 1960s (Radio Caroline, the first Radio London, etc.), but are curtailed again by legislation in 1966, and followed almost exclusively for a time by the BBC service (remodelled to accommodate criticisms and assimilate certain features of the commercial broadcasting styles of other countries). Subsequently a legislated network of hospital, factory and local commercial stations is introduced, including BBC local radio; and in the BBC there is divided audience planning and monitoring, split between the competing conceptions of commercial success as an index of popular demand, and earlier cultural valuations retained in practice for Radio 3. These conceptions reflect a longstanding argument within broadcasting in Britain over notions of culture and commercial interest. In the earliest moments, this argument resulted in controls on programming as itself a form of saturation advertising of music, dance-band leaders being restricted from using announcing microphones or repeating numbers, for example, when their concerts were first broadcast from cafés in the 1930s. But in revised schedules of the late 1960s, there is concession to the operative logic of radio popularity judged by sales, in the introduction of the playlist and sales charting.

What might be seen in these conflicting conceptions of broadcasting are certain necessary qualifications to accepted accounts of the effect of radio on musical performance and musical forms. Early certitudes that broadcasting would simply stimulate additional demand for existing kinds of concert performance, on the strength of familiarity gained in the home, need to be modified to include the acknowledgement that, alongside this undoubted effect, more general expectations of what is musical entertainment are altering, and will continue to alter, in response to the styles of radio broadcasting which are adopted.

Such alteration in response can be seen in a number of respects. Radio programmes, for example, increasingly consist of a series of linked musical items. This is a programming emphasis shifted away from approximation to concert format (continuing only in most of the 'classical' music schedules), into a primary concern for musical continuity, which is achieved through voice-over announcements (used in preference to breaks for introducing pieces), through twin-turntables, and through connecting jingle-cartridges. Musical entertainment has come to be conceived, as a result, widely as a continuously available commodity, controllable by volume and movement of the dial, rather than to be arranged and awaited, acknowledging practical constraints on music-making. And where audiences are planned for and created according to kinds of material selected for inclusion ('day-time radio', jazz and soul shows, ethnic minority programmes, and so on), musical idioms will develop at least partly in reflection of constraints of airtime.

Conventions of new musical forms follow both from technical and programming pressures. There is dynamic range reduction, to enhance the effect recordings will have when reproduced on the radio (compressors being used to even out widely varying dynamic levels of orchestral pieces); there are duration constraints, so that new compositions will not cut across programming requirements; and there are optimum record-cutting levels, frequently based on aspirations to stand out from the continuum of broadcast sound on account of volume. More generally, too, there are the calculations of memorability, reflected in 'hook' lines and musical structures of composition: conventions of a 'popular' music created in response to technical and institutional pressures as much as to audience demand.

3. Later than both gramophone and radio broadcasting in its development, tape recording alters mechanical musical reproduction over a range of the practical processes of music-making, as well as with regard to distribution and consumption. First technical explorations come very early, with the Dane Valdemar Poulsen's realisation in 1899 (the 'telegraphone') of existing theoretical conceptions of French inventor Paul Janet. But it is not until the later development of the electronic amplifier that tape machines become workable for their envisaged professional and domestic application. Indeed, the most extensive exploratory work is conducted during the 1930s and 1940s—with a view in the United States to the film industry, and in Germany under Fritz Pfleumer for I. G. Farbenindustrie, with an interest concerning political applications indicated by Hitler.

Further phases of large-scale manufacture and distribution occur (substantially as an outcome of research conducted for military purposes) in the later 1940s and 1950s. Retail sales of reel-to-reel recorders from Bauer, Marconi, ITT, etc. begin in 1956, operating first with steel, then later magnetic tape. Cassettes and eight-track cartridges appear commercially much later, in the mid 1960s (following US inventor George Eash's conception of the mid 1950s and subsequent work by William Lear and by Philips in Holland). Dolby noise reduction systems follow soon after. More recently, there has been a limited move back to metal tape, for improved frequency-range response and hiss reduction.

The most immediate effect of tape recording for the listener, however, is indirect: not so much the facility for home compilation of selected material by dubbing, which comes later, as a major revision at the recording stage of the manufacturing processes employed to make discs. Recordings before magnetic tape were made on a wax disc, from which all copies were subsequently produced. Even in early forms, magnetic tape offered new technical possibilities of overdubbing, as well as of splicing together small sections of recorded material; and this extended editing facility had implications from the outset for the logistics, expected proficiency and complexity of recorded performances. At first, too, tape appears to have lowered the capital investment necessary to record music for distribution, by minimising the time previously lost in unusable recording and rehearsal. Coupled with a contemporaneous increase in demand for records, this reduced necessary capital investment led to a sudden, if unsustained, growth in the number of, and diversification between, commercial recording companies.

But with the introduction of multitrack tape machines and mixers in the 1960s, audio recording processes undergo another major shift, acquiring additional capabilities for recording musical parts independently; and there are related extensions of editing and overdubbing, refined and modified throughout the 1970s (8, 16, 24 tracks and so on). These extended capabilities reshape the recording process quite fundamentally. Musical parts need no longer all be played simultaneously, and errors can be deleted from any single part, subject to continuing problems of cross-talk between tracks. Digital recording begins in the late 1970s, overcoming some of the outstanding problems of distortion and noise, and virtually supplanting simultaneous experiments with recording direct-to-disc. And all these recording facilities are made mobile, transportable by lorry, so that recordings might be made on location; packages of special effects, too, are arranged to be portable, in rack systems. Computerised mixing desks are also devised, simplifying the multiple operations necessary to amalgamate the various musical parts in an edited overall balance.

But these extensions in the technical capabilities have effects on wider processes of music-making, massively increasing once more the investment required to make a disc. The frequent practice develops of capital reinvestment by rock musicians and others in personally owned and domestic studios. In one direction, this economic dimension of the recording process and technology leads to the famous studio designs, competition and investment of the 1970s. But in an opposing perspective, it is challenged in the initiatives of punk and New Wave music of the mid 1970s: in DIY ('do-it-yourself') record production and distribution, and in a renewed simplicity of domestic four-track and Revox recording.

It has been one insistence within these initiatives that sound quality as an aim (despite attractions of the studio editing facilities as themselves a new resource of composition) should be kept within practical limitations of budget; more importantly, too, that in the context of declining record sales during the 1970s and a corresponding contraction in the commercial recording industry, it may be only musical forms able if necessary to by-pass expensive studio technology which can retain choice in decisions concerning composition, performance or distribution—rather than handing these over to capital and policy requirements of the existing major recording companies.

Reproduction and Performance

As can be seen from these brief remarks, it is in all cases a difficult task to chart the interests and demands of capital, control and initiative, in line with which the new musical technologies have so far been organised. Yet what is evident from even these isolated observations is that variations in the means and techniques for producing music are important beyond familiar questions of royalties and copyright, or of diminished opportunities for musicians of live employment.

Whilst these questions retain significance and urgency, they lead in two directions, which, often confused, block much present thinking and activity. In one direction there is the need to protect music-making as an activity against patterns of social forces increasingly accentuating an expanded market for music centrally produced and distributed. This direction leads importantly towards needed initiatives concerning new and more numerous institutions for performance, as it does, too, into complicated questions of reward and property which arise when music is considered as primarily a commodity. In the other direction, there is the seemingly conflicting urgency to acknowledge and meet the challenge of possible extensions and redirections of forms and relations of music which may be brought about by drawing on new techniques and equipment during a moment of major transition. Such responses will most importantly direct–as well as contest or block–changing conditions of interest and practice.

Tensions between the directions of argument will only be negotiated through future activity and deliberation. These cannot be foreseen in any detail. For the moment, what seems crucial is to avoid two opposing dangers of simplification. On the one hand, there is the simplification of seeing the mechanical, technological innovations as exclusively and decisively progress (for the musician, the fetish of the latest instruments and effects, and for audiences, the changing fashions of new sounds–fuzz and wah-wah in rock music of the 1960s, syndrums and drum-machines, synthesisers, etc.). On the other hand, there is the simplification of renouncing new instruments and recording machines on the basis of an idealising view of fixed or 'natural' means of making music (imported 'ethnic' instruments, or the 'natural' human voice accompanied on acoustic guitar; principled disregard for editing or overdubbing techniques, on the grounds that these modify performance; categorical preference for overhead pair as opposed to 'close' microphone procedures, etc.).

Differences between performance and reproduction are more than simply those between a transcription and an original. What distinguishes them is importantly the precise inscription in recording, but not in performance, of coordinations and intonations of the body and voice, movements exactly caught and represented in a stabilised, reproducible form. It is this relative fixing of relations and contradictions of performance which most clearly signals that recording has largely taken on functions long served by notation: now recording also creates–out of movements and activity–the impact of a fixable image, whether of the performer (as often in 'popular' music), or of the work (as most often in 'classical' music). The first record to sell one million copies comes as early as the 1920s; and significantly this is simultaneous with a major commercial contraction in sheet-music publishing. Together these produce as regards the record—as earlier in respect of notation—a transition from a primarily *mnemonic* form (preserving songs already known through performance) into a formative or *prescriptive* one (announcing new songs and making them known).

As products for sale and for distribution, records become relatively unimportant individually, both as artefacts (they are simply multiply-produced pressings), and as musical occasions (they are directly exchangeable, by selection on the turntable, and are frequently heard in a continuous sequence or programme—as on the radio or in discotheques). But it has been one of the importances of jazz and rock music to make evident and explore divergences between processes of production, manufacture and consumption by way of recording and editing, and performance constrained by importantly different pressures (such as those of municipal regulations governing the hiring of halls, of transporting equipment, or of advertising). Divergence and discrepancy between the contemporary forms of making music continue to be frequently obscured, nevertheless: at once by expectations that musical 'works' are devised primarily to express the human 'experience' of the composer rather than in relation to any material conditions of production or address; and by a continuing overlap between performance and recording which is often designed to reinforce advertising and sales.

This latter pressure is especially significant. Despite all evident contrasts between them, live performance and recording are repeatedly made to coincide or overlap, in a virtually complete reversal of understandings of the disc as 'record' or remnant of performance. What is represented on stage can become primarily a version of something that can be heard on disc and is for sale: songs or musical pieces, with accompanying gestures as embodiment of a performing persona, exactly a 'set' of rehearsed numbers and images. Extravagant embellishment and extension in live music are accordingly often derived from, and return to, known pieces—whose anticipated melodies, figures or riffs are frequently acknowledged in apparently spontaneous applause and appreciation. These familiar themes which serve to introduce extemporisation can indeed be valued for their capacity to serve as creative impetus. But alternatively, they can be heard, when coupled to improvisatory digression, as merely disappointing failures to live up to a pristine virtuosity, balance and finish of the record. Themes, lines and the familiarity they can produce underscore one dominant kind of live performance of music. Without the familiarity they provide, on the other hand, there is currently little social impact for 'live' music; and in this sense, recording and broadcasting contribute to a continuing, major redefinition of performance and improvisation.

Forms in Transition

Much of what is currently understood as *form* in music depends upon technical and institutional conditions of performance and reproduction such as these. Organised frequently around constraints of envisaged application, musical forms involve figures of repetition, contrast and similarity planned and executed with regard to anticipated patterns of perception and memory. As means of hearing works far more frequently than in earlier circumstances of performance, and in exactly repeated form, mechanical reproduction of music has created new possibilities for familiarity with past works and forms–organised initially though these may have been for different occasions and kinds of attention. On contemporary musical forms and experiment, it has also imposed new and different bearings and constraints, such as those of radio format, or the duration restrictions necessitated by fidelity deterioration on disc.

These properties of recording, at least partially determining contemporary musical forms, have been scarcely acknowledged as such within conceptions of artistry and expression prevailing in representations of 'classical' music, however. In these, they are usually alluded to only in the context of an increased range of comparison between those versions of works which *have* been made available by the technology: Solti's Wagner, Boult's Brahms's Symphonies, etc. These are renderings to be discriminated between on the basis of musical knowledge and taste. Yet the new range of comparison at the same time undermines something of the primacy of intention and origin to which appeal continues to be made, as especial attention is drawn to crucially defining details in the mediating processes of performance, recording and reproduction.

Listening to recorded music has clearly offered, for all such anomalies, the possibility of an increased familiarity with musical structures, making it possible to grasp arrangement and proportion through repeated listening. Indeed, this capability for familiarisation has become one important educational argument in favour of the gramophone as a teaching aid. But alongside such pedagogic application, fundamentally new potentialities for listening may also be glimpsed in tape and disc, through conceiving listening as precise recollection and anticipation: knowing sounds, movements and instrumental textures by memory and familiarity, rather than by extrapolation from perceived patterns, symmetries and learned musical structures. On the basis of this new kind of listening, musical forms might develop which are no longer dependent as before on recognisable formal pattern and arrangement. And it can be predicted that such extensions to, and modifications of, presently available forms of music will continue to develop alongside other more foreseen applications of the technology: use of tape-recorded material within the compositional process; new collaborations between recording engineer, producer and instrumentalists in mixing (the drop-in as edit; the cross-fade, panning and phasing; patterned echoes and delay effects); sounds no longer planned to conform to 'natural' acoustics, or to resemble in their stereo image the actual lay-out of performers and instruments, etc.

What it is safe to assume more generally is that new styles and genres will be created in accordance with, and in dissent from, technical resources for music-making and listening. In particular, what can be seen at present is the expansion, from origins in promotional film and television campaigns during the later 1960s, of new rhetorics of combined sound and image in the music (and especially the rock) video. Simply on the strength of comparison with earlier developments of gramophone, radio and tape recording, what seems likely is that the coming decade will witness (certainly in Western Europe, the United States and parts of South America, the Middle East and Far East) a settlement and redefinition not only of video's technical and commercial specifications, but also of the conventions and detail of its most widely adopted forms and applications.

In this current frame of argument, the important references are to the broadest definitions and conditions of the emerging forms, rather than to immediate antecedents or stylistic controversies alone. For within a diversity of local initiative and experiment also exist centring and restrictive larger pressures. And in this respect superimpositions of sound and vision in rock or 'pop' performance are exemplary. Over and beyond formal innovation and extension has existed an insistent and constraining rationale of social identification and counter-identification, linked to broader organisations of capital investment, media impact and rapid commercial obsolescence. Conflicts between these disparate interests can be traced through rock music's various forms (the single, the album, the album cover, the rock film and rock opera...). Equally, the new forms and formulae of sound and vision in the video will be met not by limitations of the technology simply, but of the technology in its more complex relations of investment, legitimation and control. Here the technical resources and their effects—as also the alternatives—are most intricately interwoven. Potentialities of practice during moments of transition will very often have to be created in opposition to first or prevailing assumptions and definitions of usage.

'Musica Practica' or Musical Image?

There is an interesting point of return here to certain of Barthes's preoccupations concerning the body in music. For Barthes, there is a transition (around the time of—and extensively through a mythology of—the figure of Beethoven), a transition away from a music of participation towards an ideal of the work. That transition, he says, has been doubled back in recent developments: 'To find practical music in the West, one has now to look to another public, another repertoire, another instrument (the young generation, vocal music, the guitar).'[9] In such terms, new music since the 1950s may be taken to have begun a partial shift away from stabilisations of the work; it may be heard less as indication of genius or inspiration, than as playing and activity, questioning investments of finance and fascination in the performing situation for a listener and a viewer. But there is also a marked movement against this shift, which needs to be taken into account. Unremarked by Barthes, this movement is clearly visible, nevertheless, in the coming of the video and video-disc. Images of identity and fashion for the performer are provided through recorded dramatic, music spectacle—through forms of what might be thought of as musical *portrait* and *portraiture*. In representations of music-making and performance of this kind, the element of play in music is subjoined to a new, contemporary investment in vision, and in technically extended realisations of the image. For the present, these may fix currencies of sounds, but they may also close eyes to music seen more broadly as practice.

Part II
Two Case Studies

5 False Relations and the Madrigal: An Alchemy of England's Golden Age in Music

Golden Age or Period of Transition?

(i)

It is frequently affirmed (but is no less striking on account of repetition) that music and song in England, rising in turmoils of the Reformation and dispersing in currents of the 1620s and 1630s that were later consolidated in the Restoration, passed through a brief period of excellence, a Golden Age. The view occupies a place in conceptions of a national musical heritage: much subsequent history of music, the reasoning goes, has its centres of activity on the European continent, and more recently in the United States and elsewhere; and in this sense an important individuality of achievement can be identified in the late sixteenth and early seventeenth century music in England, shaped as it was by forces at that time crucially different from those prevailing on the adjacent continent.

In this view, the music of Byrd, Morley, Wilbye, Weelkes, Gibbons, Dowland, Campion and others is taken to constitute a significant historic eminence. Besides marking much of the history of the solo ayre, later to develop through changes and extensions of the period into the early concert song and recitative, the period includes virtually the entire output of English madrigal writing, as well as major beginnings of instrumental music. Together, these varying developments constitute the earliest configuration of a secular, national music in England, with composition able to draw for lyrics upon poetry, according to Edmund Fellowes for example, 'at a moment when the national literature reached its actual high-water mark'.[1]

Against such an emphasis on exemplary artistic achievement, madrigals can appear to have been an innovation subject (like much contemporaneous theatre and secular poetry) to both religious and serious intellectual criticism, and indeed to have been linked more to an ideal of amateur domestic performance than to one of composition for public display. But they must be recognised, nevertheless, to have been effectively the first musical form distributed and popularised by an expanding commercial music publishing industry. And so, even in explicit insistences on participation, practice and on ephemerality (in Byrd's famous preface of 1588, in Morley, and elsewhere), the madrigal can come to seem retrospectively a decisive moment in a much larger movement towards self-consciously artistic musical composition—and so in this sense as an instance of measured individual creativity, rather than simply a transiently popular formula for entertainment.

(ii)

Originating as an isolable form in the Netherlands in the 1530s, and moving from there, by repute, with itinerant musicians into Italy where it develops throughout the century, the madrigal first appears in England in the form of copies of Italian works and collections procured by Nicholas Yonge in the 1580s, and performed daily ('for merchants and gentlemen') at his home. From these, a selection is published in 1588, including one English composition, Byrd's 'The Fair Young Virgin'. Favour is sought for the publication, nevertheless, on account of its derivation from fashionable, imported Italian models, in the title *Musica Transalpina*. And this way of claiming authority for editions is subsequently used by Thomas Watson for his *First Sett of Italian Madrigals Englisshed* (1590), as well as by Morley for *Canzonets, or Little Songs to Foure Voyces: Celected out of the Best and Approved Italian Authors* (1597). Yonge himself publishes a further collection under the same title as his first collection a decade later, in 1597.

Assessed on the basis of publication—and allowing for

irregularities such as a lag for production between activity and publication–the period of ascendency and decline of the madrigal can indeed be seen to have been brief. Only three collections are published before 1590, followed by a swift expansion, with over twenty collections between 1590 and 1610, after which occurs a correspondingly rapid diminution of activity: only nine collections between 1610 and 1620, and little madrigal publishing after this date. Yet in even so abrupt a fashion, there are intersections with other forms at a number of points, especially with existing ecclesiastical forms such as the motet, and with the secular solo song, or ayre. Indeed, within changing nomenclature, madrigals were on occasion not distinguished from these ayres–both frequently specifying alternative options for voices or instruments. It is the areas of debate and directions of initiative at points of intersection between these forms which can be made most to illuminate issues importantly involved in vocal music of the period, as well as in retrospective assessments of it. For what can be seen in these intersections is a revision of many of the techniques and premisses of music-making which, held during the later medieval period, continue to underlie even the innovative form of the madrigal late in the sixteenth century–a revision which establishes many of the directions of music later in the seventeenth century.

(iii)

The ayre alongside the madrigal, then, appears at the end of the sixteenth century combining words and arrangements in local devices and ornaments of underlaying (or 'setting') of words, as well as in polyphonic, later harmonic arrangement. Usually a song for one voice, the form has come, largely through Elizabethan and Jacobean currencies, to have strong associations with the lute. For the Elizabethans and Jacobeans themselves in turn, that connection appears to have been important as a speculated linkage with the classical 'lyre' and with pursuit of traditions of accompanied classical recitation. The lute is linked directly by Campion, for example, to the lyre and to Orpheus in a poem praising Dowland in 1595: 'ad Io. Dolandum./ O qui sonora coelites altos cheli/ Mulces, et . . .', where one of the Latin words for lyre, 'chelus', is used to describe Dowland's instrument, the lute.[2]

It is evidently this hypothesised classical origin, alongside certain technical features of the lute's construction (particularly its number of strings and resources of volume), which recommended the instrument to late sixteenth-century musicians, although the historical derivation has later been traced through Moorish influence and diffusion of Provençal music in England in the course of the late Middle Ages, rather than in descent from classical Greece.

Again to judge by publication, beginnings of the ayre as a popular form can be traced to Dowland's *First Booke of Songs* of 1597, although there appears to have been some performance of related song-forms, as well as some translation of instruction manuals in lute tablature well before, certainly from the 1570s. Indeed Dowland himself is known to have been already widely popular as a performer in the late 1580s; and in 1597 he cites existing pirate editions of his work as one pressure on him actually to publish: 'There haue bin diuers Lute-lessons of mine lately printed without my knowledge, falce and vnperfect.'[3] Significantly, too, this aesthetic innovation and new commercial speculation marked by Dowland's collection are virtually simultaneous with the acquisition by the London printer Peter Short of a font of lute tablature–the technical development clearly contributing, alongside the influence of William Barley's *Newe Book of Tabliture* of the previous year, to the sudden increase in sales of lute music and instruction manuals immediately before the turn of the century.

(iv)

Nor are such intersections between madrigal and ayre, and between these forms and the new publishing techniques and machinery, solitary evidences of combination and amalgamation in the period. The ayre itself gains currency across several earlier traditions: that of consort songs with first-part melody and contrapuntal accompaniment, later gradually transformed into the new declamatory style of Lawes and Lanier; that of earlier ballads and dance songs, including chivalric elements influenced indirectly by the Troubadours, and linking to other traditions of ballad; and that of lyrical poems (referred to by Campion in 1602 as 'such verses as are fit for *ditties* or *odes*, which we may call

False Relations and the Madrigal 123

lyricall, because they are apt to be soong to an instrument, if they were adorn'd with convenient notes'.[4] And, like the madrigal in this respect, the ayre occupies widespread but tenuous social esteem. Campion considers his songs to be too insubstantial for publication, whilst conceding to Rosseter's wish to combat existing pirating; but in publishing he nevertheless invites purchasers to improve on anything unliked. Again like the madrigal, too, in a number of collections of ayres instrument parts are provided, so that anyone wishing to join in would be able to play along.

This diffidence displayed in publication appears to indicate less any unpopularity of the forms than simply particularities of their social estimation, in contemporaneous religious, moral and aesthetic debate. As regards popular esteem, on the contrary, Dowland becomes famous throughout Europe, for example. When he is appointed lutenist at the Danish court in 1598 his salary places him among the highest members of the royal household; and many of his songs subsequently become known and widely repeated (or improvised around in 'divisions') as musical 'standards', in addition to being alluded to in correspondence of the period, in other songs and in plays. It is only in the second decade of the new century, as the fashion for the solo ayre is gradually displaced in England by taste for enlarged ensembles, for spectacle, for dancing and masques, that Dowland comes to be paid less as a solo performer on lute than either composer or set designer for the new court entertainments. And at this time, John Wilson, a composer within the later fashion, becomes analogously if less spectacularly popular, and is transported in thirty-four years across social divisions from city wait, through court musician, to Oxford professor of music.

(v)

Such brief currency of the musical forms, and their repeated intersection, indicate what is at very least a latticing in the gold of that age. Indeed what is glimpsed in the historical variation is less a patterning of ideal forms, than one of pressures and contradictions within changing social relationships, through and against which the music of the late sixteenth and early seventeenth centuries develops.

One wider view of some of the history of these musical

developments can be taken from a series of social movements in England between Reformation and Restoration: particularly in changes between two major, framing phases of social upheaval, the Dissolution of the Monasteries in the late 1530s and 1540s, and the revised land settlements of the 1640s. In the 1540s, the arriving gentry which had been created in land redistributions following the Dissolution took on some of the outward forms of position of their predecessors, whilst introducing a new emphasis upon money and acquirable indices of prestige as against more traditional prerogatives of birth and line. And that process of a symbolic, as well as economic, reordering of class relationships is continued when a largely new gentry of the 1640s is established among those buying or acquiring mortgage of royalist property, and among soldiers granted confiscated property in payment–as well as again during resettlements of the Restoration. In addition, the earliest of these land redistributions can be seen to have been contemporaneous with a major increase in demand for wool and cloth, which increased the power and influence of country houses and widely displaced the monasteries as prevailing institutions within a more general order of religious, educational and class authority. What gradually dislodge the conventions of this order, and so initiate a phase of major social and symbolic restructuring in the regions, are relations of an ascendent agrarian capitalist economy. In these, fixed income sectors of the population indispensable to that earlier social order (such as teachers, priests and fixed tenancy landowners) suffered a relative loss of position.

It is something of the changing perceptions of social relationships created in these successive movements which is negotiated in the new musical and other cultural forms of the late sixteenth and early seventeenth centuries. In a concentration of pressures and influences, a new arrangement of musical instruments, forms, institutions and audience is produced following the Restoration in the works of Purcell and Blow, evidently more modern and more familiar to present listeners than what preceded. Involving more than a series of outstanding composers and growth of individual musical forms, the alterations within the period have large-scale repercussions through later conventions and techniques of music-making, clearly discernible when the activity and achievements of the Elizabethan and Jacobean composers and musicians are seen with the relative detachment of a sufficient temporal span: transformations of musical form, of notation, of principles of harmony and accompaniment, of techniques of text-setting, and of institutions of performance and finance.

(vi)

As much close up on the musical activities of the period, as in broad comparison, changes and reforms such as these indicate a need for consideration in terms of variation and transition, rather than of achievement according to accepted and stable criteria of judgement. Representations of the Golden Age involve major idealisation, forging out of a historical period of ranging opinions and practice an image of national identity and heritage; and it is exactly material circumstances, tensions and motives—the very bases of subsequent debate, alternatives and understanding—which are obscured in the process of abstraction.[5]

There are dangers, for example, in passing without acknowledgement over relations between aesthetic conventions, such as those of Arcadian pastoral, and their surrounding material circumstances. (In this instance, what is lost is any suggestion of the direct, material force of enclosure, urban expansion and economic upheaval occurring in the cloth trade, as demand for wool—at least before saturation of available markets and relative slump of the 1550s—exerts pressure on access to open spaces and pasture, focusing unprecedentedly competing needs for 'natural' land.) In idealised renderings, broader questions of music's social currency are channelled into considerations of human expression alone. But it remains important to return that expressive or artistic human potentiality to its specific social contexts, in order to combat ways in which passing of time can expose and accentuate words and music as a collection or pantheon of isolated 'texts', when social circumstances at the time prevailing have themselves altered.

Unsurprisingly it is largely in processes of later reconstruction that much of the idealisation of a Golden Age occurs, linked directly to positions on a more general cultural and political history. Disappearing almost completely by the 1650s and 1660s, owing largely to the political effectiveness of Puritan objection after 1642 as well as to consolidated tastes for monody in music, madrigals themselves, for example, are only revived by the Madrigal Society after 1741; and it is in the century following this rediscovery that the process of reconstruction and production of the distinctive national history most actively take place, exemplified in Thomas Oliphant's editions of Weelkes, Campion and Farnaby during the 1830s, or, later again, in A. H. Bullen's *Lyrics from the Song-books of the Elizabethan Age* in the 1880s.[6] Even so, many works remain unknown until a still later period of scholarship, that of Edmund Fellowes in the 1920s. But in Fellowes's editing and commentary, too, a definite position on national reconstruction continues, that of minor canon at Windsor Castle. From this vantage a music largely of the Chapel Royal can well bespeak crucial beginnings of a national culture burnished as the gilded shell of Elizabeth and Leicester.

Whereas later unearthing of Elizabethan music might have sought less to mine gold amid dross than excavate an historical formation of important national transition, the directions of account have almost exclusively served other ends: preserved in collections notated without dynamics and for variable realisation, the musical works have come to be thought of as centrally concerned with devices of illustration, such as the famed simultaneous major and minor thirds in harmony of the 'false relations' of the madrigal. In such exclusively technical characterisation, what is immediately obscured about the madrigal and ayre is their specific responses to wider social relationships.

Madrigal and Madrigalist: Employment and Publication

> Music divine, proceeding from above,
> Whose sacred subject oftentimes is love,
> In this appears her heavenly harmony,
> Where tuneful concords sweetly do agree.
> And yet in this her slander is unjust,
> To call that love which is indeed but lust.[7]

Written by Thomas Tomkins, a madrigal composer less well known than Morley, Wilbye, Weelkes or Gibbons, 'Music Divine' was published in 1622. By this time, it is generally agreed in music histories that the madrigal's currency had passed, that achievements within the form were retrospective, even conservative–the real focus of initiative and activity having transferred to expansions of the ayre into dialogue, accompanied consort song and recitative.

Much of what is most importantly in question in the madrigal form can be read, nevertheless, from Tomkins's piece, published in his only collection of secular songs. But in order to see the forces and directions in comparison with which Tomkins's madrigal has come to be considered retrospective, or the innovations, still recent in 1622, which it belatedly records, it is useful to append to this opening statement two more detailed parentheses:

1. 'Written by Thomas Tomkins, a madrigal composer . . .'

Born in 1572 in Pembrokeshire, in the family of another Thomas Tomkins, father of two sons both called Thomas and organist at St David's Cathedral, Tomkins the composer of 'Music Divine' is himself known to have become organist at Worcester Cathedral in the late 1590s. In 1621 he was made organist of the Chapel Royal. Later, after madrigal composition in England is effectively

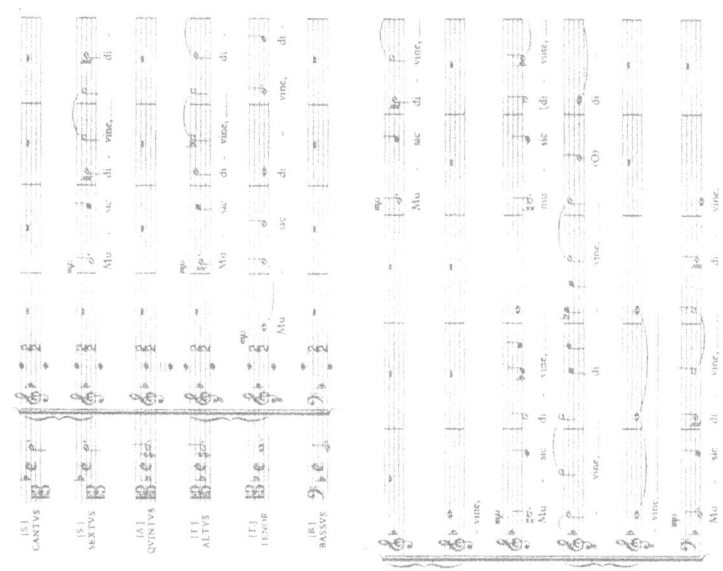

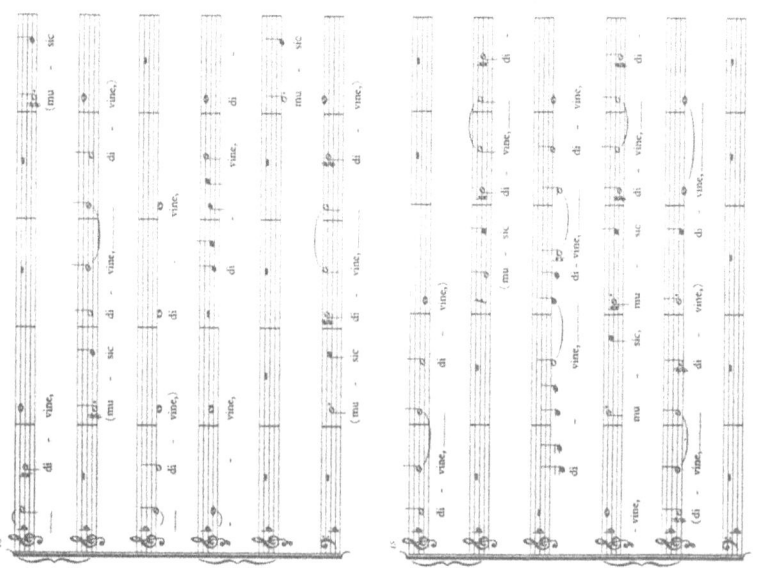

False Relations and the Madrigal

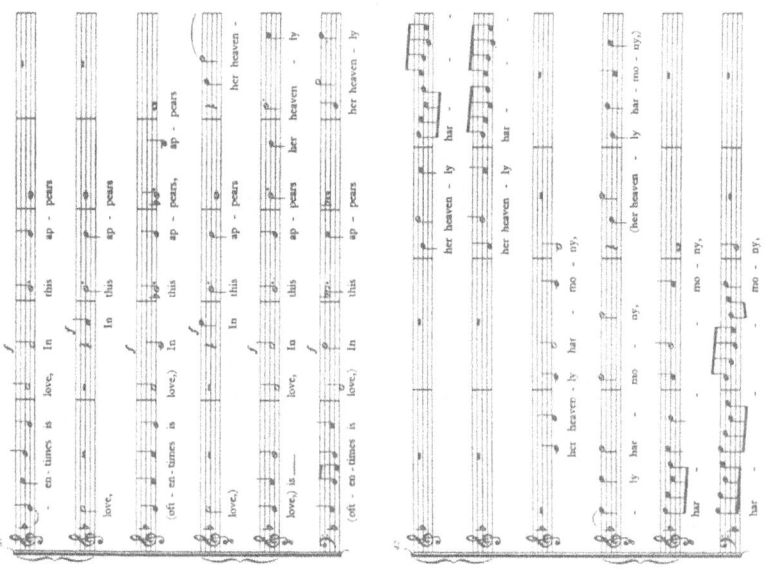

Conditions of Music

False Relations and the Madrigal

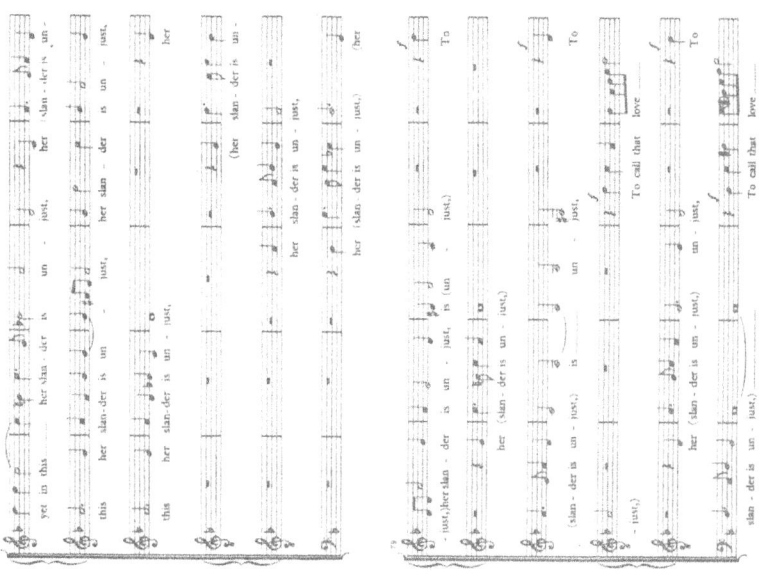

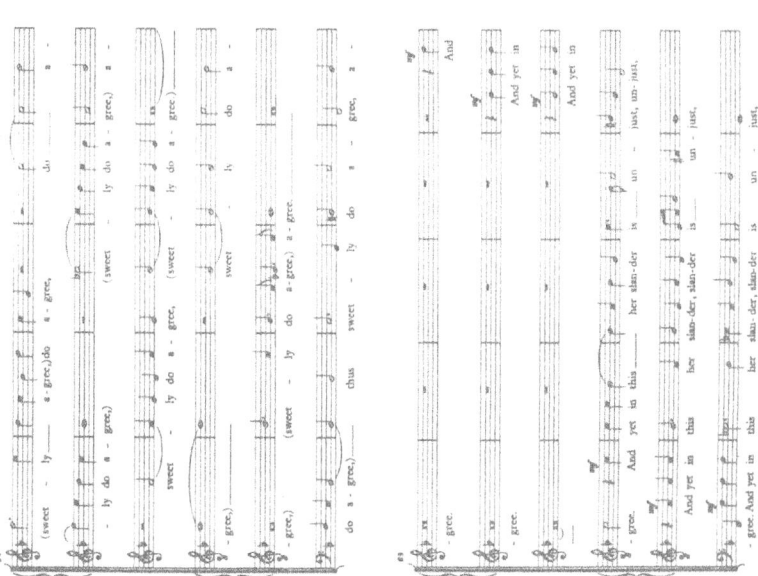

over, Tomkins becomes Composer-in-ordinary to Charles I in 1628, dying well into the mid seventeenth century in 1656.

Several details merit consideration in even so minimal a sketch. The successive redistributions of wealth and major social realignments of the period between Dissolution and Civil War had a direct and major impact upon conditions of musical employment, and so on the kinds of music musicians were expected to make. Changing conditions of music can be seen to have been met with a variety of responses, precipitating new musical forms. It is one direction of these responses which leads into the popularity and commercial success of the madrigal towards the end of the century. And so, since madrigal composition occurs in England only within this narrow historical period, it is possible to speak of a 'madrigal composer' only in respect of certain quite specific social and institutional relationships.

There is a pattern, frequently repeated throughout the late sixteenth-century and early seventeenth-century music in England, in Tomkins's professional career as a musician. A significant decline in musical activity can be identified between the 1540s and the 1580s; but this is followed by the new influence of madrigals, established through different institutions from those of earlier music—so contributing to a movement increasingly away from ecclesiastical ceremony towards secular entertainment for the country and city houses.

Although church music continues to be referred to as the most serious and respected musical activity, there is also increasing activity in other areas: in the theatre; in 'catches' or three-part rounds, often enfolding sexual double meanings in the changing vocal textures of their polyphony; in the improvisatory 'fancy', and extemporisations of 'divisions' on familiar melodies; and in music for civil occasions performed by municipal waits (originally watchmen who incidentally played—usually shawm or hautboy, sometimes sackbut—but who appear to have gradually become, by the end of the fifteenth century, musicians who incidentally watched). Indeed it is only in the later historical constructions that the new secular music of the madrigal and ayre, and instrumental forms for virginals, viols and lute, come to be considered of more significance than the fancy, or Catholic and Anglican church music.

The major reorientation of music-making brought about in these social transformations occurs unevenly between the existing professional and amateur groupings of musicians, however. A number of prominent religious musicians, for example, are displaced from their earlier employment in years following the Acts of Dissolution, from 1536 onwards (Henry VIII's, 'Forasmuch as manifest sin, vicious, carnal and abominable living, is daily used and committed amongst the little and small abbeys, priories and other religious houses of monks, canons and nuns...'[8]) But many of these musicians are later absorbed in court employment in the Chapel Royal (a 'chapel' being a vocal group, usually an itinerant ecclesiastical entourage for a noble or monarch, with The King's Musick the royal instrumental counterpart). Tallis, organist at Waltham Abbey until it is dissolved in the 1540s, then joins the Chapel Royal, and is recompensed for his redundancy; William Byrd, organist at Lincoln Cathedral, joins the Chapel Royal in 1569, despite his Catholicism. And the pattern of professional movement continues later in the century, with Thomas Morley, organist at St Paul's Cathedral, joining the Chapel Royal sometime after 1592, and then later, Tomkins himself, moving from Worcester. Crossing over in this way between church and state appointment, the English madrigalists were involved in an important professional amalgamation. Unlike their Italian counterparts, who in general enjoyed security of academic musical employment—and with a notable exception in England in Wilbye, who was retained as a regional, domestic musician—the English madrigalists frequently worked for the court while continuing to compose for the church. For them, writing madrigals itself remained in almost all instances a subsidiary or even recreational occupation.

In addition, the disruptions of the 1540s and 1550s had effects beyond those of immediate redundancy. Music in general suffered a wider decline in terms of the education of choirboys in schools; and so there is a consequent deterioration in singing proficiency in the church. But despite this contraction, there are simultaneous signs of expansion. Teaching of music continues in the universities (at Oxford and Cambridge music becomes an isolable topic in the curriculum around the mid fifteenth century, with many of the sixteenth-century composers, such as Dowland, Morley, Farnaby, Gibbons, Pilkington and Tomkins himself, holding degrees). Outside the formal institutions, musical education also continues, in direct supervision: most famously Morley and Gibbons under Byrd, and Byrd before them a pupil of Tallis.

Alongside these movements of influence and tuition for church, court and university, there is a broader reorganisation, too. What can now be seen as in general a transition from liturgical and feudal relations of music-making into the new court and aristocratic entertainments of madrigals, dancing and masques, can also be observed across more local pressures: that, for example, of diminishing busking and itinerant musical work, with minstrels (although having formed a company or guild in the course of the sixteenth century) increasingly compelled to seek domestic service in country households of the growing rural nobility, as well as, more frequently, in musical employment as waits, following the practical restrictions of required licensing enacted by the Vagrancy Laws of 1572 and 1603.

2. '... "Music Divine" was published in 1622'

Conditions for circulation of madrigals reveal further changes in relationships of music-making, in this case ones brought about by changes in the means through which the new audience of court and country houses was addressed from these altered positions of composition. If it reflects a rise in estimation of music in England that signed compositions are rare before Dunstable (still exceptional in this respect in the early fifteenth century), patronage and sales widen during the sixteenth century nevertheless to include an enlarged rural nobility, government officials and merchants and entrepreneurs. Almost without exception, madrigals are dedicated to nobles and courtiers, with an exemplary dedication in Morley's *The Triumphs of Oriana*, 1601–3 to Elizabeth I, each madrigal ending, 'Long Live Fair Oriana'. And Tomkins's own *Songs of 3, 4, 5 and 6 Parts* of 1622 are not only dedicated as a collection to Lord Pembroke in the conventional way, but each piece is also dedicated individually, including to a number of fellow composers.

But although publication of collections of madrigals marks a significant innovation in circulation of music (music publishing having begun in England on a smaller scale much earlier in the century), this extended distribution is not without restrictions imposed by monopolies awarded by Elizabeth: in particular, by one granted to Tallis and Byrd in 1575 ('Knowe ye, that we for the especiall affection and good wil that we would have and beare to the science of Musicke and for the advancement thereof, by our letters patent dated the xxii of January, in the xvii yere of our raigne have graunted ful priviledge and licence unto our welbeloved servaunts Thomas Tallis and William Birde two of the Gentlemen of oure Chappell, and to the overlyver of them, and to the assignees of them and over the survivor of them for xxi yeares next ensuing, to imprint...'[9]).

The monopoly in practice included both the printing of notated music ('so many as they will of set songe or songes in partes, either in English, Latine, Frenche, Italian or other tongues that may serve for musicke either in Churche or chamber, or otherwise to be either plaid or soonge...') and–at the time of greater commercial interest–control over music paper ('they may rule and cause to be ruled by impression any paper to serve for printing or pricking of any songe or songes, and may sell and utter any printed bokes or papers of any songe or songes, or any bokes or quieres of such ruled paper imprinted. Also we straightly by the same forbid...'[10]).

Exploitation of the monopoly appears intermittent, however. Tallis and Byrd engage printer Thomas Vautrollier (who himself becomes involved in a series of litigations concerning publishing projects other than those of music), and publish *Cantiones Sacrae* in 1575, including seventeen pieces by Tallis. But they publish little after this. When Tallis dies in 1585, the monopoly passes indirectly–and after a lapse of two years–to Thomas East (sold by Byrd, the 'overlyver'). Later again, it is awarded to Morley, in 1598 ('Wee geue and graunte fulle priviledge and licence vnto our welbeloved servaunte Thomas Morley one of the gentelmen of our Chappelle...'[11]).

Such details of publication suggest at least a general correspondence between control of publishing and the efflorescence of the madrigal in England, and indeed it might be said that it is during the lag between Tallis and Byrd, and then Morley, that maximum activity occurs. After this peak of publishing, there is some reduction; but despite currents of parliamentary hostility to monopolies from around 1597, reaching greatest impact in the proclamation of 1603, there are further dispensations regarding music, including one to William Barley in 1606, as an assignee of Morley. Yet if music printing became suddenly profitable between 1590 and 1610, when secular works and especially the madrigal begin to be circulated in England (Scotland following a different and later development in this respect), there is nevertheless a lull between about 1610 and the 1660s, followed by the new and distinct phase of activity around John Playford and others, in the reign of Charles II.

The Madrigal and Religious Controversy

(i)

These changing conditions of musical employment and distribution are clearly a minimum necessary reference within which to be able to speak at all about Tomkins's 'Music Divine' as part of an age or fashion of madrigals in England in the late sixteenth century. Equally clear, however, is that the particular social and aesthetic changes which 'Music Divine' directly addresses are neither of these. On the contrary, the madrigal is conspicuously more concerned with renegotiations of position taking place between the religious and the secular in music. And so to broach questions either of its form, or of its effects and later revaluations, it is necessary to consider this concern more directly.

When 'Music Divine' is considered peripheral to the mainstream of development of the madrigal, it is not taken to be simply late–with only the one significant collection published after it, Pilkington's *Madrigals and Pastorals of 3,4,5 and 6 Parts*, of 1624. More than this, 'Music Divine' is often viewed as somehow an interesting but refinable impurity, at the very limits of the madrigal form. As such, it is often only Wilbye and Weelkes who seem the 'great' English madrigalists, because they are most 'purely madrigalian'. And in such a perspective, there are indeed clear elements of corruption and crossover in 'Music Divine', in its explicit and accentuated overlap with music of religious celebration. But equally within such a perspective, of course, it is difficult properly to identify madrigals at all, unless by appeal to Italy, and to origins: compositions by William Byrd deflect into psalmes and songs; those of Gibbons appear to have been intended and composed as consort songs, later rearranged for voices; and those of Morley are by convention mainly balletts and canzonets.

But such pursuit of essential attributes of musical form can obscure everything that is most interesting and exceptional about Tomkins's piece—namely, that at the very end of the period of madrigal writing in England, it crystallises elements of what had been a troubled combination throughout: differing conceptions of formal properties, purposes and practical relations of music compounded when earlier secular and religious musical forms (such as the popular ballad, the motet, the round and the Catholic mass) intersect with imported Italian influences to produce the short-lived phenomenon of English madrigalian polyphony.

(ii)

Tomkins's composition is not only a dramatisation of this intersection, and the conflicts across which it is formulated, however. It is importantly a taking of position, defending a long-standing doctrine of music as of direct divine provenance against the then recent view of musical activity as appropriate to secular purposes.

The point of argument is clear in the madrigal's closing lines,

And yet in this her slander is unjust,
To call that love which is indeed but lust.

In this detail, 'Music Divine' reiterates what is already, in 1597, an active concern in Morley's dialogue of instruction, *The Plaine and Easy Introduction to Practicall Musicke:*

Master: '... for you must understand that few of them compose Motets, whereas by the contrary they make infinite volumes of Madrigals, Canzonets, and other such aireable music, yea, though he were a priest he would rather choose to excel in that wanton and pleasing music than in that which properly belongeth to his profession, so much be they by nature inclined to love ...'
Polymathes: 'You play upon the homonymy of the word 'love', for in that they be inclined to lust, therein I see no reason why they should be commended.'[12]

Disagreement such as this around meanings for 'love' is marked in philosophical and literary disputation throughout the sixteenth century, in reworkings of medieval scholastic arguments, and in humanist (avowedly 'classical'), intellectual positions. By changes taking place in meanings of the word 'slander' in the late sixteenth century, however, Tomkins's defence of the religious conception of music has subsequently been slightly obscured. Present senses of 'slander'—as malicious misrepresentation or defamation—coexisted in the sixteenth century with at least two other senses; and although already obsolescent, these produce what is now a seeming ambiguity in Tomkins's composition. The two earlier senses in question are, first, 'slander' as fame or rumour in general, unprejudiced by connotation of injury or malice, a sense not widely recorded after the middle of the sixteenth century; and second, 'slander' as shame, discredit or source of dishonour. It is only the adversative effect of the clause beginning 'and yet', and the elliptical adverbial implication of 'but' in 'but lust' as 'merely' or 'only', which continue to make clear Tomkins's position: that use of music for secular, 'lustful' subjects is a discredit to divine music.

(iii)

It is arguably this defence in 'Music Divine' of sacred composition as opposed to treatments of pastoral and sexual love, which can make the madrigal seem retrospective by the 1620s. By this time, the main impetus of debate in music appears to have moved from such concerns, crucial in the mid sixteenth century, into consideration of declamatory style, on 'classical' principles, for music in masques and as accompanied dramatic dialogue.

But it is not so much Tomkins's position itself which is surprising or interesting, as the ways in which conflicts and contradictions surrounding the madrigal form in general, and in question in the madrigal's intersections with other contemporaneous musical forms, are enacted within it. Consider, for example, the first twenty-one bars, setting the words 'music divine', before the madrigal advances with 'proceeding' in the first soprano/cantus part in bar 22. It is only later in the lyric that preference is specified between at least three at this stage ambiguous, available senses of the opening two words, 'Music divine . . . ': first, that music comes from and so reflects God, that is, the medieval Christian doctrine of a music of the spheres; second, that the music being performed is religious, devotional music; third, that music is metaphorically 'divine', that the opening bars themselves give exquisite pleasure. The ambiguities of the phrase are also underscored in opening harmonies, as initial motions within G major collide on the second uttered syllable of 'divine' with an altus part E♭ in the third bar, suggestive of a minor key against the simultaneous C in the second soprano and G in the tenor (an effect with approximate correspondences in bars 6 and 9).

(iv)

What is crucial in Tomkins's suspension of ambiguities—in distinctions between 'love' and 'lust', as in these senses of 'music divine'—is more than verbal felicity. The play on multiple meanings reflects not only the 'homonymy' of wit suggested by Morley (though it certainly does this), but also an important conflict of meanings concerning social and religious considerations of music.

Certainly a range of positions characterise sixteenth-century musical argument and practice with regard to music's relationship with religion. Extensive condemnation of music and musicians can be seen to have followed the Dissolution of the Monasteries, for example. But if music was widely associated with, and condemned alongside, supposed excesses of the Catholic Church, against this are simultaneously put forward a succession of general cultural arguments, as well as specifically musical ones. In this way, there were arguments throughout the later sixteenth century, extending into the seventeenth century, not only concerning what music should sound like, but in what circumstances and to what purposes there should be any at all.

Whilst in general the new ecclesiastical positions of Reformation England served primarily to extend earlier requirements of musical simplicity demanded, in other forms, by the Catholic Church for nearly two centuries, when seen in comparison with the newer humanist positions, the arguments also involved a contradiction between conceiving Italy as the seat of Papism, or as a new secular, 'classical'—and so refining—influence. Within the agitations for reform and restriction themselves, in addition, there were distinct and frequently conflicting currents: Anglicans requesting an amount of simple singing and accompaniment; Puritans in favour of monophonic, syllabic, rhythmically static, vernacular metrical psalms and use of familiar congregational melodies; Calvinists against all music except psalm-singing. And each variation was itself subject to controversy within the religious movement. In later and more direct prohibitions and restrictions, Puritans seek to suppress elaborate church services and to disband choral groups, but–as well as appearing to have suffered a general reduction in support during the 1590s–fail in 1617 to obtain compulsory suppression of Sunday sports and music (the throne itself moving in favour of these entertainments). Indeed the Puritan opposition to music only regathers its political force later, in the 1630s, and only later still acquires dominant influence over music, during the Civil War years.

Music by Metaphor and Rhetoric

(i)

Disagreements over religious use of music indicate that there is more in question than 'homonymy' in the opening line of 'Music Divine'. But the ambiguity which suspends the social divisions and arguments appears to be itself resolved in position in the second line, in the words 'proceeding from above'. These constitute a conventional appeal to a divine origin of music–an appeal reflected in the literalism of 'above' being consistently set, between bar 23 and bar 28 (with one exception in the tenor part in bar 26) as a rising interval, either a full octave or fifth, indicating that music from heaven issues from a higher plane.

Such illustration–perhaps the best-known feature of madrigal composition–clearly accords with suggestions in Part Three of Thomas Morley's *Plaine and Easy Introduction to Practicall Musicke*. In the section 'Rules to be Observed in Dittying', Morley describes techniques by which music should be 'disposed' or 'framed', according to the nature of the words: in respect of musical properties such as pace ('... if the subject be light you must cause your music go in motions which carry with them a celerity or quickness of time, as minims, crotchets, and quavers; if it be lamentable the notes must go in slow and heavy motions as semibreves, breves, and such like...'); or in respect of harmony ('... when you would express any word signifying hardness, cruelty, bitterness, and other such like make the harmony like unto it, that is somewhat harsh and hard, but yet so that it offend not. Likewise when any of your words shall express complaint, dolour, repentance, sighs, tears, and such like let your harmony be sad and doleful').[13]

Indeed, with regard to the setting by Tomkins of 'proceeding from above', there is a specific instruction in Morley,

> Moreover you must have a care that when your matter signifieth 'ascending', 'high', 'heaven' and such like you make your music ascend, and by the contrary where your ditty speaketh of 'descending', 'lowness', 'hell' and others such you must make your music descend; for it will be thought a great absurdity to talk of heaven and point downwards to the earth, so will it be counted great incongruity if a musician upon the words 'he ascended into heaven' should cause his music descend, or by the contrary upon the descension should cause his music to ascend.[14]

When considered in comparision with earlier forms of imitation in music (dominantly in medieval England that music should reflect proportions inscribed in the world by God), this form of literalism in 'Music Divine' as in madrigals generally–now seemingly a form of extremely conventional symbolism–takes on importance as a decisively new individualism of expression. Whereas in earlier religious music ordained scales and intervals would indicate God's harmony, in the techniques of Tomkins's madrigal compositional devices create a musical demonstration or argument in defence of the divine conception of music. In this sense both a religious traditionalism, and a degree of modernism, can be seen in the position Tomkins is adopting.

(ii)

That critical divide between an order of sounds determined already by God, and one to be established and directed by human creativity, has a wider social currency in the period, too, than as a technique of composition alone. It serves as a recurrent metaphor or rhetorical figure of wider dilemmas and conflicts of social order, a figure which lies behind much of the allusion to music in Shakespeare, and which continues, linked to new accents concerning the human voice developing in the solo ayre, into later writers, including Milton. Richard II, for example, famously laments,

> Musicke do I heare?
> Ha, ha? keepe time: How sowre sweet Musicke is,
> When Time is broke, and no Proportion kept?
> So is it in the Musicke of mens liues:
> And heere haue I the daintinesse of eare,
> To heare time broke in a disorder'd string:
> But for the Concord of my State and Time,
> Had not an eare to heare my true Time broke.
> I wasted Time, and now doth Time waste me... (V.v, 41–9)[15]

What is rhetorically in play in this passage is a movement of argument from disorders in practical techniques of music (errors of timing and pitch or 'proportion') to conceptions of social order and kingship which are similarly prey to disruption. Unsettlement of musical aesthetic is taken to illustrate a far wider breach in social relationships. Correspondingly, alongside appeals to this earlier order can be found rhetorical arguments that outside or beyond a 'concord' and consequent moving effect of 'music' lie only cacophony and revolt–for example in *The Merchant of Venice*, when Lorenzo, discussing properties of music with Jessica, affirms:

> ... naught so stockish, hard, and full of rage
> But musicke for time doth change his nature, —
> The man that hath no musicke in himselfe,
> Nor is not movd with concord of sweet sounds,
> Is fit for treasons, stratagems, and spoyles;
> The motions of his spirit are dull as night,
> And his affections darke as *Erebus*
> Let no such man be trusted: marke the musicke. (V.i, 81–8)

What becomes clear in such divisions around conceptions of music is that the apparent modernisms of the madrigal figure only contradictorily, across dilemma and nostalgic retrospect. Indeed, perhaps the most celebrated English madrigal of all, Orlando Gibbons's 'The Silver Swan', ends in one such retrospect to a more stable and worthy age, 'More geese than swans now live, more fools than wise.' Or again, the uncertainty of the period can be illustrated by Morley's complaint against performance of motets for their musical qualities, but without their words. This appears to have been one response in practice to problems of adapting already existing musical compositions either from ecclesiastical to secular function, or from Catholic service into a reformed national and religious identity linked to a new national language of religion and culture, English.[16]

(iii)

Around such varying viewpoints, what happens in the successive constructions of the new national, secular music is that existing conventions and practices are combined and reformed alongside more remembered fashionable, imported forms. When there is said to have been an unprecedented consciousness of 'humanity' and 'nation' in the sixteenth century, what lies behind this, as regards processes of secularisation in music and in the madrigal in particular, is a range of concerns: on the one hand, concern with a broad 'political' view of national identity (exemplified in Morley's collection *The Triumphs of Oriana* being brought together at the very end of Elizabeth's reign); on the other, a more local preoccupation with the individual's existence and with reproduction, in representations of sex and death visible everywhere in Elizabethan lyric and song. And the two frames of perception meet incidentally on occasion, as in madrigalian allusions to virginity (e.g. in Byrd's 'The Fair Young Virgin', 1588). Such allusions make simultaneously a reference to sexuality, to religion (Mary, the virgin mother), and to political succession (Elizabeth, the unmarried monarch).

Imitation and Ornament

(i)

Musical imitation or illustration as argument, rather than simply as secondary reflection, is one practice, then, of a significantly new articulation of individual, church and nation in the madrigal. In contradictions and conflict it combines Italian influence with a reworking of existing medieval traditions. And it is the display of such tensions and amalgamations—more than appeals to a stable perception of music or of divinity—which is most interesting in Tomkins's madrigal.

Ambiguities of the opening words 'Music divine . . .' are resolved within the first line itself. But a contradiction between cultural meanings for divinity, love and music continues nevertheless, in collocation of 'sacred subject' and 'love' in the second line, where possibilities of divine and sexual love are equally in play. It is clearly this ambiguity which is drawn upon later, in the last line, in order to achieve the resolving distinction, when remonstration is made against calling 'that love which is but lust'. Moreover, this later move from suspension of meaning in ambiguity to resolution can be seen musically in details of the setting of 'love'. In all instances before bar 42, and in all five parts, 'love' is set to a single, undecorated note. After the decoration of 'heavenly harmony' with an elaborate melisma in and after this bar, however, 'love' is set without exception by a melismatic quaver decoration, whereas 'lust' is set with a single note value. This creates a consistent distinction—from the middle section of the madrigal onwards—between the divine and the secular sense of 'love', in properties of setting as well as in implied value.

(ii)

This form of musical 'literalism' or 'imitation', working as an important source for distinctions of meaning and value, is clearly significantly different from that simply of pace and pitch suggested by Morley, which appealed to familiar lexical meanings. Tomkins's settings constitute a resource for distinguishing senses of words, rather than simply for reproducing a stable property of meaning in a secondary, conventional device.

Such a constitutive agency in what is usually taken for incidental aesthetic decoration can be seen elsewhere, too. There is a play established between meanings for words of the lyric and the music's immediate sensory effect, for example. This play, between a level of established reference and a reflexive allusion to the practical enunciation of sounds, has the effect of creating an entertainment of performance in suspensions between those levels. It has already been illustrated, in the first line's third sense of 'music divine': that music is metaphorically divine in precipitating exquisite pleasure. It can be discerned, too, in the long quaver sequences of 'heavenly harmony', which in a parallel motion in thirds are the first quaver movement of the madrigal, and appear after an accentuatedly homophonic setting of 'in this appears', so acting out musically the argument about music they conduct. It can be detected, again, in the homophonic and rhythmically regular successive chord progressions (F, B , single harmonic pivot chord of Dm modulating into A, then D, G...), which set 'where tuneful concords'. These lead, by way of this series of concords, into the following sequences and parallel motion of 'sweetly do agree', closing by way of a plagal cadence (already connotatively ecclesiastical in the late sixteenth century) back into F.

(iii)

It is clear that such devices of setting involve considerations more than simply those of pronounced illustration of a musical harmony specified in the lyric. Shifts between a level of reference and one of enunciation create for the madrigal a suspension and lack of finality analogous to that created by the relative dissonances or 'bindings', or by the false relations themselves. The differing kinds of suspension serve collectively to accentuate the subsequent resolution and taking of position which is achieved in the final close.

This property of the madrigal can be clarified by referring again to the couplet which especially plays between the levels of enunciation and reference to produce what is for the piece an important oscillation of meanings,

In this appears her heavenly harmony,
Where tuneful concords sweetly do agree.

These lines can be heard or read to mean two importantly different things. First, that, in principle, where there are circumstances in which pleasant concords are produced, then a celestial harmony is indicated. (In such an interpretation, 'this' is taken to be functioning as a cataphoric co-reference to the entire relative clause 'where tuneful concords sweetly do agree', and 'where' is considered in a function, more frequent in the sixteenth century than later, as a relative pronoun approximating to 'when . . .' or 'in circumstances in which . . .'.) Alternatively, the lines can be taken to mean that there is in the actual production of the specific concords of Tomkins's composition the epiphany of a sponsoring, celestial harmony. (In which interpretation 'this' is taken to be functioning deictically, referring not forward to the relative clause and so to the fact or condition of God's harmony, but exophorically, to the very music which is being made; 'where' introduces not a restrictive relative clause specifying circumstances or detail which identify 'this', but a non-restrictive relative clause, amplifying an already established deixis.)

The distinction is not an unimportant or gratuitously technical one. What is significant about use of musical illustration to cross between imitation of meanings in the lyric, and appeal to direct demonstration of properties enacted in enunciation of the words, is that the revelation which is to underpin Tomkins's traditional 'divine' conception of music as God's creation is referred to different auspices. In the first interpretation, it is referred to the divine order; in the second, substantially to an achievement of the human creativity of the composer. Importantly in this second construal, it is the active, human agency of the musician in his service of God, rather than a general property of sounds which reflect God, that creates the effect of revelation. Meanings for word and voice are less pre-given by authority and ordained harmonic proportion (as they were dominantly in plainchant and other medieval musics), than established through the composer's own production of meanings in discourse. And instead of offering music directly to God as celebration by way of reflection, this play of levels generates interest or pleasure in the very process of making meanings, as well as in alternating between suspension and irresolution, then later meaning and definition. In movement between these two conditions, it is not only meanings for words which are unsettled and remade, but also the positioning, within larger social frameworks of meaning, of the performer. Paradoxically, it is this property of entertainment explicitly in making and remaking meanings which has been remoulded in contemporary, complacent appeals to meanings stable beyond revision or reform: the national musical treasure.

(iv)

Exploration in the madrigal of suspensions and resolution through dimensions of composition other than those of harmony is not confined to Tomkins's singular genius. It can be seen in numerous other pieces: as for example in Wilbye's setting of 'Adieu, Sweet Amaryllis', where a definite focus of contrapuntal embellishment attaches to the setting of the words 'to part'. These words indicate both the disruption or partition of an otherwise settled contentment of the lover lamenting loss of his mistress, and also the active singing in parts which leads towards compositional resolution.[17]

Alternating between dissonances and cadence, this recreation of meanings for the self can be seen to work as a formula for reclaiming selfhood from disruptions of pain and desire. So it is unsurprising to find in Morley an emphasis on an important role for cadence in establishing resolution: 'Lastly you must not make a close (especially a full close) till the full sense of the words be perfect.'[18] And in madrigalian practice, phrases are overlapped and rhythmic devices utilised, so that no suggestion of an end prevents this concluding moment; for this purpose too, false cadences are used, 'which we commonly call "false closes", being devised to shun the final end and go with some other purpose'.[19]

Whilst deferred resolutions of this kind in madrigals need to be seen alongside continuing interest in fa-burdens and other elements from the earlier forms which intersect in madrigal composition, what is evident, nevertheless, is that the resolving and resettling effect is primarily for performers. Madrigals create a very particular position of appreciation. Active performance is required to understand the words, on account of simultaneous occurrences of conflicting syllables on any isolated beat. It is largely this effect, like that exploited in the catch or created in the syntactic disruptions introduced by dislocated repetition of phrases of the lyric, which propels the madrigal towards cadential resolution of its counterpoint, where the overlapping parts, at times contradictory in sound and meaning, are made to rejoin in sense and agreement.

In conditions of performance in the late sixteenth and early seventeenth centuries, actual 'reading' of madrigal lyrics is likely only to have taken place during singing; and in this respect, madrigals appeal to a limited position for the individual within an overall musical arrangement which only emerges when the partbooks are brought together in collaborative performance. Whilst it seems almost certain, despite this, that the lyrics did become widely known through repetition and reputation, it is only with the ayre, with ceremonial masques, and later with opera and concerts, that the seemingly required position of active, communal participation is widely replaced by one of specialised performance and spectation.

Madrigal, Ballett and Ayre

(i)

As conventional, symbolic imitation, the madrigal's illustrative devices appear individualistic and humanistic in comparison with earlier techniques. Meanings arranged in composition, more than appealed to as part of a superordinate cosmological system, most distinguish the madrigal as an innovative form. But this new linkage of music with the person of the composer is itself undergoing forms of revision during the late Elizabethan and Jacobean period, revisions brought about by technical innovation in the ayre and monodic declamation.

It seems paradoxical, of course, that concerns of the individual which are explored musically in the madrigal should appear initially in properties of overall composition and for group realisation, rather than in solo activity within the group. It is really only in developments of the solo ayre that expressive compositional techniques are made to correspond closely with features of a leading, single musical part; and in this movement of style, the madrigal's inclusion of the individual voice as a subordinate element of composition and group realisation is gradually displaced from its short-lived eminence. Yet in detailed comparison between madrigals and ayres, important relations between the points of argument surrounding the role of the individual voice, and larger notions of music, society and religion within which these arguments emerge, can begin to be revealed.

(ii)

Points of contact and divide between madrigal and ayre can be approached by considering the famous madrigalian techniques of using dissonance to express pain. These are well illustrated by a series of suspensions in the first line of Weelkes's, 'O Care, Thou wilt Dispatch me'; or, to make a comparison again with Wilbye's 'Adieu, Sweet Amaryllis', by the setting in that work of the words 'O heavy tiding'.[20] But to indicate important differences between the kinds of illustration employed in the madrigal, and those of the ayre which effectively displace them during the first three decades of the seventeenth century, it is perhaps best to consider another piece (again one which hardly conforms to idealisations of the madrigal style, but one which is nevertheless composed and influential early in the history): Morley's ballett, 'Fyer! Fyer!' (1595).

(iii)

Published in a set of balletts dedicated to Sir Robert Cecil in 1595, 'Fyer! Fyer!' occurs within a collection based closely but not exactly on Italian works, mostly by Gastoldi, but in this case, on Marenzio's 'A la Strada', of 1584. Not all of Morley's compositions in the collection incorporate features which have come to be associated with the ballett, features such as the fa la refrain or interlude, or the regular dance beat. And so, within the composer's own titles and designations, can be seen intersection and variation (Morley, it seems, in a corresponding gesture added accompaniment parts to his pieces of 1597, and published a collection entitled 'ayres' in 1600 to coincide with directions of changing popular taste).

What it is more interesting to notice in the piece, however, is the way in which certain techniques at that time becoming popular in the madrigal are combined with others, seemingly precursors of later currents. Techniques common in madrigal writing can be seen, for example, in illustrations of pain by dissonances within the polyphonic texture, as in the passage which sets 'Ay me! I sit and cry . . .'. Here, suspensions are accentuated in tied notes and in underlaying.[21] But this form of illustration coexists— even two years before Dowland's first collection of ayres—with a form of imitation now more closely associated with developments of the ayre mostly after 1600, and leading (in expanded form and with extended instrumentation) into the music of masque, recitative and finally into opera and musical concert. Consider the setting of the passage, 'Fyer! Fyer!' itself, or 'O help!', 'O I burn me!', and 'Alas!'. These illustrations, relatively homophonic, are clearly imitative less of senses of words than of the intonational contours and phrasing of exclamation in English; they link performance to declamations of the singular feeling body, rather than to a set of conventional symbolic imitations.

(iv)

What can be traced in this intersection between kinds of musical illustration is one crucial point of transition between madrigal and ayre. More widely, too, a linkage is visible between vestigial patterns of medieval musical practice (continuing nevertheless far later, particularly in church music), and new, humanist developments of the sixteenth and seventeenth centuries (traceable further back to some extent, nevertheless, especially in ballads).

Even the number of vocal parts in the madrigal appears to have enforced a kind of conservatism. In sixteenth-century music, beats were not stressed, as in later European music they have come to be (in a four-beat bar or measure, particular stress will fall on the first and secondary stress on the third beats). Without accented beats, there were no circumstances in respect of which the madrigal required bar markings (these, significantly again, were mostly a development of the early seventeenth century, evidently in response to larger musical ensembles and development of continuo accompaniment during this period). In the madrigal, each musical and vocal part produces local correspondences between vocal accents in the lyric and placings of ictus or stress in the musical phrase. In textures of polyphonic writing, with parts entering and overlapping repeatedly, musical arrangement produces an effect of counter-movements of stress between respective parts which are subsequently resolved at the end of the line or piece.

For performers of madrigals in the present, this variation in vocal and musical stress between the parts engenders the frequently acknowledged difficulty of phrasing, against what have subsequently become conventions of regularised musical accent within the bar. In techniques of the ayre, contrastingly, there is frequently a pronounced correspondence between stressed beats in the lyric and ictus in musical phrase. In a usually singular vocal line, contours are marked out for the progression of discourse according to intonational pattern; and this tends to displace local devices of accentuating and interweaving lexical felicities into a compositional unity across the parts. In this sense, what develops in the ayre is a new technical emphasis: on the one hand, continuing concern with the older kind of overall compositional unity linked to local, lexical illustration (particularly in the 'classic' techniques of Dowland and Danyel); on the other, techniques of simulating properties of intonational and syntactic progression (particularly in later styles and theory of Campion and others). But of course the detail of that transition is historically far more complicated, occurring as it did alongside experiments with and debates surrounding a reconstructed quantitative metrics for English, with accompanying theories of setting by syllable length–subsequently abandoned.[22]

The Ayre and the Singing Voice

(i)

In order to elucidate some of the contrasts in direction between the madrigal and the ayre (and in further comparison with Morley's ballett), it is useful to consider Campion's 'Fire! Fire!', from his *Third Booke of Airs* (1617?).[23] This is an example chosen again late in a movement or fashion–in this case, that of the solo ayre, rising in popularity in England after Dowland's *First Booke of Songes* in 1597, and declining gradually sometime after about 1612, by which time musical interest and experiment appear to have been more directed towards consort performance (especially of viol groups), virginals music and larger ensembles arranged for dancing and festivity.

False Relations and the Madrigal 153

Thomas Campion: "Fire! Fire!", *Third Booke of Airs* (1617?).

Photo by kind permission of University Library, Cambridge.

154 Conditions of Music

Fire, fire, fire, fire!
Loe here I burne in such desire
That all the teares that I can straine
Out of mine idle empty braine
Cannot allay my scorching paine. 5
  Come Trent, and Humber, and fayre Thames,
  Dread Ocean, haste with all thy streames:
  And, if you cannot quench my fire,
  O drowne both mee and my desire.

Fire, fire, fire, fire! 10
There is no hell to my desire:
See, all the Rivers backward flye,
And th' Ocean doth his wavs deny,
For feare my heate should drinke them dry.
  Come, heav'nly showres, then, pouring downe; 15
  Come, you that once the world did drowne:
  Some then you spar'd, but now save all,
  That else must burne, and with mee fall.

False Relations and the Madrigal   155

(ii)

Several points of immediate contrast will be noticed in comparison with Tomkins's 'Music Divine', points more of contact with Morley's 'Fyer! Fyer!'.

First, different techniques of illustration in setting are employed. If in his theoretical work Morley recommended for the madrigal the decoration of lexical and phrase meanings by 'dittying', the illustrative devices of Campion's 'Fire! Fire!' need to be referred rather to new and contrary emphases. In a famous passage 'to the reader' in the first *Booke of Ayres*, 1601, written with Philip Rosseter, Campion opposes Morley's suggestions about illustration and imitation:

> But there are some, who to appeare the more deepe and singular in their judgement, will admit no Musicke but that which is long, intricate, bated with fuge, chaind with sincopation, and where the nature of everie word is precisely exprest in the Note, like the old exploided action in Comedies, when if they did pronounce *memini*, they would point to the hinder part of their heads, if *video*, put their finger in their eye. But such childish observing of words is altogether ridiculous, and we ought to maintaine as well in Notes, as in action, a manly cariage, gracing no word, but that which is eminent, and emphaticall.[24]

What Campion appears to be emphasising in the phrase following 'manly carriage' is a technique within composition of illustrating the voice by way of features of stress and intonation ('no word, but that which is eminent, and emphaticall'), rather than according to madrigalian devices of an older, conventional lyricism. Language, for Campion it seems, is to be underlaid according more to supra-segmental discursive properties than to lexical ones. This shift of interest in setting can be seen clearly in the opening bars, 'Fire! Fire! Fire! Fire!'. Here, the melodic contour underscores the line's exclamatory character, approximating not to a representation of fire, but to the speaker's cry of 'Fire!'.

(iii)

Other revised techniques of illustration are evident throughout the Campion song, too. Consider the ways in which the words 'burne in such desire' are set in line 2, or 'scorching paine' in line 5; or again, the later 'heav'nly showres, then, pouring downe' in line 15, or 'with mee fall', the last line of the lyric. What is noticeable is that the indications of pain or desire, or of upward or downward movement, do not necessarily correspond with dissonances on the one hand, or with symbolically imitative pitch contours on the other. Indeed there is a harmonic resolution on the word 'paine' in line 5, a perfect cadence from D to G; and similarly, the first stanza resolves and ends strikingly on the word 'desire'.

Related to these differences in setting between the madrigal and the ayre are concerns surrounding repetition of the accompaniment for further stanzas of lyric. If setting is to underscore words in the madrigalian manner, repetition of this kind necessitates that words of similar affect must feature in certain slots in each stanza, to reinforce the correspondence between words and their musical imitations. And in certain early songs of Dowland, such as 'Sleepe wayward thoughts' (no. 13, in the *First Booke of Songes*), the stanzas *do* correspond at successive illustrative points in the setting. But consider again in the Campion piece the word 'paine' in line 5. In the second stanza of the song, this cadence corresponds with that of the words 'drinke them dry'—words incongruous with setting if 'paine' were illustrated in the first stanza in the manner recommended by Morley. Or again, 'drowne both mee and my desire', in the last line of the first stanza, occupies what becomes the position of 'and with mee fall' at the end of the second.

Or consider harmonic movements in the song. In the madrigal, as again recommended by Morley, cadence is deferred until the end of the piece, or, if occurring at the end of a line or section, is usually a false close or interrupted cadence, or else is disrupted by techniques that maintain overlap and continuity with a following section. In Campion's 'Fire! Fire!', by contrast, harmonic structure is used not to coincide with overall compositional design to which each vocal part is subordinate, but to support the local syntax (and so relatedly the intonation) of the lyric.

Such concern with using harmonic arrangement to support movements of discourse in melody, rather than to create moving effects of polyphony, can again be traced theoretically. Preeminently, there is Campion's own concern with deriving counterpoint from a bass line, to produce accompaniment systematically according to degrees of the musical scale and underlying structural progression. With this kind of use of harmony to underscore syntax in mind, consider again lines 2–5 of the first stanza. 'That all the teares that I can straine/ Out of mine idle empty braine/ Cannot allay my scorching paine.' These three lines form a result clause, containing a relative clause also introduced by 'that' ('that I can straine out of mine idle empty braine'). This clause (and so also the relative which it embeds) is dependent upon the 'such' in line 2, 'Loe here I burne in such desire . . . (that)'. The accompaniment to these five lines involves a series of harmonic movements which depart from the tonic of the first line (in this case a chord of G), across a series of progressions (in the second line, chords of A min, D,(E), B, E; in the third line, E, A min, E; in the fourth line, A min,(F), E,A; and in the fifth line, A,D,(B),D.(A),G, only returning by way of a perfect cadence, or 'full close', to the tonic at the end of line 5, with 'scorching paine'. Suspensions or passing dissonance function in this way not as an aspect of conventional illustration, but as a property of musical discourse in syntactically structured accompaniment.

In this sense, although the beginning of the stanza has a syntax as complicated as that of any madrigal (and enjambement following each of the first four lines), the musical arrangement works quite differently. It appears less an attempt simply to maintain a propulsive overlap or continuity between lines, as in the madrigal, than one to underline and reinforce syntactic and intonational relationships between words as parts of the speaker's discourse, by way of relations between harmonic progression and features of continuous speech.

(iv)

It is this style of setting which develops in the ayre, and continues into works by Lanier, Lawes and others. Later, too, it continues into conceptions of musical recitative, or simulation of the intoning human voice, in the Restoration composers. Seemingly, it is for qualities of this kind of setting that Milton praises Lawes in the sonnet, 'To Mr. H. Lawes, on his Aires', celebrating accents and formal arrangements of language as discourse, more than according to the communal abstractions of metre,

> Harry whose tuneful and well measur'd Song
> First taught our English Musick how to span
> Words with just note and accent, not to scan
> With Midas Ears, committing short and long ...
> ... the man,
> That with smooth aire couldst humor best our tongue.

Milton's praise for Lawes can be seen in one reference as a reflection on the earlier debates over English prosody of the 1580s. But it can also be seen to have further implications, when considered in terms of the newer techniques of setting words to music. For reflections of divine harmony are put at one remove by inscriptions of human speech in music. That remove occupies a significant place in consolidating certain new definitions of art and politics developing during the seventeenth century, created as human discourse and interpretation are increasingly acknowledged to be active agencies that might challenge a mediated institution of sound and the word.

The Period and its Prospect

(i)

It is combination, then, between properties of the madrigal and those of the ayre (and incorporating elements from the fancy, anthem, service and instrumental music) which produce the new compound forms of early years of the seventeenth century, and lead later into concert and opera. What in general this series of transitions can serve to indicate is a way in which England's Golden Age of music involves a network of conflicting lines of force, rather than a special moment of equilibrium and achievement. And just as that pattern can be followed backwards across the sixteenth century, it can also be pursued forwards, in several ways, across the Stuart years towards Civil War and Restoration.

1. In changed form following Campion and others, the song appears to have acquired the possibility of extended accompaniment, one voice leading, without obscuring words or rhythm. Introduced in England fully in 1612, in Robert Dowland's collec-

tion *The Musical Banquet* (including works by Notari and Caccini), the fashionable early seventeenth-century Italian style of monody on 'classical' principles becomes popular in court circles, more than among a temporarily declining rural aristocracy. Based on a single line sung in free declamatory style with simple instrumental accompaniment and vocal inflection conceived to intensify emotional expression, recitative makes its earliest appearances in England in this form. The process of transition, of course, has a quite specific history. As early as 1601, Rosseter and Campion dedicate their *Ayres* to Sir Thomas Monson, already an advocate of the newer Italian fashions (it is Monson who subsequently educates Dowland's son Robert, later in turn the collector of the first major publication in the new style); and again, records of the King's Musick throughout the period show a high proportion of Italians employed as musicians—frequently between one third and half the total number.

Capable of increased volume on account of extended instrumentation (making 'broken music', that for mixed groups of instruments), the new accompanied consort song for the masques and court entertainments gradually displaces the more polyphonic madrigal. It also displaces the earlier, polyphonic techniques of the solo ayre as developed by Danyel or Dowland. Indeed, Dowland's own spectacular popularity suffers a decline between 1610 and 1620 (recorded as early as 1612, in Henry Peacham's, 'How few regard thee, whom thou didst delight,/ And farre and neere, came once to heere thee sing;/ Ingratefull times, and worthles age of ours,/ That let vs pine, when it hath cropt our flowers', in *Minerva Britanna*[25]). In later ramifications, the style can be identified by increased ornamentation of melody, by rubato accommodating the increased ornamentation, and by accompaniment created, as in Campion, from a bass line—in elementary harmonisation by chords. Finally, the new musical styles of the later seventeenth century arrive properly in England with basso continuo and improvised accompaniment, figured basses being first adopted around 1630.

2. Whilst in the ascendant in this period from late beginnings, instrumental forms remain extensively imitations of already existing vocal forms, or arrangements of dance music such as the pavanne or the galliard (as in the numerous variations on Dowland's *Lachrymae* of 1604). Little attention appears to have been

paid in the earliest instrumental pieces to phrasing, preference being given instead to arpeggios, fast trills and other devices which could outstrip the voice, as well as to chromaticism and displays of technical virtuosity. Whereas there appears to have been only a small market for instrumental music (the pieces generally only circulating among professional musicians), the techniques and practical requirements of instrumental music are extended during the first half of the seventeenth century. But many of the most influential transformations only occur after the Restoration, nevertheless, accommodating new established tonal music for dancing and revised patterns of musical theatre. Some new instruments appear, and there is even a programme of organ-building during the 1630s, simultaneous with rising counter-currents of religious prohibition; there is music for viols (including for lyra viol, in competition with the lute in the first decade of the century, and advocated by Tobias Hume among others, but seemingly disliked by Dowland); there is music for virginals (a seventeenth-century instrument similar to the harpsichord, with strings plucked by plectra). And it is largely the virginals, then harpsichord, which gradually displace the lute in popularity, and so consolidate the move away from earliest instrumental associations and influences of the ayre.

3. These changes in music-making can be seen to be linked to wider alterations in demand, and in institutions of performance. Almost immediately in the new century, for example, in economic conditions of declining incomes among the rural aristocracy and so pursuit of speedy preferment at court, an emphasis of musical activity transfers from the country houses back to London (excepting years such as 1603, when severe plague appears to have depopulated the capital of classes able to travel). Whilst continuing regionally in increasingly elaborate festive occasions, it is mainly in the capital that the new institutions of performance develop, especially through changes in use of music in the theatre.

In the 1590s, vocal proficiency in singing, as well as in rhetoric, was almost certainly an indispensable professional requirement for acting. And there appear to have been fewer than ten specialist musicians attached to any theatrical company, with further assistance recruited as necessary either among court musicians or the city waits. Indeed, it may well have been this practical consideration which established the exceptional degree of overlap between court, municipal and theatrical musical forms in the period.

Even within these conditions of the drama, however, music played changing parts. It linked backwards with antecedents in the mysteries and miracles, whilst being simultaneously reshaped in response to the new tastes for declamatory song and spectacle. The public theatres themselves prefaced performance with a musical concert, and maintained traditions of short interludes between acts, as well as incorporating musical dumbshows within the action (and occasionally a jig for cast and audience after the epilogue)–in these ways appending musical entertainment to the course of dramatic action. In continuation and yet reworking of existing symbolic conventions, too, theatrical music also retained connotative functions: music from below could still indicate infernal provenance (a visual imitation loosely corresponding to illustrative devices of the madrigal); music might signify celebration ('revels' in the comedies, and stage directions, 'Strike up Pipers. *Dance*', etc.); music might herald power (again, the directions, 'Sennet', 'Tucket' or 'Flourish'); or music might indicate strong passion or sexual appetite (as in Cloten's, 'I am advised to give her music a-mornings; they say it will penetrate' in *Cymbeline* (II,iii, 11–12)).

But if the period of public theatres combined existing traditions of music and spectacle, it was itself a brief interlude. (The successive movements have perhaps only come to be so much obscured because of the continuity across them of the Shakespearean corpus.) After 1609, Blackfriars is run by Burbage as a more socially exclusive theatre than the Globe or other public theatres, and it is composers of the newer vocal styles, such as John Wilson and Robert Johnson, who are made resident composers with the King's Men. It is also in Shakespeare's later plays that the new directions of musical taste and experiment become most evident: even the long-standing notion of a music of the spheres is reworked figuratively, as an emblem of social and aesthetic rather than religious design–as presiding power and mystery in celebratory rituals linked to the remote and the exotic, dramatised in song, dancing and spectacle.

Against the background of Stuart masque and drama of the private theatres or other court entertainments, what becomes apparent is a general movement in music away from performance and activity for amateur enthusiasts. Active participation in singing is frequently reduced to that of simply dancing, in a context of more elaborate and prepared techniques of staging. Indeed, something of the scale of these increasingly professionalised performances can be seen in details of Campion's accounts of dialogue and stage machinery, as here of the Lord Haye's masque, of 1607:

> Presently the *silvans* with their foure instruments and five voices began to play and sing together the song following, at the beginning whereof that part of the stage whereon the first trees stoode began to yeeld, and the three formost trees gently to sincke, and this was effected by an Ingin plac't under the stage ... the trees were sodainly convayed away, and the first three Maskers were raysed againe by the Ingin.[26]

In comparison with the traditions of the private theatre and court entertainment from which they emerge, what is distinctive about such masques is the small place occupied in them by narrative, or by direct reference to specific occasion. Rather, they celebrate, in dance and in disguise, the courtier participants themselves, through certain conventions of occasion: performers enter in disguise heralded by a declamation; they dance with each other; they dance with spectators, then they depart. It is centrally these new accents—on scale of performance, visual attention and costume, and dancing—which can be followed through into the new musical entertainments of the Restoration: especially into the concert and opera (with arguably the first being Davenant's *The Siege of Rhodes* (1656), 'A Representation by the Art of Perspective in Scene and the Story sung in Recitative Musick', music composed by Henry Lawes, Matthew Locke and others). The institutions of this music appear themselves to date from slightly earlier than this production, from the late 1630s, when Davenant, poet laureate succeeding Ben Jonson in 1637, is granted royal licence from Charles I to open a theatre for music and masques, becoming governor of the Cockpit Theatre in 1640. But the designs are only implemented (as in the later, Duke's Theatre after the Restoration) under renewed patent, following Davenant's own internment as a Royalist until the mid 1650s.

False Relations and the Madrigal 163

Performance and Contemporary Cultural Argument

(i)

All this evident heterogeneity in Elizabethan and Jacobean musical activity is rarely neglected, exactly, in treatments of England's Golden Age in music. Frequently, even the irregular and haphazard nature of performance and publication is put into active service, and made to affirm that the period was such as to allow artistry to impinge directly on human experience, without mediating institutions of invested value in music to identify or promote its worth. As often, this is the watershed: versions of the past along these lines come accompanied not infrequently by criticism of contemporary forms and practices which are not thought to be 'golden', which can be seen to be troubled by practical problems, divisions and technicalities.

Yet contradictions remain outstanding between taking without detailed explanation the conditions of one period as enhancing creativity and achievement, while considering those of another merely to obstruct, limit or devalue it. Against such filling out of historical preference into often entrenched critical position, it is useful to outline ways in which madrigals and ayres were also responses to larger social and historical processes. Within these, the very breadth and pressure of debate and opinion reveal an important awareness of circumstance and alternative which disappears in images of a 'Golden Age'. When forms such as the madrigal and ayre are represented as being exemplary by comparison with later and current developments, a certain amount of historical fidelity evaporates in the abstraction. But more than this, such selection and preference also contribute to broader positions on a national culture; and these wider understandings in turn underpin usages of the preference to comment on priorities and directions in the present.

(ii)

An unreliability in applying evaluative comparison between past and present of this type can perhaps be illustrated by considering one detail of contemporary realisations of the madrigal and ayre, on disc and in performance: the widespread use of received pronunciation (RP) and close variants on it.

It is often said that domestic performance of music and song was ubiquitous in Elizabethan times; but this appears to need substantial qualification, when levels of literacy, and circumstances of leisure outside the social groupings of court, landed aristocracy and ascendant merchant classes, are taken into account. Often, too, it is observed that there was a significant overlap between musical forms (motet, madrigal, ballett, fancy, division, catch . . .), as well as in practicalities of performance (musicians for court frequently being also musicians for the theatre, and theatre performers overlapping again with minstrels). But even to this, it is necessary to add a reservation: not only did the majority of the English population of the later sixteenth century probably not sing madrigals or accompanied solo ayres, they most likely (certainly outside London and the immediate influence of the theatres) did not hear them either, unless in indirect and copied forms.

(iii)

So the image of the 'Golden Age' recedes. Rather, indeed, there is important continuity between the age in question here and earlier periods of English history. In these, a large proportion of successive generations had only indirect contact with the earlier Latin, French and Anglo-Norman musical forms, when, speaking English only, they were broadly excluded from words and music–the wider participation and influence in many forms only able to begin on any scale after the mid fourteenth century, when English is made the language of court and law. And whilst the cultural exclusion is quite evidently far less clearly marked in the late sixteenth century than in these earlier periods, music was still emphatically determined by a range of social divisions which are far removed from any ideal union of a musical or social Golden Age.

(iv)

If it was language which produced much of the social exclusion

False Relations and the Madrigal 165

from musical activity during the later Middle Ages, there remain of course still active forms of social division in language; and these continue to pass into music. Indeed the obstacle presented by language in earlier periods was not that of a temporary blockage before later certitudes of English and the English. Rather, it involved successive phases in a continuing process of construction and direction. Only later can a single important moment, here the late Elizabethan period, be reviewed as first instant of a specific and now secured national identity. What is interesting about madrigals in particular in this respect is the way they have become attached, arguably more than Elizabethan and Jacobean theatre or lyrical poetry, to representations of a national culture associated with certain forms of class and education. Repeatedly, this has tended to determine the accents and circumstances in which they are reproduced.

Almost exclusive use of received pronunciation, and closely related accents, in recordings of the Elizabethan madrigals and songs becomes problematic in this context. It cannot be maintained that adoption of these accents serves the purpose of a measure of historical authenticity, in the way that usages of replica instruments for early music do. English phonology has changed to the extent that 'authentic' reproduction would entail substantial departures from most contemporary forms of pronunciation of English, and indeed lead to local difficulties of comprehension. As an alternative to this view, nevertheless, it might be suggested that the accent corresponds in terms of social connotation in the present to that of the Elizabethan classes who produced madrigals (simulating not the actual acoustic forms of the address, but its social force as a class voicing). This view, however, undermines much of the very social conservatism to which it appeals. Specifically, it neglects two important considerations: first, the changing regional and class constituency of the Elizabethan and Jacobean courts (the actual *detail* of the revered past); and second, the whole *history* of English language and accent, whose forms and attachments of social valuation were themselves during this period undergoing fundamental reorganisation.

So the problem is a difficult one. Yet perhaps in retreat from the argument's abstraction, an easy resolution might be thought to exist: that contemporary accents in performance do no more than reflect the particular people who are interested in performing the music. But even this appeasing view falters, when brought into comparison with acknowledgements of accent and language as major forces of representation within virtually all other kinds of musical performance, as especially in opera. Significantly, too, the view has to move towards rescinding that most admired property of the English madrigal and ayre: their ability to convey, in music, an important sense of individual experience within stable, overarching definitions and eminence of the English nation.

(v)

It is not clear what solutions might be adopted for these problems of accent in actual performance, other than enjoining at least variety to declare that definition of what is culture or nation is not a single, decisive event, but a continuing process of renegotiation and reform within which present musical practices are an important defining activity. To distinguish patterns of contradiction, debate and change within music of the past is to open avenues for consideration of present activities and their relationship with directions of contemporary society. No model of music isolated from that frame of reference, on the other hand, can serve as an adequate cultural paradigm.

6 Rock Today: Facing the Music

Diversity of Forms and its Implications

(i)

Even provisional definitions of the music which is often referred to as rock (or contemporary 'pop') music, it is usually agreed, are surrounded by diversity and division. There is diversity in respect of genre, in distinctions between rock and roll, rhythm 'n' blues, soul, new wave, reggae or funk (as well as in evidently more evaluative definitions: progressive, punk or underground). There is diversity, too, in respect of the agents or performers involved in these kinds of music, in distinctions between superstar, revolutionary artist or mere popular entertainer. Surrounding these there is, in turn, a more consequential diversity in respect of wider frameworks of explanation: massive extension of an existing consumer leisure industry; radical communication and appeal, and so revolutionary force; or again, rite of adolescent passage into adult life.

It is seemingly variation within local definition and detail which leads towards a familiar disintegration of categories in broader arguments over rock music. Dissolved by discrepancies of musical style, circumstances of consumption and participation, or even anticipated response (domestic listening, dancing, mass audience hysteria . . .), arguments and positions are frequently only restored in failing generalisation. What appears to happen in the conflicting larger frameworks is that against forms of singular and decisive theoretical explanation arise repeated, troubling difficulties of detail, change and contradiction. Through movements and revisions within a single society, as well as in influences between one society and another, what emerges is that the musical forms of what are taken collectively as rock music have interacted, constituting new audiences, and repeatedly acquiring new and altered significances. As a result of these processes, the difficulties of definition reflect a genuine variety of practice, purpose and future possibility. And here the need for thinking about rock music most clearly emerges: importance as regards arguments concerning the music's general cultural position and evaluation, wherever that level of generality is invoked or engaged—as in broad, comparative social argument; importance, too, as illumination of points of detail crucial in structuring practical or technical developments which underlie present and future musical choices, simultaneously exposing an inappropriateness in the singular term 'rock' as a homogeneous and static category.

(ii)

When thinking about rock or 'pop' music what is in question is not simply a well-established corpus of records, performances, groups or images. Unlike television, film or arguably theatre, the forms of this music irreducibly involve an intersecting range of practices, without an obviously assured primary discourse or text. To take the gramophone disc as the 'text' of rock music is to marginalise or dismiss a wide range of activities (such as domestic improvisation, or live performances by pub and club bands) which never accede to reproduction by way of the recording process; it is also to neglect the way in which rock's musical forms have importantly diffused through a variety of technical means other than gramophone recording—'live' performance itself, cassettes, television and film soundtrack, currently 'promotional' videos.

Whilst perplexing as regards establishing an easily identifiable central 'discourse' for consideration, this varied realisation has contributed extensively to rock music's importance as a contemporary cultural form. It is this diversity which ensures that rock music has effects both as a particular corpus of individual works, and as a more general pressure of adaptation and alteration felt in other contemporary forms, such as those of film and television, or advertising and fashion—as well as in the range of musical pieces that come to be widely imitated and adapted as musical

Cut, take and show: 'As regards rock music there is no single, primary discourse or text...'

'standards'. Each of these areas apparently contingent to rock is altered in property of connotation and relative position by movements of a wider 'pop' or 'rock' culture, a culture consisting of clothing design and rhetorics of gesture and linguistic mannerism, as well as of a range of ways of perceiving and formulating human purpose and social relationships.

Regional Comparison: Disco Music in Jamaica, India and the USA

(i)

This broader rock culture is so pervasive–it is often considered 'worldwide' or 'universal'–that it can really only begin to be grasped by way of international comparison and reflection.

It is well known that record distribution and performance (and the markets which accompany them) gradually extended during the 1960s and 1970s, from earliest locations in the United States, Europe and the West Indies, into other countries of Western Europe and elsewhere in the world. This expansion took the form of extended 'world tours' incorporating parts of Asia and Africa, as well as transmitted television coverage and record sales themselves. It is largely on the basis of this expansion that it is sometimes believed that rock music–developing as a 'popular' music, and through an established technology of production and international transmission by radio and gramophone–has created, or is in the process of creating, a potentially universal language or medium of communication, for all people and peoples.[1]

(ii)

As a preliminary, regional bearing on rock music, then, something of a pattern of influence and aspiration operating between countries and cultures can be grasped in particular ways in which a distinctive idiom of disco music becomes popular and of interest in the 1970s in many countries, but across a layered and uneven regional diffusion.

Rock Today: Facing the Music 171

To focus details of this process, a comparison between three recorded tracks is useful: one from the United States, one from India in the East, and one from the West Indies. The three tracks are, first, a recording by the Bee Gees, 'Stayin' Alive' (1977), released as part of the soundtrack of the film *Saturday Night Fever*, produced by the Robert Stigwood Organisation in the United States, and internationally distributed; second, the song, 'Jane Jaan, O Meri Jane Jaan' (1982), composed by R. D. Burman and sung by session-singer Asha Bhosle and actor Kamal Hasan, as part of the soundtrack to the Hindi film *Sanam Teri Kasam*, produced in Bombay for Indian release, with restricted overseas distribution, mainly through Indian expatriate film networks; third, 'Oriental Taxi', by Sly Dunbar, from the album *Sly, Wicked, and Slick* (1979), a solo album recorded in Kingston, Jamaica, by the session drummer more widely known outside the West Indies for performances and recordings with Peter Tosh, Culture, Black Uhuru and Grace Jones, than for recordings in his own name.

(iii)

Certain conventions of musical style associated with the specific idiom of disco music are evidently common to these three recordings—similarities of necessity established in (and important in respect of) instrumental arrangement, rather than, as has become almost without exception the standard in analyses of rock music, in terms of lyrics.

Some of these recognisable paradigms might usefully be isolated as illustration:

(i) a loosely common tempo and rhythmic pattern (crotchet around 140 per minute), establishing a pace selected for dancing, and on occasion generated in recording by a drum-machine for precise speed; that pace sustained largely by a bass drum pattern of four beats to the bar (and in this respect distinguishable from many counterparts in rock and roll forms, where it is usually the first and third beats of the bar which, subject to variation, are accentuated); remaining constituents of the drum pattern made up in variations of Puerto Rican salsa figurations (semi-quaver/sixteenth-note hi-hat; snare drum on beats 2 and 4 of the bar), though again with certain important counterpointing variations, usually linked to structural changes such as movement between verse and chorus of a song.

(ii) certain textures of instrumentation, such as the use of phasing and flanging effects on guitar and/or bass guitar; electronic synthesising drumheads (syndrums) producing percussive notes descending in pitch after an initial attack (an evident relative modernism signalled by the technical availability of these effects only during the early 1970s).

(iii) occasional use of repeat echo effects, frequently linked to the rhythmic pulse, and developed extensively initially in reggae 'dub' music from the early 1970s onwards.

(iv) particularities of musical phrasing, such as phrases beginning and ending on unstressed beats or between beats, as already in many kinds of Latin American music, and in jazz at least from bebop in the 1940s onwards.

(iv)

These are selected, paradigmatic features of 1970s disco music. But with regard to these and other conventional stylistic elements, the three tracks can be noted to differ in a number of significant respects. The Hindi film song utilises conventions of this style evidently developed first in the United States (syndrum effects, style of bass riff and aspects of bass pattern—elsewhere in the soundtrack, phased guitars and bass). But equally, these stylistic elements are superimposed upon existing properties of arrangement, such as the distinctive melismata of Hindi singing, as well as upon Western musical idioms incorporated at an earlier date, largely by way of previous Hollywood soundtracks. (This would apply, for example, to features such as the horn arrangements, resembling those of big band styles of the 1930s, or to the drum breaks, which differ from those usually employed in disco music; or again, to the recurrent espressivo unison melodic string-writing or upward chromatic modulations before the final verse.)

What is in general clear in the kind of amalgamation indicated here is a development of musical styles which does not take place exclusively on the strength of preference and selective imitation.

Forces are clearly involved beyond ideals of international communication or 'appreciation', which are terms stripped of specific positions of understanding or response, and reduced to undifferentiated 'reception'.

In one sense, the disco music style is for the Hindi soundtrack simply one more in a series of adaptations of Hollywood and other American cultural forms. Yet because of locally existing resources and institutions, each successive incorporation serves to produce distinct new musical forms within India. As a compound of influences, the film music differs not only from the Hindi soundtracks of earlier periods, but also from Hindustani ragas, as well as from more recent, 'ghazal', forms of the late 1970s.[2]

In such processes of amalgamation and combination, musical styles do not simply import meanings or associations for forms intact; they recreate these through patterns of local influence and cultural aspiration. In this illustration from India, for example, influence through imitation and cultural aspiration can begin to be grasped in relation to the lack of indigenous institutions of rock music, as well as in the context of wider national and political circumstances. The latter include policies of import restriction, and insistences upon 'independent' cultural self-generation, which have one effect of enhancing both the economic and symbolic value of such cultural forms (including examples of rock music) as *do* come to be imported from the West.

(v)

Contrastingly, whilst there is in the Sly Dunbar recording stylistic resemblance of a different kind–direct quotation of a musical phrase from the Bee Gees' 'Stayin' Alive' (eight bars, introduced twice)–this does not appear to indicate cultural imitation in a corresponding way. On the contrary, the exact, repeated quotation in 'Oriental Taxi' appears to function as a satirical interjection, within a musical form where it comes to appear incongruous and insubstantial. Rather than seeming a slavish imitation of the disco music style of the Bee Gees, the musical quotation functions as a kind of assertive renunciation or rejection.

The incongruity created by the quotation can be traced in details of musical form. The quoted figure or riff is the only instance of guitar-playing in the musical track, and intervenes without context in the performance and final recorded mix (the track is otherwise played on drums and percussion, bass guitar, piano and synthesiser). In addition, the quoted riff enters in double-time in relation to an otherwise unvaried rhythmic pulse, so appealing—by way of existing rhetorics of musical pace—to an effect of lightness against a slower, counterpointing, solidity. Furthermore, the end of the repeated figure from 'Stayin' Alive' is punctuated musically by a crash cymbal stroke which anticipates by a quaver/eighth-note the beginning of the following bar and section of the composition. This is in a manner common across a range of styles of reggae, but in this particular instance the cymbal clips and cuts short the end of the Bee Gees quotation.

Culturally, that incongruity or element of rejection can be understood with regard to wider social relations, too. Unlike the situation in India, Jamaica's recording industry and traditions of musical performance have in this century employed similar, if frequently less technically developed, instruments and means of recording as those of the United States. But those means have been used to produce a variety of national styles and forms that have themselves actively shaped aspects of contemporary American and European music. Indeed, certain formal elements of Caribbean music feature within the disco music style itself—elements from calypso and reggae as well as from salsa, and including recording techniques such as those of extended 'dub' versions produced by mixing and tape-editing of a recorded track, and utilised for 12″ disco single reproduction.

Again, unlike the Hindi film song, Sly Dunbar's music occupies internationally what can be seen as a position of cultural and commercial ascendancy, in two respects: first, as part of Afro-American or 'black' music (restricted circulation 'race' record labels, from the 1920s to the 1950s in the United States, having increasingly gained a more broadly racially based circulation, as is especially clear concerning jazz, Tamla Motown and soul music); second, as a part of reggae music in particular, expanding in the West Indies to become one of Jamaica's largest capital investment industries by the mid 1970s, and gaining currency relatedly in the United States and in Britain under especial influence of Jamaican musicians such as Bob Marley or Jimmy Cliff, as well as in indigenous initiatives (such as those in Britain of Steel Pulse, Aswad, Black Slate, Dennis Bovell), and in amalgamated (or 'cross-over') musical forms such as Two-tone.

Yet for all this contemporary influence and expansion, reggae appears to have developed exactly in national opposition to, or counter-identification against, imported soul music from the United States. The early sound-systems or mobile discotheques in Jamaica in the late 1950s and early 1960s interspersed indigenously produced records–at first of mento, later ska, rock-steady and reggae–within a dominant continuity of imported American recordings and styles. In contact with such racial and national identification, the Bee Gees' use of musical elements from jazz, soul and Caribbean music can well appear, within a Jamaican frame of reference, less an ideal to be aspired to or imitated, than an appropriation to be distanced from and renounced.

(vi)

What can be seen in the comparison more generally is that it is of course inappropriate to conceive rock music as the universal musical 'language' of an age of worldwide technological transmission, creating its meanings, styles and aspirations unequivocally from centralised positions of the recording studio or the record company boardroom. Far from this being the case, rock music has its significances created and recreated variously and unevenly, in relation to local and temporally specific circumstances of being played and played back. Conceived internationally, indeed, the way cultural aspirations and points of renunciation are established across the processes of distribution and circulation involved would seem to be far less misrepresented by being likened to the patterns of trade, political control and cultural influence of imperialism: as subordinations of national self-definition and purpose to priorities agreed and promoted elsewhere (in the instance of rock music dominantly in the United States as well as extensively within Britain). But correspondingly, too, the processes can be seen to be linked as much to possibilities and conditions for reasserting and redefining those local and national forms of identification and purpose.

176   *Conditions of Music*

Changing senses of words and music: Bob Marley and the Wailers, 1979, 'Lively up Yourself', ... and *Vivas,* sales to the tune of reggae beat (ITV, 1981/2).
Photo by permission of Elida Gibbs Ltd.

Meanings and Options in One Place

(i)

These, then, are geographically and culturally *dispersed* and varying responses to musical forms. But it is equally possible to perceive such contrasting patterns of response with a *single* social or cultural formation. Where these occur simultaneously and in the same place, what becomes apparent is that it was not geographical dispersal alone that was crucial to the above illustration. Rather, within such regional movement exists a range of alternative modalities or options concerning musical activity and response, options which represent past and present choices and directions, as also lines of opportunity for change and initiative in the future.

(ii)

Consider British rock music in these terms. All impressions, here in Britain, of rock's spontaneous national origin and insular independence are certainly illusory: it is beyond doubt that rock music's forms have been successively interwoven with US models and antecedents. In the early 1960s, the Beatles play existing American songs as well as pieces of their own composition, with these compositions themselves influenced by American rhythm and blues recordings in their lyrics, harmony and instrumentation. Subsequently, the Beatles and others return versions of these forms to the United States as part of the then distinctively British form 'Merseybeat', during the 'British invasion' of 1964. Around the same time, the Rolling Stones are reproducing imported American blues and rhythm'n'blues material; and later, British mods appeal to American soul and Tamla Motown music in the later 1960s, as again during the late 1970s. And for many British listeners to jazz, a particular cultural value is attached to what has become an acknowledged special category for advertising, review and collecting: that of American 'imports'.

Dependence and imitation of this kind are frequently levelled as 'sufficient' or self-explanatory criticism of British rock music. Where this is the case, however, it is interesting to set against the view the comparison that rock in this respect simply repeats well-established patterns of cultural influence and imitation, such as Britain's successive copying of Italian musical forms in the late sixteenth and early seventeenth centuries, or a later influence of German musical forms and expatriate musicians in the early nineteenth century.

But more important than this historical comparison (or than the more specialised criticism that contemporary rock forms simply corrupt pure origins of blues, gospel and country and western) is to establish directions and purposes of influence or imitation in whatever interchanges *do* follow from origins. Much of a celebrated alternative or revolutionary character for rock music, for example, is taken to follow from its suggested rejection of values or dominant representations of a culture or a society; yet such rejections are mostly so entangled with changing meanings of the displaced and displacing forms, that the impulses of dissent and the cultural directions of preference cannot themselves be simply assumed or read off. What is especially striking, with regard to this difficulty, is that questions of imitation and appropriation are quite as crucial in respect of British rock music as they are concerning cultural forms of Jamaica or India.

Movements of influence work, it seems, reciprocally: reworking and reshaping first inscriptions of style and value, and trading images of person, nation and social aspiration backwards and forwards. Forms and images become fixed in valuations only in context of specific local circumstances, for a particular time, place and audience; and their 'meanings' exist only in relation to these. Yet it is a small range of musical pieces which circulate most widely on this international scale—hence for these, a plurality and oscillation of meanings and significances. And that circulation and recirculation is in turn organised and purposefully managed across wider economic pressures, for the producing record companies, of extendable markets—with US record sales and concert attendances significantly larger than those in Britain.

(iii)

That this circulation is indeed one of meanings rather than exclusively one of pressures of investment, advertising and sale, can be readily established. Where on occasion rejection in British rock music is made of embedded English currencies (in identifications against what is most often designated educationally and discursively to be 'culture'), appeals are frequently made, in the form of accentuated contrast, to US cultural models: the authentic 'heritage' of rock and roll in Buddy Holly imitations, hairstyles, images of Cadillac and Studebaker cars, Confederate flag insignia and baseball jackets. In other instances (as in strands of punk in the mid 1970s, and in some counter-currents within European jazz and 'classical' music), appeals of rejection are made precisely *against* imported or supra-national values, according these images, insignia and idioms a significance or attachment of value which they bring *with* them, rather than which they acquire by their new relations with surrounding discourses on arrival. Against such forms and forces are mobilised notions of local activity and autonomy of production and distribution, concerns which run across both the circulation of music and also what elements of genre or idiom will be taken as antecedents and models for future innovation.

(iv)

Where this complex patterning has been most explicitly in question in rock music is in respect of vocal mannerism. Circulation of musical forms prior to the widespread commercial availability of the gramophone in Western countries depended upon publication of a score and its subsequent realisation in performance. Discs were distinctive in introducing the possibility of exact inscription of details of voicing beyond merely those of pitch, notated dynamic and phrasing, tracing articulatory or phonational attributes. This new resource has evidently been central to the vocal styles of, among others, Marvin Gaye, Captain Beefheart, Kate Bush, Joni Mitchell and Robert Wyatt. Discs further introduced the capability for reproducing precise intonational contour and stress; and largely as a result of this, an emphasis in composition of rock music has come to be transferred from melodic and harmonic arrangement into replicable details of precise enunciation, such as local inflection of the voice and exact adjustments of volume or vocal setting.

Such new areas of interest and experiment are often taken simply as a distasteful lack of tunefulness, in comparison with earlier melodies (as of popular songs of the 1940s and 1950s). But where this is the case, it is again useful to bring to the view an historical comparison: that what is in question in such a transfer of interest is effectively one more (in this case at first technological) movement in long-revered pursuit of a musical inscription of the speaking voice as melodic contour, as *recitative*.

But what is important here, however, about inscriptions of the voice on disc is that details of vocal accent and intonation come to carry distinctions of meaning and value alongside aesthetic pleasures of differing voice qualities. Widespread use has been made in rock music, for example, of extended or improvised vocal techniques of 'strained' voicings and conventionally unaesthetic or dissonant singing, creating new orientations of social position and value. It is such distinctions around meaning and value which appear to cut through aesthetic dimensions of vocal performances by Bob Dylan, Lou Reed, Johnny Rotten, Siouxsie (Banshee), and many others. In addition, this duplicating capability of recorded music also created conditions for rock's extension of the varieties of linguistic dialect and register which might be published and transmitted: when compared with earlier singing styles, rock music has incorporated into patterns of vocal enunciation elements of regional and class accent, as well as significant dialectal and register variations in lexis and syntax (e.g. Bob Marley's 'No Woman No Cry' or 'Lively up Yourself'). And reproduction itself creates other new effects, too: notice in the inscription of the singing voice a way in which vocal mannerisms (such as those of intonation and stress that might collectively signify certitude or assurance) are retained despite displacement through varying social circumstances of reproduction—even where any sponsoring context for such certitude is removed.

In these inclusions of accent and linguistic variety, however, several contradictory strands of attitude and aspiration exist. Whilst voice quality, register and dialect may begin as indications of local origin or identity, they acquire through their regional and temporal displacement new properties of representation, as conventions of a particular cultural style or form. This movement in accent and meaning can be especially clearly seen in the extensive simulation in Britain of American forms of pronunciation, through almost all periods and idioms of British rock music, but widely challenged and explicitly renounced in much punk and

New Wave music following 1976. Usages of the American accents lead in two, seemingly quite opposed, directions: on the one hand, towards revered American origins for rock and roll, through an imitative respect for 'authenticity'–taking accent as an integral constituent of idiom or form; on the other, towards exactly playing on connotations of a cultural devaluation associated with American currencies relative to certain traditional, British cultural positions and investments. Of these conflicting directions of cultural impulse behind the single accent, one involves a dependence on representations of social relationships elsewhere (and, as regards rock and roll origins, increasingly from another period); the other represents a challenge to definitions of social relationships in an immediate environment. But what they indicate together, as discrepant purposes overrun identical material, is that forms of identification and rejection which have become the customary opposing motifs of rock music are not so simply separable or distinct from one another; they continually overlap and intersect.

(v)

At those intersections can be exposed something of a reductiveness in much orthodox 'sociological' thinking on rock music, which explains it as exhaustively either capitalist exploitation or subcultural dissent. Markings of revolt for one audience can be simultaneously planned creations of an industry and a market in another, whilst the two disparate frameworks frequently share identical 'texts' and agencies. Significances of manner, accent, lyric and musical style alter as they are shifted from audience to audience, region to region, or between nations. It is accordingly only on the basis of such specific processes and contradictions (themselves in a pattern significantly altering as rock occupies different positions as a cultural form), that the reworkings of social esteem frequently argued over as regards rock music can begin to be engaged.

Identification and Revolt

(i)

With these various acknowledgements and qualifications, the alternative or variant responses can now be projected in their more familiar form, as opposing terms of abstract argument.

Frequently, rock has been taken to be organised around forms of fantasy and escape, with these in turn considered as major constituents of leisure. Behind this view lie ideas both of aspirations on the basis of assumed likeness or resemblance, and of an element of compensatory idealisation (evident in elements of decoration and glamour developed in much nineteenth-century popular entertainment and visibly carried over into soul, Tamla Motown and disco, as well as into cabaret and a range of other forms of musical spectacle). Drawing on these properties of identification and appeal, rock then represents in leisure either an actual condition of social mobility (as exemplary industry for realising ambition and so actual escape), or else is considered merely to disguise material alienation and oppression, by offering temporary escape from it. The point of consequent division between these accounts is then exactly whether idealisation and fantasy channel into passive acceptance of existing social relations which are only appeased in fantasy, or whether they lead into movements towards action and interaction carried through in initiatives of musical improvisation and performance, or in wider social practice.

These understandings of perception and response are linked in turn to larger arguments about social structure and cultural production. Fashionable identification can be seen as part of a logic of consumer spending, geared to accelerated obsolescence and a substitutive creation of new markets. (And here arises one generally assumed importance of sales charts and record plugging.) As an example of this view, 'revivals' (of fashion such as that of mods, or of records such as the Beatles' 'Love Me Do') might be considered primarily as fresh revenue from records otherwise deleted from sales catalogues, without certain further production costs being incurred (there would be no further recording).

In these terms, rock's creations of fashion need to be considered as importantly and primarily linked to sales and advertising, in directly paid-for publicity on behalf of performances and recordings: in magazines, on television and in shop displays. Moreover, much interest in a surrounding 'rock culture' would need to be thought of as linked equally, if less directly, to advertising techniques arguably first developed to promote film and entertainment stars of the 1930s and 1940s—tours coinciding with record releases, and controversial action or statement, or style of dress or new romance, attracting coverage as 'news'. Indeed, it can be argued within this framework that rock has been simultaneous with, and indeed frequently directly linked to, expansions and innovations in the field of advertising (itself a form of representation interwoven with changing attitudes and moral condemnation, with fast money and with American influence). To this extent, rock music's concerns can sometimes seem very close to those of advertising itself: the validation, by accentuation of a social positioning in fantasy linked to a particular purchase, of an object for sale (a performance, a record, finally, the persona of the performer).

And here in the framework looms a particular threat in rock music. Contemporary advertising genres are largely organised around narratives, sketches and songs and music disposed around a commercial product. In rock, correspondingly, it might be argued that the various forms (the single, album, video, etc.) focus on a product which consists in a set of relations between image, voice and movements of the performer or performers. Collectively, these elements produce what is a kind of musical portraiture and self-portraiture, a selected and enhanced set of images of selfhood ('facing' the music). In this aspect of the genres of rock, the threat lies in that a trade of images which are addressed across powerful forces and vested interests can create, directly through representations of the body or person itself, idealised versions of voice, gesture, position and social identity.

(ii)

Such a view of rock interlocks continually, however, with another familiar version, seemingly its opposite: rock as an important creation of 'alternative' perceptions and meanings. Even where the means of production of rock music are acknowledged to conform extensively to prevailing relations and controls of capitalist production, a capacity for change can still be held to exist. That capacity in representation can in turn be believed to feed into social reform and redirection, including reform of the means of production themselves, means both specific to music-making and extending beyond. Such a potential for reform might be thought to exist primarily in the form of direct rhetorical appeals (Pink Floyd's 'We don't need no education' in 'Another Brick in the Wall', Peter Tosh's 'Legalize It', or Plastic Ono Band's 'Give Peace a Chance'); or it might be regarded to occur by indirect influence and broader social transition taking place in 'rock culture' seen in much larger terms.

Accordingly, much value has been ascribed to rock music on the strength of notions of revolt against the prevailing directions of a social formation, declaring a dissenting social identity or counter-identification. Rock is seen in this light as a challenge to a 'dominant' culture, a 'parent' culture, 'straight' culture, authority, normality, the 'system' etc; and in such terms, the music marks up graffiti of dissent, creating in general style as well as in specific protest songs meanings which undermine other existing, dominant meanings, and promote alternatives to them.

Clearly there need to be certain immediate qualifications to such a view. These are not related to the traditional rebuttal that a musical form largely created within capitalist relations of production can finally have no oppositional potentiality; that criticism relies upon a reductive collapsing of the difference between forms of representation, finally believing these to be exhaustively determined by their form of production. Rather, the qualifications concern conceiving rock music as successive subcultural forms or movements for a youth audience only, rather than forms which are addressed through particular (if often specialist) institutions of a social formation, and to which varying responses are made (an acquired active audience arguably becoming specific, youth, only as a consequence of this, and not prior to it). The distinction is not unimportant. The view of rock as exclusively a 'youth music' immediately restricts the significance and seriousness of that music to positions and interests assumed to exist already. Such positions and interests are merely reflected in the music, rather than differentially constructed by it, across it and in opposition to it. This point of division has important ramifications, as regards conceiving rock as cynical exploitation and condescension, or as regards the elitist praise

Rock Today: Facing the Music 185

that it is a music intelligible only to one social grouping who can 'relate' to it.

Again, it is an incidental historical comparison which begins to bring out the narrowness of reference, and the limits of the polemic. Implicitly, the criticism of rock as restricted to a small and selective audience advances social division and selectivity as major reduction of importance, despite clear analogies for such 'limitation' with that of many earlier, revered cultural forms of music and literature, which also, in this sense, addressed very specialised sectors of a population. Alternatively, the praise of rock for the same selectivity fails to look forward to moments at which the avowed taste and advancing age will come (unless the view is revised) into insoluble conflict. But in each case, the important point is obscured: music and other cultural forms are not simply a matter of predisposition and pre-existent interest; it is one effect of social institutions of production and distribution to determine selectivity of appeal, as well as governing in some relation to notions of value invested in particular selections what will be the socially dominant cultural representations at any time. As regards rock in particular, the role of circulation in generating value can be especially well illustrated: institutions of chart and radio playlist on the basis of sales have the effect that even sales to one very specific social grouping can come to be represented as popularity, 'general' currency and a national entertainment repertoire, by virtue simply of attaining a threshold for gaining airtime on 'national' radio.

Rock cannot be seen as a 'youth' music, as exclusively the music of a phase or repeated structure of adolescent rebellion to be duly abandoned in capitulation to social orthodoxies. Forces which precipitate such changes (conforming for the sake of employment, settling with family, etc.) constitute cultural options and determinations, not an exclusively 'natural' progression or successive 'socialising' stages. The important observation about these processes then is that as such they vary, and remain variable. And the history of rock makes this plain: rock music has played changing roles in a limited but unmistakeable alteration of social styles and modes of interaction over twenty years, and this shifting ground and esteem of the music undermine attempts to secure for styles a singular fixed purpose, effect or explanation. The address of rock to changing generations and audience constituencies itself produces differing expectations, redefinitions and anomalies (the Beatles are now 'classics'; parents and children attend Rolling Stones' concerts together; television incorporates rock forms, in ways which no longer frame them primarily as forms of social occasion outside the home; radio programmes include 'nostalgia' spots, often linked to repeats of radio 'news' from a particular year, etc.).

When this dimension of historical and cultural movement around rock music is submerged, in order to identify an abstract process of growth responsible for what will be a later stable identity, the music's two main and radically divergent potentialities are equally obscured: its power for change or innovation, and its liability to suffer kinds of assimilation and dilution of challenge or protest. Importance of contemporary music as specific forms, relations and directions diminishes into a presiding force of fashion or immobile and impotent dissent. In either of these ceases to exist the possibility of distinction between valuable social alternative and what is simply conventional gesture (exemplary when, in the film version of *Woodstock*, the announcement is made to the assembled audience, 'If we think hard enough, maybe we can stop this rain . . .').

The Who, 'My Generation', and David Bowie, 'Fashion'

The way the recurrent terms of 'youth' or generational revolt, and of 'fashion', overrun these opposing theoretical abstractions can be further clarified in details of two well-known recorded songs.

The Who, 'My Generation' (1966)

It is clear that this song focuses exactly on possession of an identity in time, identifying 'my generation' ('Talking 'bout my ge-ge-generation'). But who is referred to as this collective identity in any act of listening involves a crucial ambiguity. On the one hand, the phrase and title 'my generation' specifies exactly 'youth', not adults, and draws this sense from a physical presence of the performers, the Who, performing and recording in the mid 1960s, as well as from associations of the musical style with a new 'young' phenomenon of rock music, a 'youth' music. As a reference of this kind to 'youth', the song can still be taken to articulate problems of understanding between generations—between parents and teenagers, between adults and adolescents ('Hope I die before I get old . . .'). In this sense, the listeners who occupy that position of identity in the present, as 'my generation', are the 'youth' of today.

On the other hand, the phrase and title 'My Generation' specifies exactly those (including the performers the Who themselves) who were 'young' during the 1960s, and draws this sense from associations of the musical style of the song with a period (1960s rock music), as well as from frames of perception, reference and experience shared between any group of contemporaries. In this sense, those occupying the position of identity, as 'my generation', are presently those who, young in the 1960s, are still a generation, but now—at least in relational terms—a different generation, an older (or 'the older') generation.

These distinctions across the song (between the physical age of 'youth', as a generation in relational terms, and the social generation of a historical period) clearly cut across any simple, general structure of subcultural dissent. Indeed, in the most familiar currencies of the rock press, the distinctions are passed over altogether: 'My Generation . . . an anthem that blasted past its derivations, totally a part of the moment in which it was conceived and in the process, totally eternal, because it captures that moment so completely.'[3]

A further important point emerges in this illustration, too. Consider,

Why don't you all f-f-fade away,
And don't try to dig what we all say.

Two familiar observations might be made about these lines: first, that they reflect a pressure, during the late 1950s and 1960s, around the varieties of English able to enter national networks of distribution such as radio, television and film; second, that ways of concealing words and idioms against censorship, such as those devised in 'f-f-fade away' have a history in a variety of symbolic conventions in earlier blues and rock and roll music.

But what is more important than either of these observations, in the context of arguments concerning rock as a generation's music of protest, is the way in which the sense of 'generation' in

'My Generation' is directly appealed to on the basis of a desired control over, and exclusion by way of, a circulation of meanings ('. . . and don't try to dig what we all say'). That relationship acknowledged in the song between verbal and musical forms on the one hand, and positions within and against a social formation on the other, offers kinds of social alignment which explicitly depend upon acts of positioning in relation to meanings. But at the same time, such positioning can only take place across complications of reference produced by the relational character of definitions of personal identity, a relational character which is further emphasised by the subsequent displacement of the recording from any 'original' supporting context.

What becomes clear in 'My Generation' is a significance for rock music more complicated than either of the abstract models above: not the significance of a new and decisively altering world (the music of the 1960s, 1970s and 1980s has changed and is changing everything); nor yet that of an unchanging world (the music of the 1960s, 1970s and 1980s changes nothing). Rather, the significance is of continuing conflicts in meanings and social relationships which are articulated through musical forms of one period, then inherited—but with differing relations between the forms and their range of possible reference and implication—by subsequent generations.

If this variability of reference and identification in rock music between successive periods is thought to be inconsequential, one further, related observation might be made. Musical rejection and dissent in rock in 1976 surrounding punk and New Wave music marked a range of challenges to a decadence, capitulation and collusion considered to have developed within rock music itself. As a result, divisions were not so much between rock musical forms and an external 'society' in comparison with which rock music might be taken as protest and opposition, but between differing versions, and changing meanings, of rock music itself.

David Bowie, 'Fashion' (1980)

It is clear that in an importantly changing social formation much is lost by categorising as opposing entities a homogeneous culture and an array of fractured subcultures and countercultures.

What disappears in such formulations is primarily the active processes of interpretation and negotiation which shape response and social positioning.

The extent to which positions of interpretation have to be actively organised can be seen especially clearly in David Bowie's 'Fashion'. This song is explicitly addressed to the way processes of fashion operate in rock music in styles of dancing ('There's a brand new dance but I don't know its name/ That people from bad homes do again and again', or 'Fashion, turn to the left . . . Fashion, turn to the right . . .'). But alongside such apparent critique of the regimentation of fashion, the song also occupies a place within it–as an influence within what have come to be called traditions of 'glamrock' (especially as these passed, when linked to influences from surrealism and pop art, into New Wave music: the Ramones, Blondie, Iggy Pop . . .).

What is particularly interesting about this song is that it works criticisms of processes of fashion ('There's a brand new talk . . . it's loud and it's tasteless and I've heard it before . . .') into its own continuing existence within an idiom of fashionable dance music. As a consequence, an evident ambiguity of address is created between the possible constructions of position on which fashion relies. This ambiguity creates a variety of available positions for interpretation, positions which are related not simply to qualities of lyrical or 'poetic' expression, but which depend upon wider circumstances of the record's distribution and consumption.

In the lines, 'They do it over there, but we don't do it here', for example, two senses are conveyed simultaneously: on the one hand, that unfortunately the new dance has not reached 'here' yet–wherever 'here' is taken to be; on the other, that while the new dance may be acceptable elsewhere, it is unwanted 'here', and can be disdained. Interpreting the 'fashion' either way is precisely a taking of position, one way or the other, an identification. But repeatedly in the song suggestions for such positioning remain contradictory–there to be articulated but not passively assumed.

Wherever a directionality in the rhetoric appears to become clearer, it remains subject to ambiguity, nevertheless. If 'we are the goon squad and we're coming to town, beep, beep!' seems to imply criticism, this line needs still to be seen in relation to contemporaneous 'fashionable' idioms of self-designation as 'punk', to stylistic 'cloning' and reworkings of clothing styles utilising discarded material, and to styles of robotic dancing. These are fashions in which earlier signs of disregard, deprecation or abuse are adopted as exemplary terms of resistant identification and decoration. Nor can the contrast of 'bad homes' in the first verse and 'good homes' in the second be taken to indicate simple preference, given ways in which 'bad' acquires, by inversion in certain social dialects and contexts, the sense of 'good', as well as in view of implicit criticisms in each verse of activities from either kind of home.

Or, again, consider the melisma on the word 'the ' in the last line of the second, final verse ('Shout it while you're dancing on the-e-e dance floor'). Enunciated first of all on the last quaver/eighth-note of one bar, this word is extended as a slur over a quaver phrase on an especially accented beat, a first beat of a bar. This is extremely unusual for a closed-system word in virtually any musical idiom, especially for the definite article, 'the', / /, it being usually open-class words which, on the premiss that they supply relatively more information, are made to correspond with metrical stress.

This accentual displacement of the 'the' suggests an investment of weight in inappropriate places, placements crucial for a dance music. In this sense, the song evidently conveys a note of condemnation or contempt. Indeed, such misalignment or irregularity in setting of the lyric can be seen in other aspects of musical arrangement, too. Although 'fashion' begins with a relatively dissonant drone pulse and includes extensive, punctuating fuzz guitar playing, it also incorporates throughout the song a riff (with partially damped 'string' sound) very close to those used in many disco records of the same period (and especially clear in Michael Jackson's 'Don't Stop Till You Get Enough', on the album *Off The Wall* (1979)). This riff accompanies the repeated chant throughout the extended fade, seemingly taking up the last line's 'Shout it while you're dancing on the dance floor . . .'. The fade has the effect of explicitly reaffirming for the song, for all its polemic, a function as dance music, layering ambiguity and discrepancy over continuing currency as a fashionable form.

Groups

(i)

Shortcomings in the terms of account mentioned so far make it clear that to begin to grasp in rock music indications of cultural value or direction will necessarily involve attention both to musical forms and to their organisation and circulation. It is only on the basis of such interwoven attentions that it will be possible to begin to understand relations between kinds of musical effect and pleasure in rock music, or to grasp—between these and the properties of other musical forms—broader relations that are the basis of comparative cultural argument.

(ii)

As a first reference on relations between rock's musical forms and the arrangements in which they are presented, it is worth considering associations of rock music with the celebrated format of the musical 'group'. Here notions of musical practice and enjoyment, of original identity and interest, and of learned conventional idiom importantly intersect.

The three-, four-, five- and six-person rock group appears a new phenomenon of the 1950s and early 1960s, and emerges in part as response to the increased commercial availability of electric guitars and amplification. These appear to have extended capabilities for producing volume without corresponding increases in personnel. So it is again a development within the technology of production which stimulates, indirectly, a transition in forms and modes of presentation. For subsequently the group format develops away from early conventions of solo performer and sidemen in the smaller jazz bands and rock and roll groups of the 1950s, and, in this newer form, has become established as what seems now the 'classic' organisational framework for rock music. It is only in the mid 1970s that this format becomes in turn subject to major revision and challenge, following performances of all-women groups of instrumentalists, and new combinations of instruments which further modify practical requirements for performing and recording (instruments such as synthesisers, prepared tapes and drum-machines).

(iii)

Frequently traced to local youth fraternities—and so often also to a group psychology of collective identity—the formation of the musical group can be traced to a variety of practical origins: as exactly this banding together of friends; as pursuit of alternative forms of art and expression, especially in rock groups of school and art-school background in the 1960s; in calculated creation, when session musicians, already professional entertainers, combine as a group in order to do live performances, or when groups are devised to embody an image of an already calculated social demand (the Monkees, Bucks Fizz, etc.); or again, especially in the later 1960s, when 'supergroups' (such as Emerson, Lake and Palmer, Humble Pie, Blind Faith or Crosby, Stills, Nash and Young), are formed as compounded virtuosities, at a time when rock music was being increasingly considered in terms of exceptional musical or 'artistic' ability; or still again, when political factions and other extra-musical groupings (e.g. Hare Krishna devotees, church youth groups, football teams) utilise influential rock forms as a platform for rhetorical declamation, often in accompanied singing and chanting, or in music theatre.

Yet for all the deficiency of failed comprehensiveness, the model of local, sociable groupings merits continuing attention. This is less because of its faithfulness to a practical reality than owing to its continuing currency far in excess of other models of formation and origin. The model itself is familiar: groups of acquaintances, especially associations of men, sometimes in the first instance incorporating members without any musical proficiency, and playing and singing for entertainment gained from the physical activity of music-making itself as much as from ambitions elsewhere. In this respect, the formation of groups is in part an extension of forms of association, frequently linked to emphases on shared rebellion or migration ('You see—instead of throwing a knapsack over your back and getting out on the highway to learn about life, we were able to do it together. We were protected by one another. We were secured by one another'[4]). And within the perspective, the group identity can be taken to provide either a single, inclusive point of reference, or (as most celebratedly in respect of the Beatles) to provide a form of composite persona, in which the identifying group image includes multiple complementary characteristics (particularly clear, for example, in the Beatles' early film, *A Hard Day's Night*, 1964).

(iv)

What it is important to acknowledge in this context is that collectivity of this kind is always more than origins alone. Images of group identity always stand in some relation to conventional representations or mythologies of association and social identity. Regional or class origins themselves are passed into, and projected as, conventions of forms and styles. Central to rock's importance—as also to its difficulty—is again the peculiarity that the formal conventions are worked so closely over images of body and voice, that they can as a result carry extremely powerful notions of an actual or absolute identity, social position and interest.

Groups are not origins or pre-existent identity and interest alone, nevertheless. Indeed such notions fail particularly to explain the group format in view of rock music's celebrated social and economic mobility. Impetus, for example, to move from locality and immediate audience to larger performance arenas and into record distribution is not determined exclusively by attractions of increased income or fame; it follows in addition from a broader institutional framework in which the dominant definitions of musical success for rock music have been established and accentuated on the basis of sales charts and of radio exposure focally organised around programming on the strengths of sales, in selective playlisting. It is one of the effects of movements for performers in and through such institutions of rock music that definitions of early practice (of any kind) will require successive revision, as changing pressures of demand and opportunity, or setbacks and restrictions on aspiration, force changes in response, planning and self-definition. Indeed, that very image of mobility becomes itself conventionalised, as is especially clear when categories of employment for musicians (amateur, semi-pro, pro) gain currency less as reflections of actual or immediate occupation, than as prospective categories of commitment.

So what is involved in rock's musical groups, then, is less a singular decisive moment of identification than a continuous dynamic. In this light what becomes important about reconceptualisations of the musical group during whatever is the course

Conditions of Music

Photo by permission of EMI.

Photo by permission of EMI.

Image matters: '... images of group identity always stand in some relation to conventional representations or mythologies of association and social identity.'

of its development is that the development cannot be reduced to exclusively psychological or economic redefinitions (loss of sight of 'real origins', 'selling out', etc.). Rather, the successive redefinitions are made across relations of material opportunity that are created in prevailing musical institutions, coupled with a (not necessarily corresponding) range of representations of those relations, especially those surrounding rock stardom.

As symbols of a passage for notions of identity and interest through larger institutions of rock music, group names themselves attest points of collision between the social conventions and references back to an assumed prior identity. Simultaneously, the names are definitions of selves in relation to a social context, and yet interventions also within a conventional genre of group names: Duane Eddy and the Rebels, the Animals, the Beatles, the Band, the Who, Them, Pink Floyd ('the band is really fantastic, that is really what I think/ O by the way, which one's Pink?'[5]), Frank Zappa's the Mothers (becoming on record company instruction, the Mothers of Invention), the Sex Pistols, the Slits, XTC, The Au Pairs, Television, Talking Heads, Siouxsie and the Banshees, Spandau Ballet, Altered Images, Eurythmics, U2, Oxy and the Morons...

'Real' Experience or Conventional Genre?

(i)

Arguably it is forms of representation of identity such as these which are what is most importantly at issue in rock music. The various potentialities of the music circulate around them: on the one hand, experiment and transformation, in disturbances of existing connections between image, voice and body, and so challenge to limits on gesture and habitual perception; on the other hand, repetition and determined hold on known relations between the elements, in negations of idiom or genre as complex articulations, and countering insistence upon true origin and authenticity of voice, or on an exhaustive fixity of image and tried convention.

But a continual oscillation between the potentialities is also discernible. Valuable insistence on self-redefinition against existing currencies of representation (in gained control over names, images and details of recording and performance), is liable to shade back into concern for control and definition of experience over and against any form of representation whatever. This results in aspirations towards declaration through music waged not only against rock music's prevailing economic and institutional relations, but against *all* modes of collective or social organisation. In consequence, there can be the progression in thought and argument from experience, 'real life' or 'street credibility', into an ideal of musical performance and recording in which 'middle' processes of production are only considered in terms of successful implementation or of exploitative manipulation. In these terms, the surrounding relations and conditions of rock are reduced to a set of mere obstacles to the individual. And related larger aspirations and ready answers can come to correspond: isolated, 'creative' individualism, personally owned recording studios, reclusive communes and celebrations of rock as the form which can make anyone a star, but in which what is involved is less a devaluation of 'stardom' by that extended access than an accentuation of the competition through which it is thought to be attainable.

(ii)

The significance of discrepancies between these kinds of understanding can begin to be clarified when the variants are projected as two familiar axes of broad historical outlook:

1. Rock as 'direct' declaration or confession of life and experience, in an address unmediated by conventions of representation (in which context, it can appear apposite that even rock's PA systems take their name from 'public address' systems). Rock music as in this way transcending limitations of conventional musical or aesthetic forms, and so attaining a directness of address which makes simultaneously possible two otherwise seemingly opposite capabilities: that of a vocal intimacy (addressing a listener directly, as in romantic or sexual supplication); that of 'general' or 'universal' public address (the basis of rock's oratory and proposed social alternative). Meanings for songs considered as reflections of an immediacy of experience, rather than precipitated

diversely, through relations of circulation and reproduction.

There are a series of important moments in a history of rock music based in such a view:

(i) use in skiffle music during the 1950s of improvised instruments, or, relatedly, the later use of new and relatively inexpensive instruments and amplification. Such usages can be seen as part of an extended access to music-making and performance, and are repeated in the 'Merseybeat' group expansion of the early 1960s, as well as in emphases within punk and New Wave music on DIY ('do-it-yourself') during the mid 1970s.

(ii) adoption of technically simple musical forms in punk (three guitar chords, and learned rudiments of drum-playing such as paradiddles and flambs displaced by 'learnings' of experience such as pace and energy); dissonances employed to challenge an indulgent 'aestheticism' of 'mega-bands' dislocated from 'real-life'.

(iii) singer-songwriters, and folk traditions, bringing to music an authenticity of social experience and relevance, as in the way in which folk music of civil rights campaigns in the USA during the 1960s channelled into certain rock 'protest' genres.

(iv) inclusion of lyric-sheets with records to make clear what is being said but remains inaudible ('progressive' music as an alternative voice, linked to the 'underground' press of the 1960s).

(v) toasting and rapping, as direct speaking and appeal over a musical background, in accompanied declamation (with local toasters and DJs as members of the communities they address).

2. Rock as composition of songs according to stylistic convention and artifice: conventional lyrics, frequently referred to (usually critically) as 'moon in June' or 'blue since I lost you' lyrics, but later extended into a range of vocal idioms. Corresponding conventionalism of musical arrangement: introduction, middle-eight, chorus, coda or fade, as well as forms derived from other sources ('ballad' from musicals and film soundtracks; the 'twelve bar' from blues). Further compositional conventions established within these genres: harmonically, often a link between chord sequence and modalities of the song's lyrics—with middle sections ('middle-eights') in related, often minor, keys, and con-

structed around lyrical contingencies or qualifications, before a return to generalised formulations of chorus and title. (This can be seen clearly in the Beatles' 'Ob-la-di, Ob-la-da', for example, where the middle-eight projects Desmond and Molly from their everyday lives ('Desmond has a barrow in the market place/ Molly is a singer in a band') into a hypothetical family future together ('In a couple of years they have built a home, sweet home...').)

But again, such elements of formal convention are made the object of experiment and extension. This is especially clear in respect of beginnings and endings of songs: in performance, especially in the 1960s and early 1970s, consider extensions and variations around a drawn-out final chord, laced with drum fills and guitar figures; or in many recordings, a gradual fade-out repeating the chorus, or on the tonic chord or in alternation between tonic and sub-dominant. At first, techniques of the fade appear to be linked simply to the recording process (producing endings without decisive cadence or resolution); but they are gradually extended (e.g. in the Beatles' 'Hey Jude', and often elsewhere with a mantric quality in the late 1960s), until that extended fade intersects with emphases in many Afro-American, Caribbean and Latin American forms upon repeated harmonic and rhythmic cycles that establish a continuum for embellishment and variation, central to dancing and to genres such as funk and disco.

The element of conventionalism is especially evident, too, in references back to earlier songs, usually in one of two forms. First, as reflexive local allusion to elements of genre (as clearly in Arthur Conley's 'Sweet Soul Music'); or to a band or singer's own past and images (as clearly in the Beatles, 'And here's another clue for you all/The walrus was Paul' alluding to 'I am the Walrus'[6]). Second, in the form of stylistic imitation, as musical 'standards' or cover versions, frequently referred to as 're-makes'. These sometimes take the form of duplications which link rock with wider structures of an already established entertainment industry (as in Radio 2 orchestrations of 'pop' songs); sometimes they take the form of simulation—as technical education or apprenticeship (in the 1960s, for example, many groups in early stages of development repeat the changes of Cream's, 'Sunshine of Your Love' or Eddie Cochran's 'Summertime Blues'); sometimes they take the form of allusive re-creations or inflections of style of presentation (the Sex Pistols' 'My Way', etc.), referring to genre not as authority for present activity, but in order to comment upon it, criticise it or merely make money out of it.

Equally, there are a series of important bearings and references in versions of rock history on these lines:

(i) Songs by the Beatles, Dylan, etc., as developing or extending imaginative lyricism during the 1960s into extended song-forms.
(ii) the 'concept album'; excursions into music theatre, film and video; inclusion of rock lyrics as a kind of poetry: all these as extensions of medium and scale of formal resource.
(iii) punk as a displacement of existing idioms, by modifying habitual representations of songs, clothes, gestures, etc., to produce a new range of stylistic options.
(iv) toasting and rapping, as new versions of recitative or rhetoric, linking rock musical forms back with traditions of oral poetry.

The Rock Song I: Radio

(i)

These are two distinguishable frameworks for considering voicing, song and music-making in rock. What is immediately evident about them is that almost identical turning-points are invoked in each, to support radically different terms of reference and interpretation.

In order to begin to locate and clarify points of discrepancy and major divergence between the conceptions, it is useful to consider developments within conventions and usages of one particular, central idiom, the rock 'song'.

Rock musical forms developed initially within traditions of popular song, and from antecedents in existing forms such as the blues, folk song and gospel music. But more is evidently in question with regard to songs than stylistic, technical or institutional origins alone. Relations of the song-form with a technology of production and distribution through which the expansion and rapid diffusion of rock music has taken place provide one exemplary instance of this. For what can be seen in such relations is that important considerations exist beyond those of traditional accounts of rock's origins—such as the one according to which disc jockey Alan Freed moves from Cleveland to New York in 1954, and in doing so extends his already established predominantly white audience for rhythm'n'blues records (previously restricted in currency by the distribution network and prevailing social connotations of 'race' recording labels).

(ii)

One reason accounts of origins such as this are insufficient is that the radio format itself subsequently exerts important pressures back upon rock music's forms and innovation. Consider Britain again as example. The practice of radio playlisting begins, on US precedent, in the early 1960s, on the basis both of market research concerning advertising on commercial stations, and as part of a restructuring of BBC programming that ensues from cultural debates surrounding radio 'piracy'. In each case, the policies of selective programming are caught up in arguments about taste and demand being indicated by sales, despite the evident circularity that repeated exposure in airtime can actively establish taste, and so produce the increased sales which the programming is taken to reflect.

As regards development of the song-form in rock, however, what is important is that in radio's sequence of recordings is established a continuity of programming that makes an individuality of any composition largely subordinate to a format of their controlled sequence or succession. This continuity establishes many of the constraints of genre. Musical forms are circumscribed, for example, by programming constraints both of envisaged listening circumstances (driving, washing-up, serious evening listening), and of limitations imposed by acknowledged disparities in the audio fidelity of various types of equipment for reproduction (stereo tuners, car radios, portable transistors, etc.). Indeed to accommodate that disparity, the dynamic range of radio output is frequently at some stage reduced (by appropriate composing, by compression in recording, etc.), so that where loud passages will not be too loud, quiet passages will nevertheless not become inaudible.

In this respect, sequence of records as programme format actively shapes elements of rock's forms. At the same time, too, it imposes limits on the range of recordings or compositions that will be admissible within the defined table of entertainments (as regards playlisting on the basis of sales 'charts', what will be played will be primarily records currently conceived to be 'popular'). As a result, what is established through the radio playlist is a temporary stability of known records; and this provides a degree of familiarity immediately available whenever 'popular music' radio stations are switched on. Currently selling (and therefore repeated) records are interspersed with records declining in popularity and with new ones selectively introduced–with that turnover regulated both by patterns in sales themselves, and by controlled programming emphases ('golden oldies', previews, favourites, etc.). And whilst in 'specialist' programmes there are different audience constituencies, and so differences in what is taken to be familiar and what is not, these in effect assist in creating additional genre subcategorisations. Indeed, the finer distinctions feed into further divergences and subsequent stabilisations of forms–forms which largely reflect aspects of the 'radio' institutions over which they are propagated. As a longer-term consequence, new pieces of music come to be devised partly in response to established convention and acceptance, whilst simultaneously projecting into these some degree of compatible novelty.

The Rock Song II: 'Shifters' and the Terms of Address

(i)

These varying points of pressure upon rock's forms are not merely of historical or technical interest. They impose significant, continuing conditions upon ways in which the songs of rock will be understood. They affect, too, the terms of perception and debate outlined above concerning rock's general cultural importance, exposing complexities beyond either of the familiar frameworks. Regarding conceptions of songs as conventions to be employed in effect without engaging ways of referring to or defining experience, the recurrent problem is exactly of reducing rock's innovation to a mere formalism. In this view, no significant reorientation of experience or social relationships will be possible through musical experiment or change alone. Regarding direct expression on the other hand, it can never be more than delusion that meanings are directly exchangeable across complex relations of medium and performance without a whole range of constitutive and modifying relations intervening.

(ii)

Evidently, understanding rock's songs will not follow from either approach in isolation. There is a line on a Bob Dylan live album (*Bob Dylan at Budokan*), when—introducing the song 'Simple Twist of Fate'—he announces, 'Here's a simple love story . . . happened to me'. This laconic introduction plays ambiguously between the two traditional conceptions: between a conventionalism of the romantic song, and autobiographical or experiential confession. And this interlinking can be traced through senses of the word 'lyric' itself: first, a sense deriving from things recited or sung (originally, to the accompaniment of the lyre), hence arrangements of words whose material properties possess qualities of unusual or enhanced aesthetic interest; second, expressions of innermost being or reflection on experience, a sense made especially eminent with regard to poetry and song of the late eighteenth and nineteenth centuries.

(iii)

Rather than in development of either single framework, the effects of musical forms and lyrics need to be engaged in particular relations between performance, reproduction and response. Such relations can perhaps best be approached by considering the occurrence in rock songs of pronouns and other linguistic 'shifters'. These are words whose property of reference varies according to who is speaking, when and where. Self-evidently, these are especially crucial for any notion of expression of experience or direct address within a song-form.

Shifters appear straight away of especial significance in rock music. A density of second-person pronouns and imperatives in particular appears virtually without parallel in song-forms of any earlier periods, occurring elsewhere seemingly only in three forms which differ fundamentally from the rock usages: in dance music, where the address figures as reflexive instruction; in contextually specified dramatic dialogue between characters (as in opera and musicals); in devotional songs and hymns, as supplication with God. In many song-forms, singers refer to themselves as singer or as a collectivity of performers in first-person constructions ('I'/'we'), but there is seldom the suggestion of an addressee unless as a named apostrophe–usually linked to third-person, rather than second-person, reference ('my baby/ Daphne, etc., . . . she'). It consequently appears to be largely the suggestion through second-person pronouns of an unspecified or general direct addressee which underlies notions of an immediacy of address established in rock music, enabling it to transcend limitations of a mere formalism.

(iv)

In this unusual property of rock music there is an interlocking of the song-form with conditions of the surrounding technology, institutions and ideology of records and radio, shaped as these are in turn by a broader contemporary mythology of communications. Largely sharing conventions of actual performance with antecedent forms such as blues or popular song, rock seemingly acquired its aspiration towards a directness of address in a superimposition of notions of communications (between individuals across a mass medium, along the lines of telecommunications) on existing notions of the conventionalism of other cultural forms.

It is such directness of address (exemplary already in the Beatles' 'From Me to You' in 1963) which can be seen to be anomalous because of shifters. For perhaps what is most extraordinary about first- and second-person pronouns in rock songs is the possibility of identification they evidently establish: the possibility to superimpose the person of a listener on the 'I' of the singer, in an identification which creates the effect of the rock singer speaking out on an audience's behalf; or alternatively, the possibility of the listener occupying the position of second-person addressee addressed by that 'I' of the singer. These processes of positioning are in turn central to larger questions of pleasure and value which surround rock music. Whilst in conversation there is relatively little likelihood of failing to distinguish the referent of pronouns, in rock musical forms a whole set of additional relations to do with pleasure and fantasy cut across considerations of reference alone. Nor do these follow exclusively from displacement of the song from an imagined original context of enunciation. Rather, they are articulated and continually redefined within larger structures of the music's institutions and industry, focally around images of the performer as rock-star. In this can be distinguished one important dimension of the continuing eminence of musical linkages between voice, body and image: songs seemingly articulated in reference to particular experience are passed into conventions of genre or form (the song as 'text'); but these are taken up in listening often less as 'text' or locally identified speech act (Mick Jagger said; Diana Ross invoked; Sting importuned ...), than as sites of imaginative entry and identification—hence their peculiar attachments of pleasure and desire.

(v)

Consider, in relation to such questions, the way in which the 'you' in rock can engage a listener across at least four distinctions or divisions: (i) address to one specified individual (contextually clear in the song), 'Angie', 'Oh Carol', etc.,[7] in dramatic monologue or apostrophe; (ii) address to any singular listener ('you'), in an intimacy of address which, however, does not discriminate between the many possible individual listeners to whom it may appeal ('Hey! Hey! You! You! Get off of my cloud!'[8]); (iii) address extending this sense to a 'general' or 'universal' listener ('you' overlapping with 'one'), or to a collectivity of each and every singular listener, 'you all' (The Rolling Stones', 'We Love You'); (iv) address to an addressee determined by the listener himself or herself, upon occupying the imaginary position of the singer.

The way divergence between senses such as these can affect interpretation of individual songs might be illustrated by Carly Simon's 'You're so Vain' (1973). Here, the first 'you', of a specific addressee, can be ascertained, by autobiographical anecdote, to be Warren Beatty, James Taylor or Mick Jagger, as the song is referred for its intelligibility to the experiences and confessions of its composer. The singer reproduces a previous 'direct' address in a simulated second-person form to be 'overheard' by a third party, the audience. The second and third kinds of addressee (each, but any singular listener) become whoever is listening, and the song is interpreted in relation to circumstances of being heard rather than circumstances of being written or performed ('You're so vain... I bet you think this song is about you, don't you?'): the singer addresses an audience 'direct' through channels of communication such as performance, radio and disc reproduction. The fourth mode, as appropriated or 'borrowed' address made by the listener occupying the position of the singer, constructs its addressee again in relation to conditions of listening, but these are imagined as conditions of (simulated) performance. Evidently, these are importantly different modes of interpretation, and correspond to radically different kinds of pleasure.

(vi)

Consider, alternatively, first-person constructions. These play a major part in rock's creation of senses of identity, group identity, and collective subcultural or social identity (as in the Who's, 'My Generation', Chicago's 'I'm a Man', James Brown's, 'Say it Loud– I'm Black and I'm Proud', or Dire Straits', 'We are the Sultans of Swing'). Again, the properties of identification and avowal these usages suggest are subject to a number of complexities.

These might be illustrated by considering the song 'We are Family', by the American vocal disco group, Sister Sledge. The chorus of this song is as follows, 'We are family/ I've got all my sisters with me/ We are family/ Get up everybody and sing ...'. The proposition 'we are family' clearly divides here between two forms of reference, which depend upon the shifting property of the first-person pronoun, 'we'. In the first couplet, 'we' refers to the particular persons in the band, and the second line expands and explains the assertion made in the first. In the second couplet, contrastingly, an extended reference for this pronoun–referring to both the group and the audience, or to the group and humankind in general as being 'one family'–is superimposed upon the first kind of reference to the members of the group alone. (In this extended reference, 'We are family' also becomes what everybody is to get up and sing, as the chorus is repeated.) This extension of the 'we' modulates the significance of the chorus from that of affirming an identification of the band simply, into claiming a general social unity or community. Linked to the imperative 'get up', it takes on the conventional role within disco music of exhorting the audience to get up to dance and sing (to 'get down') in order to confirm a worldwide human solidarity.

The Rock Song III: Position, Polysemy and Innovation

(i)

These various anomalies of shifters indicate that whilst there can be no privileged access to self in rock's forms of address, processes of appealing to senses of identity are indeed central to many of rock's songs. Indeed, consideration of shifters confirms as a general modality for rock music the kinds of relational framework for response and identification which seemed necessary in construing the particular songs, 'My Generation' and 'Fashion'.

That relational character of response does not, however, make it the case that interpretation is, as a consequence, merely open-ended or indefinite. Limits are imposed upon interpretation by specific institutional arrangements or conditions. That this is so is apparent, for example, in discrepant conventions of address, in certain genres and periods, between songs sung by men and songs sung by women. Whilst in many rock genres there are decisive and emphatic declarations of identity in first-person constructions, in a number of songs by women it is possible to see exactly a corresponding process of identification, but within fundamentally different relations of address. This is perhaps most clear in Carole King's 'You Make Me Feel Like a Natural Woman', where identity is consistently determined not by self but by another (e.g. 'Look what you've done to me ... You make me feel like a natural woman').

There is, of course, a difficulty in statements of this kind: that of positing for sake of comparison an imaginary equivalence of genre. The difference in address might alternatively be accounted for as a difference between idioms—that between rock number and ballad. Yet it is perhaps precisely this question of idiom or genre which is the important distinction. Restrictions on individual performance and interpretation, for men and for women, are created in conventional forms and genres which importantly *codify* social possibilities, rather than which simply follow from gender-specific differences of disposition or interest *reflected* in the differing styles. Roles for men and women in rock have developed along largely separate lines (especially as regards women's recurrent prominence as singer or dancer, but—until recent changes—long-standing absence as instrumentalist); and these respective positions are not unconnected to larger relations of production. A spectrum of images of women, for example, is first significantly challenged exactly as women themselves enter performance in rock music as instrumentalists, and in doing so confront and begin to displace a range of earlier representations which had otherwise fixed terms of sexual difference.

(ii)

Subject to such constraints on positions for utterance and interpretation, however, it seems that much of the pleasure and purchase of rock songs is created precisely in a play between possibilities of placement and displacement. Whilst pronouns are of especial significance as regards locating the centrality of categories of person and identity to the song-lyric, the variety in response they engender is not confined to such features alone.

On the contrary, a range of other properties also contribute. Consider, for example, line-breaks and local repetition within song-forms, and the pauses in enunciation through which these are usually represented acoustically. In such temporal lapses can occur a breach of connections, and on many occasions temporary or intermediary senses are established before the lyric resumes: David Bowie's, 'Make me, baby . . . Make me jump into the air . . . ', in 'Moonage Daydream', links sexual supplication with a subsequently resumed more general sense of giving pleasure (and in this way is related to other techniques in rock of sexual innuendo); or consider the correspondingly ambiguous chorus line and title 'Love I never had it so good' on Quincy Jones's *Sounds . . . and Stuff Like That*, where 'love' can be either a (vocative) term of direct address, or else an object of 'I never had . . .' co-referential with 'it'; or again, there is the Sex Pistols', 'We're so pretty, O so pretty . . . vacant', in which the initial syntactic role of the word 'pretty' as adjectival complement is transformed into that of an intensifier premodifying the adjective 'vacant'–so combining a convention of rock narcisissm ('We're so pretty') with its subversion by an alternative self-definition ('We're so pretty vacant').

These effects of a temporary polysemy produced by separation between vocalised lines in rock songs constitute more than an interesting area of formal experiment. That area of what *is* exclusively formal experiment does exist, and is everywhere apparent. (It might be illustrated here, for example, by the homophonic effect in the Temptations', 'Papa was a Rolling Stone', that when papa died, all he left his family was 'alone' ('a loan'); by the chorus of Peter Gabriel's 'Biko', which is organised centrally around play on the sound /biː/, 'Bi-ko, Bi-ko, be-cause Bi-ko'; by the closely similar effect in Marvin Gaye's, 'You're a Wonderful One'; or by local details in Paul McCartney's, 'Maybe I'm Amazed'–as for example in symmetries between corresponding line beginnings, 'Baby I'm amazed . . . ' and 'Maybe I'm a man . . . '. In these lines, not only does 'baby' rhyme with 'maybe', but both the affix and the indefinite article 'a' (the almost always unstressed 'schwa', / ə /) occupy identical metrical position and are each followed by stressed /m/.

Although important as recurrent local felicity of rock songs, such phonic play is nevertheless clearly distinguishable from the effect of pauses and line-breaks indicated above, in which what is crucial is that some provisional or temporary meaning is created before following words recreate or cancel any such sense out.

Consider, in addition to these effects, ambiguities which can occur in moments of transition between the often relatively specific frames of reference in verses of a song and the equally often general formulations of a song chorus. In the Beatles' 'Let It Be', for example, the lines 'There will be an answer, Let it be' can either invoke activity towards solution and change, or propose exactly an opposite passivity, because there will be a solution towards which no action is required. Or again, consider the effect of transition in Lou Reed's 'Take a Walk on the Wild Side', where the imperative construction that constitutes the chorus ('Hey babe, take a walk on the wild side') is, as regards the lyric as a whole, uttered by one specific voice within a narrative; but where, too, as the general formulation of a chorus, that imperative construction can reach outside the narrative, as a general exhortation to the audience.

(iii)

Collectively, these effects of interruption and disruption create the range of positions for interpretation that are made available in the songs of rock music. This applies both to kinds of response in which the song is considered from an exterior or disengaged position (taken to represent virtues of poetry and artifice, or to stand as expression of a singer's experience), and to processes of identification in listening liable to be induced by the special effect in rock music of shifters ('he/she is really saying this to me'; or, 'this, ideally, is what I would say to him/her/them').

Within such a range of possible responses, specific interpretations are created in connections and disconnections across the lyric, and in surrounding elements of fantasy and memory. In this way (and since there cannot be for any song a singular or exhaustive listening relation), responses engage and construct pleasures and desires as much in displacement and disconnection as they do in perceptions of coherence.

Within such movements of pleasure and desire, even so, emerges an important point of division. To clarify this, distinction might be made between two kinds of listening. In one kind, dislocations are indeed registered, as meanings come in and out of focus, but they are contained under a coherence guaranteed by the resuming generality of title and chorus. Chorus and title offer a certitude of vocal address, punctuating a flux of movements with an assured pleasure in communication and declared position. Disjointed relations of words and phrases unheard, of fragmented senses and false starts, occur in verses like counterpoint and embellishment–there only to be restored with a subsuming and directed speech act.

But there is another kind of pleasure that also attaches to disjunction and displacement, and can exist in the rock song. For such a pleasure, the possibilities of that containment are overrun, and an oscillation in response causes a loss of position, rather than simply forestalling such coherence during verses only for it to be regained in a chorus—and often confirmed in successive repetitions of that chorus as conclusion and fade.

Indeed, the very promise of stability in title and chorus can be itself undermined. This is perhaps most remarkable where contradiction or incongruity continue to protrude in the lyric, as when Stevie Wonder's appeal for a day of public holiday in reverence to Martin Luther King is heard simply as its chorus salutation, 'Happy Birthday to You'.

Consider, in this respect too, Bob Dylan's 'Rainy Day Women # 12 and 35'. In this song, the degree of disconnection or contrast that can appear between verse and chorus in song-forms is accentuated, with a resulting unresolved irony or contradiction. In the verse, the sense of the verb 'to stone' is 'batter', 'destroy' or 'make to suffer' ('They'll stone you when you're riding in your car/ They'll stone you when you're playing your guitar'). But in the chorus, a passive construction of that same verb creates another sense, that of intoxication: 'Yes, but I would not feel so all alone/ Everybody must get stoned.' In this movement between verse and chorus, 'everybody' itself becomes ambiguous. It can be either a third-person inclusive generalisation from the verses (everyone who drives a car; everyone who plays the guitar . . .); or it can be a second-person address, through the song-form, to the audience (i.e. 'You must all get stoned'). Ambiguous between these senses, the song overall can constitute either a general, philosophic proposition concerning the difficulty of sustaining human life, or else an equally conventional rock performer's entreaty to enjoyment. What is important here is that the incongruity between these possible senses is left, for the song-lyric itself, unsettled.

(iv)

Distinction such as this between a kind of pleasure linked to restoration and coherence, and one created in displacement of stability, has ramifications in rock music's cultural and commercial currency. Arguably, 'Rainy Day Women' gained its wide circulation precisely by way of the possibility of recuperation produced in the song's chorus, rather than from any displacement of settled position or meaning. In this respect, the song might be thought to correspond with the fashionable circulation of David Bowie's otherwise equally ambiguous 'Fashion' discussed above, indicating less an undercutting property of unresolvable irony or contradiction, than a way in which even contradiction within a song-lyric can be restored to coherence in performance and listening.

That critical explanation of 'Rainy Day Women' gains some support from comparison with many other songs which explore word associations, homophones and puns—techniques nowhere more apparent than on the album *Rock Bottom* (1974), by Robert Wyatt, produced by Nick Mason of Pink Floyd. Where no resolving position can be established along the lines of a chorus address, a far more extended range of fragmentary, unstable relations is precipitated, overspilling any settled overall position of speech act or speaker. Within current priorities of production and assessment, nevertheless, such experiment and creations of pleasure are usually accorded a far reduced machinery of recording and distribution, and are as often condemned as gratuitous poeticising or aesthetic whimsy. But in view of the complexities of songs indicated here, it is difficult to regard this neglect as being unrelated to the threat such pleasures pose to the conceptions of address and communications described above, on which the majority of rock-songs appear to have been predicated.

Albums I: *Sergeant Pepper* and *Dark Side of the Moon*

(i)

Details of the song-form suggest that whilst in general rock music is governed by surrounding forces at work in its production and reproduction, such conditions can also lead into exploration and initiative. The ways in which pronouns specify positions for performer and listener, for example, have been seen simultaneously to offer possibilities for innovation and alternative. In rock groups' sets of pieces for performance, too, the very element of sequence and continuity which in radio programming seemed to indicate restriction and control is decided—in relation to conventions of a dynamic of concert performance (introductory numbers, finale, encore...), and subject to agreement with promoters and varying municipal regulations—by performers themselves as an evening's sequence or programme of entertainments. And the rock album form is exactly another instance in which the two directions or pressures—that of restriction and that of initiative—clearly intersect. So in order to chart ways new formal potentialities are created in active response to, as well as in reflection of, surrounding aesthetic, technological and institutional conditions, it is worth considering aspects of development and controversy surrounding experiment with the long-playing record.

(ii)

The album features within the recording process as a distinct innovation, but also as a continuing anomaly, able to represent either a new musical form, or simply a collection or accumulation of smaller, separate pieces. Technically, the album becomes available, as the long-playing microgroove record at 33 r.p.m., from the early 1950s. But at first it remains for rock music without exception a succession of songs ('album' as exactly a collection of images, usually between five and ten per side). It is only in the course of the later 1960s, particularly with the emergence of the 'concept' album and with experimentation in stereo following more widespread commercial availability of stereo equipment around 1968, that the album takes on its appearance as a distinct, compound musical form. Before this period, it is only in 'classical' music (and to some extent in jazz—particularly in its aspirations towards a scale of form and cultural influence along the lines of 'classical' music), that use of extended playing time is widely made.

It is clear from the outset that the historical changes surrounding the album, and the conflicting directions for rock music these emphasise, must be seen in relation to factors beyond the musical forms themselves: first, in relation to changes in the social esteem of rock music and musicians around 1968, following (among other factors) social and economic upheavals related to the international commercial success of many groups and solo performers, leading indirectly towards an unprecedented 'artistic' credibility; second, in relation to technical developments in recording processes themselves, researched and implemented in part as responses to aesthetic and technical demands from performers, but also with regard to cost-saving within a then expanding popular music industry centrally and increasingly linked to record sales.

(iii)

Some necessary distinctions around these developments can be made by way of a comparison between certain details of the Beatles' album *Sergeant Pepper's Lonely Hearts Club Band* (1967), and Pink Floyd's *Dark Side of the Moon* (1972, completed in early 1973). In each of these recordings, experiment is made with interconnecting songs or musical pieces linked by an overall design or level of cohesion.

In terms of techniques of production, a point of distinction between the two records is clear. *Sergeant Pepper* is recorded on four-track tape facilities (on occasion with two machines synchronised), when EMI are deliberating whether to introduce new eight-track and sixteen-track machines,[9] and with much interest in overdubbed effects deployed in George Martin's elaborate arrangements and orchestration. As a result of this experimentation, the album finally takes up 700 hours of studio time, compared with ten hours for the earliest Beatles' LP in 1963. *Dark Side of the Moon* is also recorded for EMI and at Abbey Road studios, London, but by contrast on the later installed multi-track machines (sixteen tracks at that time[10]). Correspondingly, a point of aesthetic and historical comparison is also clear. *Sergeant Pepper* is commonly taken in accounts of rock music to have initiated the musically or thematically cohesive rock album (Frank Zappa's *Freak Out*, 1967, having claim to a prior, if lesser, cohesion); *Dark Side of the Moon* is equally frequently considered perhaps the exemplary peak of that form and aspiration, before major redirections after 1976 precipitate renewed interest in albums made up of a sequence of short songs.

The important modifications of aesthetic interest and technical capability which underlie the initiatives of these albums can best be clarified in a contrast between two interludes or 'bridges' in individual tracks. Consider first of all, the song 'A Day in the Life'. This song is credited to both Lennon and McCartney, and is remembered by Lennon as a high point in their song-writing collaboration—though also as being largely his own composition, with only the central section, already written for other purposes, added by McCartney late in the writing process.[11] The song has come to be most widely remembered for its introduction of techniques of absurdist or surrealist lyrical collage into rock music, as well as for an overall sombreness of manner ('he blew his mind out in a car/ he didn't notice that the lights had changed'), often related to allusions to drugs ('I'd love to turn you on', set across extended orchestral crescendi in the middle and end of the song; or 'Found my way upstairs and had a smoke/ And somebody spoke and I went into a dream', followed by a brief choral passage with increased reverberation). These are techniques and allusions in respect of which the song was temporarily withdrawn from airtime on radio stations in a number of countries at the time of its release.

But it is in a small detail of the section beginning 'Woke up, fell out of bed/ Dragged a comb across my head', rather than in such general lyrical techniques, or across reputation as regards differing representations of drug use, that most effective contrast with Pink Floyd's *Dark Side of the Moon* is to be made. The waking from the smoke-induced dream in this middle section is announced by a short ringing sound, as of an alarm clock, followed by a new, accelerated tempo of staccato beats, as well as by modulation from the key of E minor to that of E major. These mutations collectively produce—across long-standing programmatic conventions of rhythm and harmony—a representation of haste, with the sonority of the bell sound linked to an immediately specified frame of extra-musical reference, 'Woke up . . .'.

(iv)

Consider by contrast the musical interlude which intervenes between the songs 'Breathe' and 'Time' on the first side of *Dark Side of the Moon*, an interlude which is itself given the title 'On the Run'. The song 'Breathe' addresses a deceptive shortness of human life and consequent need for urgency of action, and ends, 'And balanced on the biggest wave/ You race towards an early grave . . .'. These lines are then followed by a section in which footsteps, airport announcements and other sounds are overlaid across synthesiser and tape tones, culminating in an explosive crescendo; after this acoustic explosion emerges a ticking pulse, then an array of chiming bells and clock alarm sounds; out of these a rhythm is established which in turn develops through sustained guitar notes and variably pitched percussive embellishment, leading into the song 'Time', which begins, 'Ticking away the moments that make up a dull day . . . '.

What is instantly clear from this description is that the interlude involves techniques far more extended and elaborate than those of 'A Day in the Life'. The elements of co-reference between the two songs—from ' . . . race towards an early grave', through the various suggestions of time and haste in 'On the Run' (the timetable or airport schedule, rapid footsteps, measured passing of time by clocks in which an alarm of awakening urgency erupts) into 'Ticking away the moments . . . '—are extended over a far greater duration than in 'A Day in the Life' (a timespan of just short of six minutes, as compared with the two seconds which pass between the clock and 'Woke up . . . ' in the Beatles' song). In this way, the scale of cohesive interrelations involved is much greater in this later record, creating and calling upon far more complex interconnections than those of *Sergeant Pepper*.

Whereas, too, in the Beatles' recording, the alarm sound functions almost exclusively as representation of the clock which wakes the dreamer to a more quotidian reality ('Went downstairs and drank a cup/ And looking up I noticed I was late . . . '), in the Pink Floyd episode, the sonorities of the clock bells function both at this level of programmatic depiction of time, and also as musical textures which produce their own relations of rhythm and timbre. The clock sounds establish a rhythm which permutates through guitar and percussion figurations and leads into the rhythmic and harmonic fabric of the following song. And there is a further contrast, too. In the Beatles' song, the alarm is a relatively quiet sound within what is overall a generally constant dynamic band. (According to at least one recollection, the alarm clock was inserted to mark a 24-bar pause to be filled later—by the orchestral crescendo—and then found to be undeletable.[12]) But the dynamic range of the sounds in *Dark Side of the Moon* requires a far greater fidelity of reproduction to be heard (to the extent that many spoken interchanges, including the final, modifying words, 'There is no dark side in the moon, really . . . as a matter of fact, it's *all* dark' disappear altogether in many reproductions), even if certain organising musical textures, such as those of drums, bass, keyboards and guitar, are mixed to be audible across a very wide range of reproduction apparatuses.

Albums II: New Form or Sell-out?

What makes comparison of techniques and scope of cohesion between these two albums of interest is that it can serve to indicate a more general shift of emphasis taking place in rock albums between the late 1960s and the early 1970s. This shift has implications for what have remained central and active controversies over rock music's claims and possibilities.

Assessment of the combined technical and aesthetic developments illustrated in this comparison has gone in two main, opposing directions, closely related to the two more general positions on rock music outlined above:

(i) that they were part of a technological, commercial and aesthetic evolution, establishing possibilities for large-scale composition in a new musical form capable of including greater integration and coherence of elements. It is this dimension–embryonic in earlier Pink Floyd albums, as in the track 'Echoes' on *Meddle*–which is extended in their later projects (from 'Everything under the sun is in tune/ But the sun is eclipsed by the moon', through machine sounds of 'Welcome to the Machine' representing machinations of the rock music industry on *Wish You Were Here*; in *Animals*; more recently, on *The Wall*). Or again, it is that level of continuity or cohesion of musical entertainment which is explored elsewhere by the Beatles, as on side 2 of the *Abbey Road* album, if with an important, exceptional precedent in the collage *Revolution No 9* on the double album, *The Beatles,* 1968 ('The White Album').

The argument over value is centrally that developments around the album produced a new degree of autonomy in selection of a table of entertainments, and potential for dialectical counterpoints within a single, composite piece of music, on terms not dictated by such 'external' pressures as radio programming; that, moreover, the album in this way represented a means for rock music of becoming extricated from traditions of a more controlled 'popular' music, and so of acquiring the extended formal resources of earlier concert-music forms, whilst establishing these stripped of existing cultural investments.

Less directly, too, the argument has been that the new recording techniques and increased social esteem at stake revolutionised for rock music the nature of collaboration and musical composition. With multitrack tape-recording facilities, a capability exists to discriminate, include or delete during overdubbing, editing and mixing, and this can be taken to have made engineering and mixing, and the kinds of collaborative discussion and reflection surrounding them, integral parts of musical composition. Composing as an activity becomes in such terms a collective process involving musicians, producer and engineer, as well as an initial composer, especially when, in music which draws extensively from jazz, blues and other participatory forms, musicians embellish, and so effectively co-compose, the music on which they play. So whilst in rock music of the 1950s and early 1960s, it is preeminently the producers, arrangers and bandleaders who stand out as the creative technicians of production, these roles become increasingly interwoven, in developments of the album and of multi-track recording studio facilities, with those of the engineer. It is undoubtedly George Martin as arranger/producer, rather than engineer Geoff Emerick, who figures for *Sergeant Pepper* as primary creative musical organiser and technician. But with regard to *Dark Side of the Moon*, a twofold process of change has occurred: a virtually total transferral of musical arrangement from orchestration to synthesiser and tape effects managed by the group themselves; and an increased importance attached to technical facility with, and creative direction of, the studio equipment. As a consequence, it is as much Alan Parsons, recording engineer, as producer Norman Smith, who goes on from *Dark Side of the Moon* to become known as 'creative' musical artist, directing in later recordings from that engineer/producer position the successive Alan Parsons Project albums. And indeed similar reputations for aesthetic, as well as technical, direction are established among recording engineers during this period: Tony Visconti, Conny Plank, Martin Rushent and others.

(ii) that, on the contrary, these developments destroyed the widely based ideal of rock music as a purposefully oppositional or anarchic form, replacing such initiative with simply one contemporary version of an élite regime of 'artists' linked to an increasingly expensive (and so to new musicians increasingly alienating) mode of production. In such terms, the concept album appears merely a capitulation to traditional aesthetic currencies, and in effect an aspiration, as earlier on occasion in jazz, towards the cultural status of musical forms such as the 'suite' (cf. the Nice, *Five Bridges Suite*, Mike Oldfield's *Tubular Bells*, Rick Wakeman's *Myths and Legends of King Arthur and the Knights of the Round Table*, etc.).

This view is able to draw upon exactly an upward revaluation of rock music which takes place at the same time as these first cohesive 'album' compositions, a revaluation which incorporates rock forms within already established and unmodified categories of aesthetic criticism. At first, rock is dominantly represented as degenerative and trivial, or made the subject of objection and occasionally panic (frequently linked to a moral propriety opposed to sexual promiscuity, subcultural violence, drugs or, later, to large assemblies such as rock festivals). In the later 1960s, however, that condemnation comes to coexist with a series of reassessments that acknowledge rock as an 'art-form', and so precipitate scholarly criticisms (of the Beatles, of Bob Dylan, to a lesser degree of Leonard Cohen, Joni Mitchell, the Doors, etc.). In this major redefinition, nevertheless, critical terms of lyricism, poetry and musical setting are staked out irrespective of rock's larger institutions and conditions of address or musical production. Explicitly opposing such views, critiques of the album might contend that if the early rock forms were major reorientations (on precedent of Latin American, and Afro-American and Caribbean musical forms) of the body and dancing into European popular music, the addition of 'concepts' to the album only displaced this emphasis once more; displaced it with concern for artifice and virtues of arrangement and composition that transferred a focus of activity from social occasions for dancing and association into more isolated, usually domestic listening.

As regards openings created by the new recording technology, the criticism might run that the album did not revolutionise creative relations of music-making at all. Concerning the claim of extended collaboration, the rebuff might be that the novelty merely disguises other continuing perceptions and interests, such as the practice of in general paying session players and studio engineers as simply executants, secondary to an initial, creative act; or concerning other aspects of the studio utopia, that, for all the innovation, the facilities of the recording studios remain largely, through payment of recording advances, directly and indirectly related to centralised record company investment and control.

Albums III: Implications for the Contemporary Scene

(i)

It is evident that the full complexity of innovation and transition surrounding the album as a form cuts across the explanatory scope of either of these two accounts.

When in the late 1960s a number of rock's forms were extended or modified–the concept album itself, the long single (such as 'Bridge over Troubled Water'), the inclusion in songs of extended sections of improvised solo instrumental virtuosity, etc.–these formal extensions simultaneously involved changes at the level of institution and cultural currency. As a result, a range of issues need to be engaged in assessing the changes: questions concerning purposes to be directed into musical and lyrical forms, as modes of address; questions concerning technology and relations of musical production; and questions concerning wider economic and cultural conditions of performance, distribution and evaluation.

As regards innovations of the later 1960s, it might be observed that a general shift in the institutions of rock music accompanied the album. Notions of concert performance, musicianship and art-work were widely enhanced in comparison with, and substituted for, earlier notions of social occasion in dancing and jukebox entertainment; and in this way a new primacy of the individually significant musical work was created, in part displacing earlier complexes of image, sound, genre and institution. The 'taking seriously' of rock music in this period, that is to say, involved transformations in a variety of relations between text, performer and expectations of listeners, not simply in alterations of forms alone.

Correspondingly, the challenges in the mid 1970s to these revised relations appeared over an analogous range of often conflicting formulations and alternatives, reflecting different strands within a complicated cultural argument: (i) as formal or 'textual' transformation: seeking to replace 'corrupt' or 'indulgent' musical forms with pristine, 'original' or 'classic' structures of rock and roll and blues, or alternatively with new dissonances (revival of the EP as indicative here of one direction of formal restoration, alongside innovations such as the 12-inch single); (ii) as 'occasional' or 'institutional' transformation for the listener: seeking a relative movement away from ideals of passive listening assumed for concert performance and away from domestic listening to hi-fi, towards an indispensable audience participation in dancing to live performance and in social gathering; (iii) as 'ideological' transformation: in favour of authenticity or 'realism' (as opposed to convention), in revolt against idiom or genre, and in favour of direct voicing and experience (this ideological transition linked to the urgency to control processes of production, often through 'independent' record companies and networks of distribution).

(ii)

What is immediately striking about these criticisms of the album associated with various musical movements of the later 1970s, is that they do not cohere as a single alternative. The situation they have produced is one of outstanding contradiction and diversity of practice and belief: punk, New Romantics, mod revival, further rock and roll revival, heavy metal, as well as explicit linkages for rock music with a full spectrum of contemporary political positions.

It is possible, nevertheless, to distinguish at least one crucial watershed within the varying objections and senses of direction and priority. Certain objections emerge as being what might be termed 'relational' or 'processive': they seek to counter one specific set of circumstances in order to create new conditions which will in turn develop and mutate; others (such as those advocating a return to 'original' forms of rock and roll) might be thought of as being 'absolute' or 'principled': they formulate or imply definitive correction according to a stable or fixed set of values.

The two kinds of position again correspond loosely to the opposing strands already described, and, like them, are most often found combined together, but across a number of contradictions. That a distinction between them remains important, nevertheless, might be illustrated with respect to arguments over the extended access to music-making brought about by rejections, through use of 'dissonances', of an alleged 'aestheticism' in rock of the late 1960s and 1970s. Within a 'relational' perspective, this challenge might be thought to have allowed members of a new generation, otherwise largely excluded from rock music, into active music-making and performance–allowing them to become performers who might later extend their musical techniques without constraint from any fixed 'aesthetic' linked specifically to dissonance or simplicity. In the 'principled' conception, on the other hand, a certain type of dissonance becomes enshrined as *the* condition of music, with any subsequently aroused interest in refinements of technique or orchestration to be regarded as capitulation from an otherwise decisive musical revolution. Felt as crisis and break-up in many bands of the period, this point of division leads into fundamentally differing perspectives on the contemporary musical situation.

(iii)

Two critical reflections on aspects of this divergence are perhaps illuminating. First, the 'principled' viewpoint presumes for dissonances a set of stable properties, despite a familiarity created by their repetition, which is likely finally to reduce the dissonant effect of *any* acoustic convention, by displacing its earliest context of comparison. In this sense, repetition and processes of generic stabilisation appear likely to undermine the aesthetic framework within which the dissonances gain their 'principled' value, and reveal them to have been, from the outset, 'relational'. Second, the initial waves of extended access to music-making in the late 1950s and 1960s applied almost exclusively to men. New Wave criticisms and innovations of the mid 1970s importantly included extended access to rock music-making, as instrumentalists, also for women. This poses major problems for retrospective appeals to a pristine value for rock music invested in forms and ideals of rock and roll. For women, extended access to music-making cannot be simply part of any restoration of an originary ideal, since there exist no 'original' paradigms for women bands to aspire to. The present situation produced by the emergence of women instrumentalists is exactly an unprecedented one, calling for consideration and activity accordingly.

(iv)

These two reflections lead out of the familiar terms of argument over rock music into a new and different perspective. Transitions within rock have provided and continue to provide unprecedented (and often unforeseen) opportunities to transform both the forms and the relations of musical practice, to create new criteria of activity and value. It is this potential which overspills, but is usually concealed by, the widespread failure of the rock argument so far. Rock music's conditions differ from those of any musical or cultural model to which appeal by analogy is made. And as the music's specific conditions have effects across its full range of activities and possible innovations, they are as a result indispensable to critical perception and explanation. The failure of the rock argument lies less in any particular position adopted, than in the fact that as yet such conditions remain almost totally unacknowledged in all the formulations of position and purpose, all the models for assessment.

The Current Prospect: Synthesisers and Video

(i)

Divergent lines of controversy and opportunity do not exclusively concern a set of finished transitions surrounding the album form and related alterations in rock music during the late 1960s and early 1970s, with these transitions challenged in turn by completed movements of punk and New Wave music of the mid 1970s. Rather, there is a continuing process of change through which rock music has been and is presently shaped and engaged.

To grasp important elements of the contemporary phase of developments, it seems necessary to consider at least two areas of pressure from aesthetic, economic and institutional innovations, which follow from recent, more specific, developments within the technology applied to music-making. To these changes, responses have not yet been decisively worked out or consolidated as conventions and idioms.

The innovations most in question are the advent of a relatively inexpensive portable synthesiser and computer technology, and applications to rock music of videotape and video-disc. It is already beyond doubt that major reorganisations of rock music's forms and institutions will proceed from these two points of pressure and stimulus. But the range of forces and interests which surround the technological innovations (as well as the already established diversity in perception and argument) make it impossible to predict the nature or dominant directions of changes which will ensue from them. It is only possible to begin to distinguish–in their various linkages, definitions and comparisons– details of rock music's conditions as a practice, conditions to which appeal will be made as basis for acceptance, dissent and transition.

To contribute to such reflection, and by way of conclusion, the following preliminary sketch of background to each might serve.

Synthesisers

The electric guitar is the classic instrument of rock. But even a classic instrument has a development that must be set against its apparent stability. Following early adaptations within 1930s dance bands, the guitar can be seen to have undergone a major phase of development and expansion in sales during the 1950s, when designs including solid-body models (and linked with amplification design and manufacture) eased certain practical difficulties of portability in relation to volume. It is largely the introduction of new and cheap instruments produced by these changes which engenders the new group format, now the 'classic' rock group format of the later 1950s and guitar-and-drums bands of the 1960s (the guitar itself coexisting during this period with the saxophone as dominant solo instrument). As regards ensemble playing, too, the guitar further codifies its melodic conventions (also dating in this context from electrification in the 1930s) around the same time, when–in many of the early rock bands–respective roles of lead guitar and rhythm guitar are

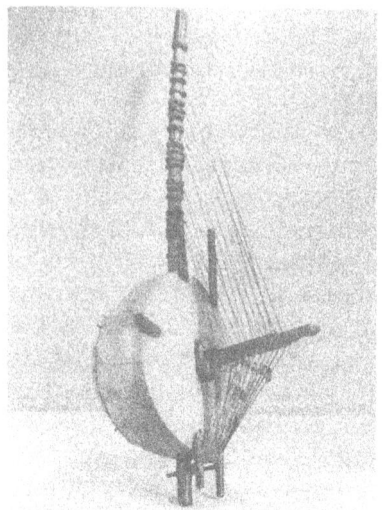

Photo by permission of the Horniman Museum, London.

Photo by permission of Keith Rowe.

Lines for string-players: the rock guitar, from Kora to Banshee.

stabilised and distinguished. Gradually guitar timbres introduce elements of variation and distortion, with a succession of devices or 'effects': reverb, fuzz, wah-wah, phasing units, talking-guitar tubes, synthesiser modules. And alongside these successive changes, there is the development of the bass guitar (exemplary as regards the importance of volume in relation to portability in its displacement of the double bass): at first it plays simply root notes, alternating fifths and riffs, but gradually extends into its present range of styles: picking, slapping, etc.

These modifications in respect of the guitar need, however, to be considered along with other levels of innovation and transformation. As well as indicating instrumental proficiency or interest, representations of the rock guitarist come to bespeak an additional range of mannerism and display. In this way the electric guitar acquires a changing range of postures for rock music: it becomes, in this respect, a source for musicians of allusion and adaptation—on occasion, merely of dependence.

It is this level of representations of the guitar (e.g. as revolt, as phallus, as heritage), as much as details of its instrumental timbre, which initiates much of the controversy around it. Consider, for example, Bob Dylan's introduction of electric instruments into his music around 1965—celebratedly at the Newport Folk Festival in 1965, and then on the album *Bringing It All Back Home*. This use of the electric guitar was widely taken to have displaced two important and valued features of folk music traditions: first, an anti-capitalist, anti-technological association of the acoustic guitar, considered to be in itself a protest against a form of mass production and a popular music industry; second, a subordination in the role of instruments to accompanying the voice, the latter being the primary source of music—enunciating truths of experience and protest (electric instruments thought to be appealing by contrast to traditions of rock and roll and jazz, in which voice and instrument enter into different relations). In such terms, the controversy surrounds a set of cultural, rather than acoustic, resonances of the electric guitar; and these cultural emphases and priorities prescribe conditions for aesthetic pleasure. At points of disagreement of this kind is exposed a special importance in alterations of musical technique and equipment. An initially technical or technological development shapes musical forms; and these in turn produce a nexus of associations, and conflicts between associations, with regard to usage.

Each of these levels is already engaged in relation to synthesisers, which have come to prominence alongside the guitar as both melodic and accompanying instrument or sound source, and have also become—across certain ranges and models—of comparable expense for the rock musician.

The various levels of initiative and argument around the new technology are important. Intersections between them, for example, emphatically undercut those forms of contemporary resistance to synthesisers which are formulated in terms simply of their usurpation of existing instruments and instrumentalists, as 'artificial' sounds are substituted for 'natural' ones. In such criticisms, differing usages and genres are considered without differentiation. Yet in order to engage questions of the synthesiser and its repercussions, it is necessary to consider usages and pressures exactly with regard to specific circumstances, genres and purposes. Whereas *some* synthesisers may be used to replace string sections, others are designed and utilised as keyboard instruction or for assisted performance, extending musical performance rather than diminishing it. Such usages are evidently incommensurate: whatever positions are taken on current changes will need to be developed on the basis of appropriate detail and distinction.

(ii)

To trace the development of keyboard synthesisers, it is necessary to make a retrospect at least as far as the early electronic organ of the 1930s. From traditionally ecclesiastical overtones and connotations, the organ gains currency both as a domestic instrument and in 'light music' ensembles such as those of Hammond organ, bass and drums. In one series of influences and directions, it enters rock music through this ecclesiastical usage, by way of gospel music, and into soul and reggae. But already subject in other genres of the 1960s to changing resonances, the organ features in the Tornados' 'Telstar' as representation of a kind of space-age future, whilst slightly later than this develops a contrasting emphasis (in the mellotron and other machines of the late 1960s that simulated string sections and sound-effects often of contextually indicated 'natural' provenance, as in pieces by King Crimson, the Moody Blues and Pink Floyd). The current range of synthesisers–refined and reduced in size and difficulty of operation–appear to have been first similarly linked to a phase of changing representations of a 'future' (in the micro computer and space revolution, as indicated in recurrent features of the music of bands such as Kraftwerk). But alongside its allusive usages, the synthesiser has become an integral instrument of composition and performance, linking such properties of social allusion with usage within conventional instrumental idioms, rather than remaining exclusively a means for generating backing 'special effects'.

With the synthesiser, and with other contemporary means of music-making, relations between voice, instrument and machine are posed as urgent questions once again. There is, for example, a current intersection between machines *making* music and those reproducing it in idioms such as 'scratching', where a machine manufactured for reproduction (the gramophone) is taken as an instrument, and used to produce sound collages over which are layered speaking or singing voices. In one respect, this idiom of 'scratching' projects much of what is at stake in synthesisers themselves. Equipment and technology can be used for a range of purposes; and these are not reducible to the means themselves. The issues surrounding synthesisers do not as a result so much concern an altered relation of human creativity to machine ('dehumanising' music in repetitious sequencing, programming the aesthetic of the future); the important relations are those between instrument and surrounding conventions, conditions and purposes. The controversies over synthesisers can accordingly be focused more as ones of genres and their effects than of threatened artistry or 'humanity'. All purposes in relation to a technology are constrained to employ, and so gain relational definition with, a surrounding network of representations and comparisons which are more importantly 'social' than they are 'human'.

(iii)

If there *is* an obstacle for music presented by synthesisers, it concerns a general way in which a compositional emphasis (linked to slow, deliberative programming of sounds of the machines) can enhance recording, over and against interactive relations and collaborations of music-making. The latter have produced long-standing demands for extended access and participation, and these need to be defended against encroachment by such emphases. But this is less a problem of any technical specification of the machines than of an array of surrounding and variable representations—whose currency will be increased, maintained, lost or altered by reflection and comment, not by 'principled' opposition or suspicion.

Moreover, that the kinds of transition surrounding synthesisers do not concern simply acoustic or formal issues can be shown by considering contingent transitions in rock's group images. With capability for extensive overdubbing in multitrack studios, a long-prevailing requirement of group collaboration or cooperation for recording ended, technically and practically. Group recordings could be produced without all the members of a musical group being simultaneously in the studio, individual musical parts not needing to be recorded at the same time or in the same place. Indeed, irregular attendances at rock recordings appear to have been already a feature of Beatles' sessions as early as 1967, and the practice has now become an accepted convention of record production. One or two musicians can play most or all of the instruments in a recording, and this has been the case for Mike Oldfield, Stevie Wonder, Paul McCartney, Roy Wood, Eddy Grant and others. Synthesiser and drum-machine mark significant extensions in this process of altering practical relationships of music-making. Contemporary rock stage-acts can incorporate techniques closely analogous to those of recording; and in consequence, the visual impact of musicians and sound sources is no longer obliged to conform to the now 'classical' appearance of the rock ensemble, as can be seen in rock performances accompanied by tape (such as ones by Grace Jones), or in those of contemporary British synthesiser duos. If in earlier periods of rock music groups who recorded without a collective 'group' image would frequently recruit mime performers for subsequent stage or television appearances, current representations of musical technology have made this no longer necessary, the equipment creating—not in itself, but through more complicated relations of its currency—a new configuration within the *visual* profile of rock music.

Images and Videos

These circumstances surrounding the new range of sound sources for performance and recording are made more complicated by relations between them and an important new discourse or 'text' for rock music: video. As album was to single, so video will be to album, the reasoning might go: video as the moving album sleeve, or transplanted rock film.

A number of immediate qualifications to this view are necessary. From the outset, the analogy of extension and enrichment

needs to be seen not with regard to technological innovation only, but rather to technological innovation contemporaneous with, and linked to, significantly declining record sales during the mid 1970s—a period simultaneously of increased investment in and sales of video tape-recorders and video cassettes.

Yet neither does the video 'revolution' correspond neatly and exclusively with a redirection of capital speculation and controls. In at least one important sense, video simply extends a process already underway in rock music as regards the gramophone disc (in respect of sound rather than of vision). For it appears to have been first the 'record' or disc which created for rock music a concern with image beyond that already established for stage performance and spectacle: a concern with creating persona as a 'set' of tracks played and recorded. This 'setting' has often come subsequently to constrain performance to conform to arrangements and balance of recording, the 'record' becoming less the recollection of a performance, than the predefining 'text' *for* it. In such terms, performance can come to be largely advertisement for records, in an inversion of earlier conventions according to which performance was the primary or dominant audience relation, when songs were considered to be tested out for response after being devised in relative isolation and solitude.

In the rock video, then, what seems in question is another shift (in this case in relation to vision rather than to sound) in a series of changing procedures for representing body and gesture. These have transformed interactive elements of gesture, carrying them over from performance and establishing temporal discontinuity or displacement between production and consumption. That temporal discontinuity in visual images of rock is itself not entirely new, of course. Record sleeves have throughout the development of rock music represented a performing source, though subject to successive changes: at first, the early, posed publicity images; then in the later 1960s, often a new and careful 'naturalism' (gardens, houses, T shirts . . .), or studio shots locating music-making as a profession of manufacture–but simultaneously elevating work in the recording studio to a defining position in the construction of meaning; further modifications to the image-making follow during the 1970s, as in usages of idioms from Pop Art less in celebration than in disfigurement of contemporary consumer societies: Peter Blake's *Sergeant Pepper* cover is transformed into punk representations of abuse, rejection and misplacement.

Alongside such revisions within conventions of 'still' photography in the course of rock's history, however, a number of further revisions can be seen which are specific to moving pictures. And certain features of the use of rock music for film and television soundtrack might illuminate the processes of redefinition.

Conventions of Hollywood scores have usually depicted,

through orchestral arrangements, states of mind and emotions or dramatic registers of incident. But usages of rock music have never simply conformed to this convention. On precedent of jazz films of the early 1950s, rock constituents of film scores appear initially to have most often represented social atmosphere (coffee bars, 'street-life', wild living), or to have continued existing traditions of 'musical' (the Elvis Presley films, those of Cliff Richard, etc.). Songs feature as performance in such films *within* the image–as mime and dance. But as rock music is more frequently used, these conventions of sound and vision have divided into at least three distinguishable modes:

(i) continuing representations of concert, in rock documentaries such as *The Concert for Bangladesh* (1972), *Pink Floyd Live at Pompeii* (1971), *Let It Be* (1970), or coverage of social occasions such as *Woodstock* (1970), or of the Rolling Stones' Altamont concert in *Gimme Shelter* (1970). When embellished, these might be usefully thought of as intersections between documentary techniques and those of the 'musical'. In both, what is crucial is that the music-making continues to be consistently represented in the image.

(ii) productions and genres in which a persona of the rock star is shifted across simply as actor, into film or television drama, with little or no direct connection to rock music itself (though often there is an element of continuity provided by associations of a surrounding 'rock culture': Mick Jagger in *Performance* (1970), Diana Ross in *Lady Sings the Blues* (1972) or *Mahogany* (1975), or Sting in *Brimstone and Treacle* (1982), as before them Elvis Presley and Frank Sinatra.

(iii) sound linked more directly to conventions of television and film soundtrack already established in and for other genres, music joined to sequences in which no music-making is actually visible. Sound is superimposed on image without visual specification, as frequently, for example, in *A Hard Day's Night* (1964), *Help* (1965), or much of *The Harder They Come* (1972); in *Easy Rider* (1969), in parts of *Tommy* (TV, 1968–70; film 1975); more recently, in *Quadrophenia* (1979), and *The Wall* (1982). Currently used as main musical style in many films and television programmes with no direct connection with rock.

In these usages emerges one difficulty, as well as one dimension of opportunity, presented by rock film and video. Existing rhetorics of sound and image developed for film and television are modified and revalued in new techniques, as an existing repertoire of conventions is faced with comparison and alternative. And again one significant intermediary in the directions of change concerning sound and vision is to be found in representations, in film and television, of juke-boxes, domestic radios and discotheques. These occupy a place between that of 'musical' itself and that of soundtrack, the sounds being indeed performed within the image, but remaining invisible because the machines themselves emit sound but do not move.

Across this local anomaly, as well as in broader terms of opportunity within rhetorics of image-making, rock videos (and video-discs) are in an important phase: important in respect both of their developing techniques, and in the availability of their necessary equipment of production. It is forms of combination between these two elements which are shaping and will continue to shape video and its cultural valuations and revaluations.

With antecedents in rock films as above (and in such record promotions as the Beatles' for 'Penny Lane' and 'Strawberry Fields Forever'), rock videos can be traced more specifically from such works as Jon Roseman's production for Queen's 'Bohemian Rhapsody' (1975) and the Boomtown Rats' 'I Don't Like Mondays' (1979); in productions of Don Letts and others; and in a surrounding range of styles and modes of production (invoking already familiar terms and problems of the established rock debates).

But alongside all the existing, unsettled questions emerge new ones, too. As initial definitions of interest, and points of pressure and controversy, these might be projected as three areas of imminent impact and influence, areas corresponding closely to the three emerging soundtrack conventions described above:

(i) In and from video will without doubt be created new genres, developed in adaptations of existing rhetorics of the image. Arguably dominant among these will be sequences stylistically based in gestures of performance at present recorded in rock documentary and musical, but gradually projected into more elaborate mime and scenario. (There is already a working guideline in the business that new groups should at first be represented always accompanied by their instruments, in order to establish for them a specific, performing identity.) Alongside these techniques, there will be adaptations from other related idioms, including the publicity photograph and existing film and television soundtrack usages of music.

(ii) Forms and relations of rock music other than those of the video itself will be affected by these transformations. Videos may become dominant within the currently wide range of rock forms, subordinating or marginalising records and performance, and leading—by way of saturation and influence—to a consequent danger of submerging active improvisation and amateur music-making as practices. More broadly in such circumstances, an aural emphasis available to early rock music (because already established during a phase of technical and institutional primacy of radio and gramophone) appears in process of mutation, leading towards a new dominance of the visual, elsewhere promoted by the increasing cultural centrality of television. As constructive reflection on this change, it is possible to conjecture new disjunctions and divergence between forms and media, in effect leading to further reclassification and resettlements of genres. These would then develop according to opportunities presented by the specific and individual properties of the materials and media employed.

(iii) New currencies of the rock video will have effects into television, advertising and film themselves, beyond actual reference to rock music—as one consequence of movements within the wider 'rock culture'. These effects will almost certainly channel into long-term expectations surrounding techniques of juxtaposing images. Yet the influence will stem from techniques at present crucially constrained by conditions within rock genres of a necessary brevity required for accompanying 'single' length songs. From such specifically motivated conventions, the rock video will have major repercussions on the culturally central currencies of television and film, in which social representations of several generations are at present being redefined.

Notes and References

CHAPTER ONE: Music and its Language

1. See, Ferdinand de Saussure, *Course in General Linguistics*, edited by Charles Bally and Albert Sechehaye in collaboration with Albert Reidlinger, translated by Wade Baskin (London: Peter Owen, 1960) p. 18. Perhaps the only major semiological exploration subsequently has been Jean-Jacques Nattiez, *Fondements d'une sémiologie de la musique* (Paris: 10/18, 1975).
2. Walter Pater, 'The School of Giorgione', in *The Renaissance: Studies in Art and Poetry* (London: Macmillan, 1912) p. 135.
3. Ibid., p. 137.
4. Ibid., pp. 138–9.
5. Ibid., p. 151.
6. Ibid., pp. 151–2.
7. Deryk Cooke, *The Language of Music* (Oxford University Press, 1959; reprinted 1974) p. 21.
8. Ibid., p. 97.
9. Ibid., p. 27.
10. Otto Karyoli, *Introducing Music* (Harmondsworth: Penguin, 1965; reprinted 1981). See especially, pp. 66–72 and p. 96.
11. For this area of contemporary development, see references to work by Leonard Bernstein, Fred Lerdahl and Ray Jackendoff, Matthew Chen and Mark Steedman, cited in the bibliography to this chapter.
12. A particular debt for this section is owed to Raymond Williams, *Keywords* (London: Fontana/Croom Helm, 1976). See especially the introduction to this work.

CHAPTER TWO: Classical Music

1. Daniel Defoe, 'Augusta Triumphans', in *The Novels and Miscellaneous Works of Daniel Defoe* (1841), XVIII. 16, and cited in E. D. Mackerness, *A Social History of English Music* (London: Routledge & Kegan Paul, 1964) p. 110.
2. For prevailing currencies of the new musical language, see, for example, Donald Mitchell, *The Language of Modern Music* (London: Faber, 1963; reprinted 1976) pp. 31–2, 52–4.
3. See, P. Pedersen, 'Perception of Octave Equivalence in 12-tone Rows', *Psychology of*

Music, vol. 3, no. 2 (1975) 3–8, and cited in John Booth Davies, *The Psychology of Music* (London: Hutchinson, 1978) p. 18.

CHAPTER THREE: Tuning and Dissonance

1. Boethius, *De Musica*, Book I, ch. 2; quoted, in translation, by Ruth Halle Rowen, *Music Through Sources and Documents* (Englewood Cliffs, New Jersey: Prentice-Hall, 1979) p. 38.
2. Quoted by Rowen, ibid., p. 90.
3. Paul Hindemith, *The Craft of Musical Composition* (New York: Association of Music Publishers, 1945) vol. I, pp. 152–6; and quoted Rowen, *Music Through Sources*, p. 343.
4. See Charles Rosen's account of the end of *Erwartung*, in *Schoenberg*, Fontana Modern Masters (London: Fontana, 1976) pp. 66–71.
5. Anton Webern, *The Path to the New Music*, edited by Willi Reich (Bryn Mawr, Pennsylvania: Theodore Presser, 1963) p. 16; quoted by Rowen, *Music Through Sources*, pp. 327–8.
6. Theodore Adorno, *Philosophy of New Music*, translated by A. G. Mitchell and W. V. Blomster (New York: Seabury Press, 1973) p. 9.
7. Hanns Eisler, an interview with Ashley Pettis entitled 'Eisler, Maker of Red Songs', in *New Masses* (New York, 26 February 1935), reproduced under the title 'On Schoenberg' in, Hanns Eisler, *A Rebel in Music: Selected Writings*, ed. Manfred Grabs, trans. Marjorie Meyer (Berlin: Seven Seas Books, 1978) pp. 75–6.
8. Adorno, 'On the Fetish Character in Music and the Regression of Listening', in Andrew Arato and Eike Gebhardt (eds), *The Essential Frankfurt School Reader* (Oxford: Basil Blackwell, 1978) p. 298.
9. Adorno, *Philosophy of Modern Music*, p. 59.
10. 'The Crisis in Music' (1935), reproduced in Eisler, *A Rebel in Music*, pp. 115–16.

CHAPTER FOUR: Performance: Sound and Vision

1. For a detailed consideration of the relations between psychoanalysis and sound and (especially) vision, see, Stephen Heath, 'Sexual Difference and Representation', *Screen*, vol. 19, no. 3 (1978) 51–112. Further interesting light is thrown on these relations by Freud's own pronouncement, in the opening paragraphs of *The Moses of Michaelangelo*, 'Wherever I cannot do this' (i.e. explain the powerful effect of works of art), 'as for instance with music, I am almost incapable of obtaining any pleasure', *The Standard Edition of the Complete Psychological Works of Sigmund Freud*, edited and translated by James Strachey, in collaboration with Anna Freud, and assisted by Alix Strachey and Alan Tyson, 24 volumes (London: Hogarth Press, 1953) vol. XIII, p. 211.
2. Roland Barthes, 'The Grain of the Voice', in *Image–Music–Text*, essays selected and translated by Stephen Heath (London: Fontana, 1977) pp. 179–89. For a linguistic

account of voice quality, see J. Laver, *The Phonetic Description of Voice Quality*, Cambridge Studies in Linguistics 21 (Cambridge University Press, 1980).

3. Richard Wagner, 'Contrast between the Present-day Theatre and the Greek', an extract from *Zukunftsmusik* (1860), in Albert Goldman and Evert Springchorn (eds), *Wagner on Music and Drama: A Selection from Richard Wagner's Prose Works*, translated by Ashton Ellis (London: Gollancz, 1970) p. 63.
4. Ibid., 'The Dissolution of the Drama', an extract from *Art and Revolution* (1849) pp. 63–4.
5. 'The Modern Theatre is the Epic Theatre' (1930), in *Brecht on Theatre: The Development of an Aesthetic*, edited and translated by John Willett (New York: Hill and Wang; London: Methuen, 1964, paperback edn, 1978) pp. 33–42. The quotation occurs on pp. 37–38.
6. Eisler, *A Rebel in Music*, p. 124.
7. Barthes, 'Musica Practica', in *Image–Music–Text*, pp. 149–54. The quotation occurs on p. 152.
8. For detailed consideration of questions which surround the relation of technology to cultural forms, see, Raymond Williams, *Television: Technology and Cultural Form* (London: Fontana, 1974), and Stephen Heath, 'The Cinematic Apparatus: Technology as Historical and Cultural Form', in *Questions of Cinema* (London: Macmillan, 1981) pp. 221–35.
9. Barthes, 'Musica Practica', in *Image–Music–Text*, p. 149.

CHAPTER FIVE: False Relations and the Madrigal

1. Fellowes, *The English Madrigal Composers* (Oxford University Press, 1921, second impression, 1950) p. 42. As regards the Golden Age, consider also, 'The Elizabethan musicians added no little lustre to that glorious page of our history which records the deeds of great explorers and the defeat of the Armada; and the golden age of English Literature was also the golden age of English Music. But quite early in the seventeenth century . . . the English school of composers and singers suddenly crumbled away' (ibid., p. 30). Or Wilfrid Mellers, 'The Elizabethan and Jacobean age is, then, one of the greatest epochs in the history of European music; and the finest things in it were created in a relatively brief period stretching from about 1600 to 1615. This period corresponds exactly with the highest point of contemporary culture in poetry and the drama; and while such parallels must not be driven too hard, one can see some relationship between the position of Byrd (1543–1623) in our musical history and that of Shakespeare in the evolution of our literature'. 'Words and Music in Elizabethan England', in *The Pelican Guide to English Literature*, vol. 2, 'The Age of Shakespeare' (Harmondsworth: Penguin, 1955, reprinted 1979) p. 386. Or again, Donald Tovey, 'No period of musical history is more important or less adequately brought before the concert-going public of to-day than the sixteenth century, though everybody knows that it is called the Golden Age of Music. In so far as it is true that the exploitation of sudden discords, and the use of instruments in ways not imitative of vocal harmony, put an end to the harmonic purity and self-contained organization of music at the beginning of the new century, the term "Golden Age" is very appropriate to the unconscious freedom and security

Notes and References 237

with which the masters of the sixteenth century said all that they wished to say', 'Weelkes: Four Madrigals', in *Essays in Musical Analysis*, vol. v, 'Vocal Music' (Oxford University Press, 1937, sixth impression 1948) pp. 3–4.
2. Diana Poulton, *John Dowland* (London: Faber, 1972, rev. edn, 1982) p. 46.
3. Ibid., p. 48.
4. Campion, *Observations in the Art of English Poesie*, 1602, Ch. 8 ('Of Ditties and Odes'), in Walter R. Davis (ed), *The Works of Thomas Campion: Complete Songs, Masques, and Treatises with a Selection of the Latin Verse* (London: Faber, 1967, reprinted 1969) p. 309. Or see Percival Vivian (ed), *Campion's Works* (Oxford: Clarendon Press, 1909, reprinted 1967) p. 49.
5. For a detailed study of representations of country and pastoral, see Raymond Williams, *The Country and the City* (London: Chatto & Windus, and Paladin, Frogmore, St Albans, 1973).
6. Concerning these developments, see, respectively, Edmund Fellowes, *English Madrigal Composers*, pp. 154–5; and Stephen Ratcliffe, *Campion: On Song* (London: Routledge & Kegan Paul, 1981) ch. 1.
7. Thomas Tomkins, 'Music Divine', in Philip Ledger (ed), *The Oxford Book of English Madrigals* (Oxford University Press, 1978) no. 25, pp. 175–85.
8. G. R. Elton, *The Tudor Constitution: Documents and Commentary* (Cambridge University Press, 1972) p. 374 (27 Henry VIII, c. 28).
9. Fellowes, *English Madrigal Composers*, p. 84; Robert Steele, *The Earliest English Music Printing* (London: Bibliographical Society, 1903) p. 26.
10. Fellowes, *English Madrigal Composers*, p. 85; Steele, *English Music Printing*, p. 26.
11. Steele, *English Music Printing*, p. 27.
12. Thomas Morley, *A Plain and Easy Introduction to Practical Music* (1597), ed. R. Alec Harman (London: Dent and Sons, 1952) p. 253. See also the facsimile edition of this text produced by Oxford University Press, and listed in the bibliography to this chapter.
13. Ibid., p. 290.
14. Ibid., p. 291.
15. See also, J. Stevens, 'Shakespeare and the Music of the Elizabethan Stage: An Introductory Essay', in Phyllis Hartnoll (ed), *Shakespeare in Music* (London: Macmillan, 1964) pp. 3–48. See especially p. 18.
16. Morley, *Practical Music*, p. 293.
17. See Philip Ledger, *English Madrigals*, no. 2, pp. 8–11, especially bars 12–17, and 28–36.
18. Morley, *Practical Music*, p. 292.
19. Ibid., p. 223.
20. Weelkes, 'O Care, Thou wilt Dispatch me', in Ledger, *English Madrigals*, no. 28, pp. 192–3, bars 1–24; Wilbye's 'Adieu, Sweet Amaryllis', ibid., p. 9, bars 18–22.
21. 'Fyer! Fyer!', in Ledger, ibid., no. 17, pp. 112–20; see especially, p. 115, bars 27–31.
22. For this debate over prosody, see G. Gregory Smith (ed), *Elizabethan Critical Essays*, 2 vols (Oxford: Clarendon Press, 1904), and Derek Attridge, *Well-Weighed Syllables: Elizabethan Verse in Classical Metres* (Cambridge University Press, 1974).
23. Campion, 'Fire! Fire!', in W. Davis, *Works of Thomas Campion*, pp. 156–8; P. Vivian, *Campion's Works*, p. 170.
24. Campion, in Davis, *Works of Thomas Campion*, p. 15; Vivian, *Campion's Works*, p. 3.

25. Poulton, *John Dowland*, p. 71.
26. Campion, in Davis, *Works of Thomas Campion*, pp. 221–2; Vivian, *Campion's Works*, p. 70.

CHAPTER SIX: Rock Today: Facing the Music

1. This view of an effortless internationalism is not shared everywhere within the rock industry. Consider, for example, this view from Miles Copeland, manager of The Police, concerning the section of their 1980 tour in India: 'If the Indians get into Western music it really means that they get into Western culture, which means that they become orientated to the West as opposed to the East... that's a side effect that in the end is a good thing.' Quoted in, Dave Rimmer, 'Music for the New Depression', in David Widgery (ed), *The Book of the Year: September 1979 to September 1980* (London: Ink Links, 1980).
2. *Ghazal*: musical forms usually for voice, sitar, jaltarang, and sarangi–genres appearing to have been derived (if originating in Urdu forms especially in Pakistan) in combinations between film music and raga. The sudden popularity of these forms is widely thought to be at least in part a result of calculated commercial stimulation by HMV and Polydor/Music India.
3. Dave Marsh, 'The Who', in Jim Miller (ed), *The Rolling Stone Illustrated History of Rock and Roll* (New York: Random House, and London: Picador, 1981) p. 287.
4. Robbie Robertson of The Band, quoted in Greil Marcus, *Mystery Train: Images of America in Rock'n'Roll Music* (London and New York: Omnibus Press, 1975) p. 72.
5. Pink Floyd, 'Have a Cigar', *Wish You Were Here* (Harvest, 1975). For details of all records referred to in this chapter, see the record list provided in the Bibliography.
6. The Beatles, 'Glass Onion', *The Beatles* (Apple, 1968).
7. The Rolling Stones, 'Angie' (Rolling Stones, 1973); Neil Sedaka, 'Oh Carol' (RCA, 1959).
8. The Rolling Stones, 'Get Off of My Cloud' (Decca, 1965).
9. See, Brian Southall, *Abbey Road* (Cambridge: Patrick Stephens, 1982), p. 113.
10. Ibid., p. 144.
11. John Lennon, cited in *The Rolling Stone Interviews*, vol. I (New York: Warner Paperback, 1971; reprinted, 1974) pp. 196–7.
12. Southall, *Abbey Road*, p. 117.

Select Bibliography

Collecting a useful bibliography for discussion of music along lines suggested in this book is subject to a number of special circumstances, which are worth recording.

As has been a recurrent theme throughout, music spans a range of forms of realisation. As a result, what will be the most appropriate document or source (and so the most useful citation) concerning one period or form will not necessarily correspond to what will be most useful as regards another. Inevitably what immediately follows from such variety in the forms of realisation is that, in order to reflect period and genre, selection of references will overrun considerations of bibliographical symmetry.

In general, however, where no distinction is being drawn that is dependent upon one particular form of realisation of a musical work, I have chosen not to isolate one: reference in the text and in notes is made, on this basis, to Beethoven's *Sixth Symphony* rather than to Solti's *Beethoven's Sixth Symphony*, for example. And since in this form titles are sufficient reference, such works are not given separate entries in the bibliography or record list.

Differences between forms of realisation merit special attention with regard to Chapters 5 and 6, however. As regards Chapter 5, sources for contemporary listeners and readers comprise primarily a group of composed texts in the form of notation. The most appropriate form of reference to these will accordingly be citation of scores (facsimile or in modernised editions), as well as reference to historical and critical studies. Citing specific recordings of such musical works can indeed suggest a misleading fixity and authority in their performance, disguising an original and intended diversity of practice — as well as an important, defining role in subsequent interpretation. Arguably it is experience of corresponding diversity in recordings that can be most illuminating here. With regard to Chapter 6, on the other hand, records occupy a different position altogether. Here little is to be gained by scrutinising notated scores, even in the relatively few instances where these exist. Notation of audio recordings does not capture purposeful and therefore crucial details of instrumental timbres or of intonation and voice quality. Rather, it is a range of records, sleeve designs, videos and films which are centrally (though not exclusively) in question. So in this case it is virtually indispensable to list particular records, as primary texts.

The bibliography is organised by chapter. This arrangement seems best suited to the above requirements, and at the same time offers some initial distinction between what would otherwise be a wide-ranging but unordered catalogue. And so that few footnotes intervene in the body of the text itself, reference to source works for historical sections of the arguments has been confined to these short supplements to each chapter.

In addition to the particular books and records listed in this way, the following more general reference texts are particularly useful:

The New Grove Dictionary of Music and Musicians, edited by Stanley Sadie, 20 vols (London: Macmillan, 1980). First edition of *The Grove Dictionary of Music* 4 vols, edited by J. A. Fuller Maitland, with an index by Mrs Edmond Wodehouse, (London, 1878).

The New Oxford History of Music, 11 vols (Oxford University Press, 1968).

Scholes, Percy A. *The Oxford Companion to Music* (Oxford University Press, 1955, 10th edn, 1978).

Chapter 1: Music and its Language

Allen, Warren Dwight, *Philosophies of Music History: A Study of General Histories of Music, 1600–1960* (New York: Dover, 1962).

Bernstein, Leonard, *The Unanswered Question: Six Talks at Harvard* (Harvard University Press, 1976).

Blacking, John, *How Musical is Man?* (London: Faber, 1976).

Brook, Barry S., Downes, Edward O. D. and Van Solkema, Sherman (eds), *Perspectives in Musicology* (New York: W.W. Norton, 1972).

Carter, H. H., *A Dictionary of Middle English Musical Terms* (Indiana University Press, 1961).

Chen, Matthew, 'Towards a Grammar of Singing: Tune-text Association in Gregorian Chant', unpublished paper, to be included in the first issue of, *Music Perception*, University of California Press, forthcoming.

Cooke, Deryk, *The Language of Music* (Oxford University Press, 1959, reprinted 1974).

Hanslick, Edward, *The Beautiful in Music* (1854), translated by Gustav Cohen (Indianapolis: Bobbs-Merrill, 1957, ninth printing, 1977).

Jackendoff, Ray, 'The Unanswered Question', *Language*, 53, 4 (1977) 883–94.

Select Bibliography

Jackendoff, Ray and Lerdahl, Fred, 'A Deep Parallel Between Music and Language', an extract from forthcoming work (Indiana University Linguistics Club, 1980).
Karolyi Otto, *Introducing Music* (Harmondsworth: Penguin, 1965; reprinted 1981).
Mellers, Wilfrid, *Music and Society: England and European Tradition* (London: Dennis Dobson, 1950).
Meyer, Leonard B., *Emotion and Meaning in Music* (University of Chicago Press, 1956).
Mitchell, Donald, *The Language of Modern Music* (London: Faber, 1963; reprinted 1976).
Nattiez, Jean-Jacques, *Fondements d'une sémiologie de la musique* (Paris: 10/18, 1975).
Nketia, J. Kwabena, *The Music of Africa* (London: Gollancz, 1979).
Pater, Walter, *The Renaissance: Studies in Art and Poetry* (London: Macmillan, 1912).
Roche, Jerome and Elizabeth, *A Dictionary of Early Music: From the Troubadours to Monteverdi* (London: Faber, 1981).
Ruwet, Nicolas, *Langage, musique, poesie* (Paris: Seuil, 1972).
Saussure, Ferdinand de, *Course in General Linguistics*, edited by Charles Bally and Albert Sechehaye in collaboration with Albert Reidlinger, translated by Wade Baskin (London: Peter Owen, 1960).
Shepherd, John, Virden, Phil, Villiany, Graham and Wishart, Trevor, *Whose Music: A Sociology of Musical Languages* (London: Latimer, 1977).
Small, Christopher, *Music–Society–Education* (London: John Calder, 1977).
Steedman, Mark, 'The Perception of Rhythm and Metre in Music', *Perception*, 6 (1977) 555–69.
——, 'The Blues and the Abstract Truth', unpublished article (1982).
Strunk, Oliver, *Source Readings in Music History: From Classical Antiquity to the Romantic Era* (London: Faber, 1952).
Williams, Raymond, *Keywords* (London: Fontana/Croom Helm, 1976).

Chapter 2: Classical Music

Baines, Anthony (ed), *Musical Instruments Through the Ages* (Harmondsworth: Penguin, 1961; reprinted, 1978).
Brindle, Reginald Smith, *Serial Composition* (Oxford University Press, 1966; reprinted 1977).
——, *The New Music: The Avant-Garde Since 1945* (Oxford University Press, 1975).
Boulez, Pierre, *Boulez on Music Today* (1963), translated by Susan Bradshaw and Richard Rodney Bennett (London: Faber, 1971; reprinted 1975).
Cage, John, *Silence* (Mass.: MIT Press, Cambridge, 1966; paperback printing, 1967).
Cardew, Cornelius (ed), *The Scratch Orchestra* (London: Latimer, 1972).
——, *Stockhausen Serves Imperialism, and Other Articles* (London: Latimer, 1974).
Cooper, G. W., and Meyer, Leonard B., *The Rhythmic Structure of Music* (University of Chicago Press, 1960; reprinted 1963).
Defoe, Daniel, 'Augusta Triumphans', in *The Novels and Miscellaneous Works of Daniel Defoe* (London, 1841).
Forsyth, Cecil, *Orchestration* (London: Macmillan, 1914; reprinted 1974).
Henze, Hans Werner, *Music and Politics: Collected Writings 1953–81*, translated by Peter Labanyi (London: Faber, 1982).

Krebs, S. D., *Soviet Composers and the Development of Soviet Music* (London: Allen & Unwin, 1970).
Lang, Paul Henry, *Music in Western Civilization* (New York: W. W. Norton, 1941).
Mackerness, E. D., *A Social History of English Music* (London: Routledge & Kegan Paul, 1964).
Partch, Harry, *Genesis of a Music: An Account of a Creative Work, its Roots and its Fulfillments*, second, enlarged ed (New York: Da Capo, 1974).
Pearsall, Ronald, *Victorian Popular Music* (Newton Abbot: David and Charles, 1973).
Pedersen, P., 'Perception of Octave Equivalence in 12-tone Rows', *Psychology of Music*, 3, 2 (1975) 3–8.
Rosen, Charles, *The Classical Style: Haydn, Mozart, Beethoven* (London: Faber, 1971; reprinted, 1980).
——, *Schoenberg*, Fontana Modern Masters (London: Fontana, 1976).
Schoenberg, Arnold, *Style and Idea*, essays selected by Dika Newlin (London: Williams and Norgate, 1951).
——, *Letters of Arnold Schoenberg*, selected and edited by Erwin Stein, translated by Eithne Wilkins and Ernst Kaiser (London: Faber, 1964).
——, *Fundamentals of Musical Composition*, edited by Gerald Strang (London: Faber, 1967).
Stravinsky, Igor, *Poetics of Music: In the Form of Six Lessons*, English translation by Arthur Knodel and Ingolf Dahe, preface by George Seferis (Harvard University Press, 1970).
——, and Craft, Robert, *Conversations with Igor Stravinsky* (London: Faber, 1959, reprinted, 1979).
Weber, William, *Music and the Middle Class: The Social Structure of Concert Life in London, Paris and Vienna* (London: Croom Helm, 1975).

Chapter 3: Tuning and Dissonance

Adorno, Theodor, *Philosophy of Modern Music*, trans. A. G. Mitchell and W. V. Blomster (New York: Seabury Press, 1973).
——, *Introduction to the Sociology of Music* (New York: Seabury Press, 1976).
——, 'On the Fetish Character in Music and the Regression of Listening', in Andrew Arato and Eike Gebhardt (eds), *The Essential Frankfurt School Reader* (Oxford: Basil Blackwell, 1978).
Aristotle, *Politics*, trans. H. Rackman, Loeb Classical Library (London and New York: Heinemann, 1932).
Boethius, *De Musica*, ed. Michael Bernard (Munich: Bayerische Akademie der Wissenschaften, 1979).
Davies, John Booth, *The Psychology of Music* (London: Hutchinson, 1978).
Donington, Robert, *The Interpretation of Early Music*, 2nd ed. (London: Faber, 1974).
Eisler, Hanns, *A Rebel in Music: Selected Writings*, ed. Manfred Grabs, trans. Marjorie Meyer (Berlin: Seven Seas Books, 1978).
Helmholtz, Hermann, *On the Sensations of Tone, as a Physiological Basis for the Theory of Music*, 3rd ed. (London: Longman, 1895).
Hindemith, Paul, *The Craft of Musical Composition*, 2 vols (New York: Association of Music Publishers, 1945).
Plato, *The Republic*, trans. and with an introduction by F. M. Cornford (Oxford, 1944; reprinted 1966).

Select Bibliography 243

Rowen, Ruth Halle, *Music Through Sources and Documents* (Englewood Cliffs, New Jersey: Prentice-Hall, 1979).
Salzer, Felix, *Structural Hearing: Tonal Coherence in Music*, 2 vols, with a foreword by Leopold Mannes (New York: Dover, 1962).
Schwarz, Boris, *Music and Musical Life in Soviet Russia, 1917–1970* (London: Barrie & Jenkins, 1972).
Webern, Anton, *The Path to the New Music*, ed. Willi Reich (Bryn Mawr, Pa: Theodore Presser, 1963).

Chapter 4: Performance: Sound and Vision

Apel, Willi, *The Notation of Polyphonic Music, 900–1600*, 4th revised ed. (Cambridge, Mass.: The Mediaeval Academy of America, 1949).
Attridge, Derek, *The Rhythms of English Poetry* (London: Longman, 1982).
Barthes, Roland, *Image–Music–Text: Essays Selected and Translated by Stephen Heath* (London: Fontana, 1977).
Benjamin, Walter, *Illuminations* (1955), ed. Hannah Arendt, trans. Harry Zohn (London: Fontana, 1973; reprinted 1979).
Borwick, John (ed), *Sound Recording Practice: A Handbook*, compiled by the Association of Professional Recording Studios (Oxford University Press, 1976).
Brecht, Bertolt, *Brecht on Theatre: The Development of an Aesthetic*, ed. and trans. John Willett (New York: Hill & Wang; London: Methuen, 1964; paperback edition, 1978).
Browne, Lennox and Behnke, Emil, *Voice, Song, and Speech: A Practical Guide for Singers and Speakers; From the Combined View of the Vocal Surgeon and the Voice Trainer* (London: Sampson Low, 1883; 16th ed, 1904).
Donington, Robert, *Wagner's 'Ring' and its Symbols* (London: Faber, 1974).
Eisler, Hanns, *Composing for the Films* (Oxford University Press, 1951).
Freud, Sigmund, *The Standard Edition of the Complete Psychological Works of Sigmund Freud*, ed. and trans. James Strachey, in collaboration with Anna Freud, and assisted by Alix Strachey and Alan Tyson, 24 volumes (London: Hogarth Press, 1953).
Gelatt, Roland, *The Fabulous Phonography: From Tin Foil to High Fidelity* (Philadelphia and New York: 1955).
Goldman, Albert and Springchorn, Evert, *Wagner on Music and Drama: A Selection from Richard Wagner's Prose Works*, trans. Ashton Ellis (London: Gollancz, 1970).
Heath, Stephen, 'Sexual Difference and Representation', *Screen*, 19, 3 (1978), 51–112.
——, *Questions of Cinema* (London: Macmillan, 1981).
Highfill, Jnr, Philip H., Burnim, Kalman A. and Langhans, Edward A. (eds), *A Biographical Dictionary of Actors, Actresses, Musicians, Dancers, Managers and Other Stage Personnel in London 1660–1880*, 8 vols (Carbondale and Edwardsville, Illinois: Southern Illinois University Press, 1973).
Laver, J., *The Phonetic Description of Voice Quality*, Cambridge Studies in Linguistics, 31 (Cambridge University Press, 1980).
Peacock, Alan and Weir, Ronald, *The Composer in the Market Place* (London: Faber, 1975).
Simpson, Claude M., *The British Broadside Ballad and its Music* (New Jersey: Rutgers University Press, 1966).
Tagg, Philip, *Kojak, 50 Seconds of Television Music: Towards the Analysis of Affect in Popular Music* (Skrifter Från Musikuetenskapliga Institutionen Number 2, Göteborg, 1979).

Williams, Raymond, *Television, Technology and Cultural Form* (London: Fontana, 1974).
Winternitz, Emmanuel, *Musical Instruments and their Symbolism in Western Art* (London: Faber, 1967).

Chapter 5: False Relations and the Madrigal

Attridge, Derek, *Well-Weighed Syllables: Elizabethan Verse in Classical Metres* (Cambridge University Press, 1974).
Auden, W. H. *et al.* (eds), *An Elizabethan Song Book: Lute Songs, Madrigals and Rounds* (London: Faber, 1957; reprinted, 1977).
Borren, Charles van der, *The Sources of Keyboard Music in England*, trans. James E. Matthew (London: Novello, 1914).
Boyd, Morrison Comegys, *Elizabethan Music and Musical Criticism* (University of Pennsylvania Press and Oxford University Press, 1940; 2n edn, 1962).
Campion, Thomas, *Campion's Works*, ed. Percival Vivian (Oxford: Clarendon Press, 1909; reprinted, 1967).
——, *The Works of Thomas Campion: Complete Songs, Masques, and Treatises with a Selection of the Latin Verse*, ed. with an introduction and notes by Walter R. Davis (London: Faber, 1967; reprinted, 1969).
Carpenter, Nan Cooke, *Music in Mediaeval and Renaissance Universities* (University of Oklahoma Press, 1958).
Case, John (?), *The Praise of Musicke* (Oxenford: J. Barnes, 1586).
Chambers, E. K., *The Elizabethan Stage*, 4 vols (Oxford: Clarendon Press, 1923).
Cowling, G. H., *Music on the Shakespearean Stage* (Cambridge University Press, 1913).
Dent, Edward J., *Foundations of English Opera: A Study of Musical Drama in England During the Seventeenth Century* (Cambridge University Press, 1928).
Elton, G. R. (ed), *The Tudor Constitution: Documents and Commentary* (Cambridge University Press, 1972).
Fellowes, Edmund H., *The English Madrigal School*, 16 vols, 2nd revised edn. (London: Stainer and Bell, 1920).
——, *The English Madrigal Composers* (Oxford University Press, 1921; second impression, 1950).
——, *The English Madrigal* (Oxford University Press, 1925).
——, *William Byrd* (Oxford University Press, 1936).
Glyn, Margaret H., *About Elizabethan Virginal Music and its Composers* (London: William Reeves, revised edn, 1934).
Hartnoll, Phyllis (ed), *Shakespeare in Music: Essays by J. Stevens, etc.* (London: Macmillan, 1964).
Kastendieck, Miles, M., *England's Musical Poet: Thomas Campion* (Oxford University Press, 1938).
Kerman, Joseph, *The Elizabethan Madrigal: A Comparative Study* (New York: American Musicological Society, 1962).
Ledger, Philip (ed), *The Oxford Book of English Madrigals* (Oxford University Press, 1978).
Le Huray, Peter, *Music and the Reformation in England, 1549–1660*, Studies in Church Music (London: Herbert Jenkins, 1967).
Mellers, Wilfrid, 'Words and Music in Elizabethan England', in *The Pelican Guide to*

English Literature, vol. 2, 'The Age of Shakespeare' (Harmondsworth: Penguin, 1955; reprinted, 1979).

Morley, Thomas, *A Plaine and Easie Introduction to Practicall Musicke* (1597), with an introduction by Edmund Fellowes, Shakespeare Association Facsimiles (Oxford University Press, 1937).

———, *A Plain and Easy Introduction to Practical Music* (1597), ed. R. Alec Harman (London: Dent and Sons, 1952).

Naylor, Edward W., *Shakespeare and Music* (London: Dent and Co., new edn, 1931).

Pattison, Bruce, *Music and Poetry of the English Renaissance* (London: Methuen, 1948).

Playford, John, *An Introduction to the Skill of Music* (1674) (Ridgewood, New Jersey: The Gregg Press, 1966).

Poulton, Diana, *John Dowland* (London: Faber, 1972; rev. edn, 1982).

Price, David C., *Patrons and Musicians of the English Renaissance* (Cambridge University Press, 1981).

Ratcliffe, Stephen, *Campion: On Song* (London: Routledge & Kegan Paul, 1981).

Reese, Gustave, *Music in the Renaissance* (London: Dent and Co., rev. ed, 1954).

Scholes, Percy, *Puritans and Music in England and New England* (Oxford University Press, 1934).

Smith. G. Gregory (ed), *Elizabethan Critical Essays*, 2 vols (Oxford: Clarendon Press, 1904).

Spink, Ian, *English Song: Dowland to Purcell* (London: Batsford, 1974).

Steele, Robert R., *The Earliest English Music Printing: A Description and Bibliography of Engish Printed Music to the Close of the Sixteenth Century* (London: Bibliographical Society, 1903).

Sternfeld, F. W. (ed), *English Lute Songs, 1597–1632*, facsimile edn (Menston: Scholar Press, 1970).

Stevens, Denis (ed), *The Penguin Book of English Madrigals: For Four Voices* (Harmondsworth: Penguin, 1967; reprinted, 1979).

———, *The Second Penguin Book of English Madrigals: For Five Voices* (Harmondsworth: Penguin, 1970; reprinted, 1977).

Stevens, John, *Music and Poetry in the Early Tudor Court*, Cambridge Studies in Music (London: Methuen, 1961; reprinted by Cambridge University Press, 1979).

Tovey, Donald Francis, *Essays in Musical Analysis*, vol V, 'Vocal Music' (Oxford University Press, 1937; sixth impression, 1948).

Warlock, Peter, *The English Ayre* (London: Humphrey Milford, 1926).

Williams, Raymond, *The Country and the City* (London: Chatto & Windus, and St Albans: Frogmore, Paladin, 1973).

Woodfill, Walter L., *Musicians in English Society* (New York: Da Capo Press, 1953; reprinted, 1969).

Chapter 6: Rock Today: Facing the Music

Bailey, Derek, *Improvisation: Its Nature and Practice in Music* (Ashbourne, Derbyshire: Moorland Publishing in association with Incus Records, 1980).

Chambers, Iain, 'Pop Music: A Teaching Perspective', *Screen Education*, 39 (1981) 35–46.

Chester, Andrew, 'For a Rock Aesthetic', *New Left Review*, 59 (1970) 83–7.

———, 'Second Thoughts on a Rock Aesthetic: The Band', *New Left Review*, 62 (1970) 75–82.

Clarke, Michael, *The Politics of Pop Festivals* (London: Junction Books, 1982).
Clarke, Sebastian, *Jah Music: The Evolution of the Popular Jamaican Song* (London: Heinemann, 1980).
Collier, James Lincoln, *The Making of Jazz: A Comprehensive History* (London: Macmillan, 1978).
Ewen, David, *All The Years of American Popular Music* (Englewood Cliffs, New Jersey: Prentice-Hall, 1977).
Frith, Simon, *The Sociology of Rock* (London: Constable, 1978).
———, 'Music For Pleasure', *Screen Education*, 34 (1980) 51–61.
———, *Sound Effects: Youth, Leisure and the Politics of Rock 'n' Roll* (London: Constable, 1983).
———, and Angela McRobbie, 'Rock and Sexuality', *Screen Education*, 29 (1978/9) 3–19.
Harker, David, *One for the Money: Politics and Popular Song* (London: Hutchinson, 1980).
Hebdige, Dick, *Subculture: The Meaning of Style*, New Accents Series (London: Methuen, 1979).
Hodeir, André, *Jazz: Its Evolution and Essence*, trans. David Noakes (New York: Grove Press, 1956; rev edn, 1979).
Kofsky, Frank, *Black Nationalism and the Revolution in Music* (New York: Pathfinder Press, 1970; fourth printing, 1978).
Lee, Edward, *Music of the People: A Study of Popular Music in Great Britain* (London: Barrie & Jenkins, 1970).
Malson, Lucien, *Histoire du jazz et de la musique Afro-Americaine* (Paris: 10/18, 1976).
Marcus, Greil, *Mystery Train: Images of America in Rock 'n' Roll Music* (London and New York: Omnibus Press, 1975).
Mellers, Wilfrid, *Twilight of the Gods: The Beatles in Retrospect* (London: Faber, 1973).
Middleton, Richard, '"Reading" Popular Music', in *Form and Meaning*, 2, The Open University Second Level Course in Popular Culture, Block 4, Unit 16 (Milton Keynes: Open University Press, 1981).
Miller, Jim (ed), *The Rolling Stone Illustrated History of Rock and Roll* (New York: Random House, and London: Picador, 1981).
Oliver, Paul, *The Story of the Blues* (London: Barrie & Jenkins, 1969; republished Harmondsworth: Penguin, 1972; reprinted, 1978).
Pollock, Bruce and Wagman, John, *The Face of Rock and Roll: Images of a Generation* (New York: Holt, Rinehart & Winston, 1978).
Rolling Stone Interviews, The, vol. 1. (New York: Warner Paperback, 1971; reprinted, 1974).
Shaw, Arnold, *The Rock Revolution* (London and New York: Crowell-Collier Press, 1969).
Southall, Brian, *Abbey Road* (Cambridge: Patrick Stephens, 1982).
Taylor, Jenny and Laing, Dave, 'Disco-Pleasure-Discourse: On "Rock and Sexuality"' *Screen Education*, 31 (1979) 43–8.
Widgery, David (ed), *The Book of the Year: September 1979 to September 1980* (London: Ink Links, 1980).

Record List: Chapter 6

The following is an alphabetical list of records directly referred to in Chapter 6 ('Rock Today: Facing the Music'). It should be remembered that many of the tracks listed here

Select Bibliography

which were released as singles also feature on albums, and vice versa (in some cases, also in other versions–such as 12 inch singles or special mixes). Where there is this diversity, only a single reference has been given. The list is *not* intended as a more general, select discography, or as an overall listening guide to rock music.

Beatles, The, 'Love Me Do' (Parlophone, 1962).
——, 'From Me to You' (Parlophone, 1963).
——, 'A Day in the Life', *Sergeant Pepper's Lonely Hearts Club Band* (Parlophone, 1967).
——, 'I am the Walrus', *Magical Mystery Tour* (Parlophone, 1967).
——, 'Ob-la-di, Ob-la-da', *The Beatles* ('The White Album') (Apple, 1968).
——, 'Glass Onion', *The Beatles* (Apple, 1968).
——, 'Revolution No. 9', *The Beatles* (Apple, 1968).
——, 'Hey Jude' (Apple, 1968).
——, *Abbey Road* (Apple, 1969).
——, 'Let It Be' (Apple, 1970).
Bee Gees, The, 'Stayin' Alive', *Saturday Night Fever: The Original Movie Sound Track* (RSO, 1977).
Boomtown Rats, The, 'I Don't Like Mondays' (Ensign, 1979).
Bowie, David, 'Moonage Daydream', *Ziggy Stardust and the Spiders from Mars* (RCA, 1972).
——, 'Fashion', *Scary Monsters* (RCA, 1980).
Brown, James, 'Say it Loud, I'm Black and I'm Proud' (King, 1968).
Burman, R. D., 'Jane Jaan, O Meri Jane Jaan', *Sanam Teri Kasam* (Music India/Polydor, 1981).
Chicago, 'I'm a Man' (CBS, 1970).
Cochran, Eddie, 'Summertime Blues' (London, 1958).
Conley, Arthur, 'Sweet Soul Music' (Atlantic, 1967).
Cream, 'Sunshine of Your Love', *Disraeli Gears* (Polydor, 1968).
Dire Straits, 'Sultans of Swing' (Vertigo, 1979).
Dunbar, Sly, 'Oriental Taxi', *Sly, Wicked, and Slick* (Front Line, Virgin, 1979).
Dylan, Bob, *Bringing It All Back Home* (CBS, 1965).
——, 'Rainy Day Women # 12 and 35', *Blonde on Blonde* (CBS, 1966).
——, 'Simple Twist of Fate', *Bob Dylan at Budokan* (CBS, 1978).
Gabriel, Peter, 'Biko', *Peter Gabriel* (3) (Charisma, 1980).
Gaye, Marvin, 'You're a Wonderful One' (Tamla Motown, 1964).
Jackson, Michael, 'Don't Stop Till You Get Enough', *Off The Wall* (Epic, CBS, 1979).
Jones, Quincy, 'Love I Never Had It So Good', *Sounds . . . and Stuff Like That* (A & M, 1978).
King, Carole, 'You Make Me Feel Like A Natural Woman', *Tapestry* (Epic, 1971).
Kraftwerk, *The Man-Machine* (Capitol, 1978).
Lennon, John, 'Imagine', *Imagine* (Apple, 1971).
McCartney, Paul, 'Maybe I'm Amazed', *McCartney* (Apple, 1970).
Marley, Bob and the Wailers, 'Lively up Yourself', *African Herbsman* (Trojan, 1972).
——, 'No Woman No Cry', *Natty Dread* (Island, 1974).
Nice, The, *Five Bridges Suite* (Mercury, 1972).
Oldfield, Mike, *Tubular Bells* (Virgin, 1973).
Parsons Project, The Alan, *Pyramid* (Arista, 1978).
——, *The Turn of a Friendly Card* (Arista, 1979).

Pink Floyd, 'Echoes', *Meddle* (Harvest, 1971).
——, *Dark Side of the Moon* (Harvest, 1973).
——, 'Have a Cigar', *Wish You Were Here* (Harvest, 1975).
——, *Animals* (Harvest, 1977).
——, 'Another Brick in the Wall (Part II)', *The Wall* (Harvest, 1979).
Queen, 'Bohemian Rhapsody' (EMI, 1975).
Reed, Lou, 'Take a Walk on the Wild Side', *Transformer* (RCA, 1972).
Rolling Stones, The, 'Get Off of My Cloud' (Decca, 1965).
——, 'We Love You' (Decca, 1967).
——, 'Angie' (Rolling Stones, 1973).
Sedaka, Neil, 'Oh Carol' (RCA, 1959).
Sex Pistols, The, 'Pretty Vacant' (1977), *Never Mind the Bollocks Here's the Sex Pistols* (Virgin, 1977).
——, 'My Way' (Virgin, 1978).
Simon Carly, 'You're So Vain' (Elektra, 1972).
Simon and Garfunkel, 'Bridge Over Troubled Water' (CBS, 1970).
Sister Sledge, 'We Are Family', *We Are Family* (Atlantic, 1979).
Temptations, The, 'Papa Was a Rolling Stone' (Tamla Motown, 1972/3).
Tosh, Peter, 'Legalize It', *Legalize It* (Virgin, 1976).
Tornados, The, 'Telstar' (Decca, 1962).
Wakeman, Rick, *Myths and Legends of King Arthur and the Knights of the Round Table* (A & M, 1975).
Who, The, 'My Generation' (Brunswick, 1966).
——, 'I'm Free' (Track, 1969).
——, *Meaty, Beaty, Big and Bouncy* (Track, 1970).
Wonder, Stevie, 'Happy Birthday', *Hotter Than July* (Tamla Motown, 1980).
Wyatt, Robert, *Rock Bottom* (Virgin, 1974).
Zappa, Frank, *Freak Out* (Verve, 1967).

Index

Abbey Road Studios, 213
acoustics and psychoacoustics, 60–2
Adorno, Theodor, 78, 79–80, 81–3
Aldhelm, Bishop, 69
Altamont Festival, 231
Altered Images, 195
Ambrose, St, 68
Animals, the, 195
Aristotle, 17, 64, 66
  Politics, 64
Ars Nova, 70, 98
Aswad, 174
atonality, 45–8, 49, 55
Augustine, St, 66, 68
Au Pairs, the, 195
ayres, 119–26, 127, 149–58, 163–6

Bach, J. S., 32, 42, 44, 68
  Well-tempered Klavier, 74
ballads, 151
Band, the, 195
Banister, John, 33
Barbarina, 97
Barley, William, 122, 136
  Newe Book of Tabliture, 122
Barthes, Roland, 90–2, 96, 100, 114–15
  'The Grain of the Voice', 90–2
  'Musica Practica', 96, 114–15
Basil, St, 68
Bauer, 107
Bayreuth, 94
  see also, Wagner
BBC, 105–6, 198
Beatles, 177, 182, 186, 192, 193, 195, 198, 199, 203, 211, 213–18, 228, 230–2
  'Love Me Do', 182
  'From Me To You', 203
  A Hard Day's Night, 193, 231
  Help, 231
  'Penny Lane', 232
  'Strawberry Fields Forever', 232
  'I am the Walrus', 198
  'Ob-la-di, Ob-la-da', 198
  Revolution No. 9, ('The White Album'), 216
  'Hey Jude', 198
  Sergeant Pepper, 211, 213–14, 215, 217, 230
  'A Day in the Life', 213–15
  Abbey Road, 216
  'Let it Be', 208, 231
Beatty, Warren, 205
Bee Gees, the, 174, 175
  'Stayin' Alive', 171, 173
Beefheart, Captain, 179
Beethoven, Ludwig van, 11, 13–14, 24, 25, 39, 40, 43, 44
Berliner, Emile, 103
Berlioz, Hector, 11, 44
  Symphonie Fantastique, 44
Bernstein, Leonard
  The Unanswered Question, 15
Bhosle, Asha, 171
Black Slate, 174
Black Uhuru, 171
Blackfriars Theatre, 161
Blake, Peter, 230
Blind Faith, 192
Blondie, 189
Blow, John, 124
Blumlein, A. D., 104
Boethius
  De Musica, 66–7
Boomtown Rats, the,
  'I Don't Like Mondays', 232
Bovell, Dennis, 174
Bowie, David
  'Moonage Daydream', 207
  'Fashion', 186, 188–90, 206, 211
Brahms, Johannes, 38, 112
Brecht, Bertholt, 82, 95
Brimstone and Treacle, 231
Britton, Thomas, 33
Brown, James,   — *continued*

'Say it Loud, I'm Black and I'm Proud', 205
Browne, Thomas, 69
Bruckner, Anton, 43
Bucks Fizz, 192
Bull, John, 32
Bullen, A. H.
  Lyrics from the Song-books of the Elizabethan Age, 126
Burbage, James, 161
Burman, R. D.
  'Jane Jaan, O Meri Jane Jaan', 171–3
Bush, Kate, 179
Buxtehude, Diderik, 32
Byrd, William, 11, 119, 120, 134, 135–6, 137, 144
  'The Fair Young Virgin', 120, 144

Caccini, Giulio, 158
Cage, John, 56
calypso, 174
Campion, Thomas, 119, 121, 122–3, 126, 152–8, 159
  'Fire! Fire!', 152–7
  and, Rosseter, Philip, *Booke of Ayres*, 155, 159
  Lord Haye's Masque, 162
Cannabich, Christian, 38
cantabile, 38, 42, 93
  see also, voice
Caruso, Enrico, 27
cassettes, *see*, recording
Cassiodorus, 66
catch, 133, 148, 164
Caxton, William, 25
Cecil, Sir Robert, 150
Chalcidius, 66
Chapel Royal, 126, 127, 134, 136
Charles I, 133, 162
Charles II, 33, 137
Charles, Ray, 86
Charpentier, Marc-Antoine
  Règles de Composition, 75
Chicago
  'I'm a Man', 205
Christian, Charlie, 102
Civil War, 133, 141, 158
Cliff, Jimmy, 174
  The Harder They Come, 231
Cluniac reforms, 71
Cochran, Eddie
  'Summertime Blues', 198
Cockpit Theatre, 162
Cohen, Leonard, 218
composer, 12, 25, 26, 39–40, 49–50, 51–2, 54, 55, 105, 111, 149
composition, 18, 23, 25, 32, 56, 120
  see also, standards
concert and concert-hall, 18–19, 23–4, 27, 30–1, 72, 73, 75, 78, 83, 86, 87, 89, 96, 101, 103, 106, 149, 151, 158, 162, 211–12, 220, 230
Concert for Bangladesh, 231
concerto, 18, 38
conductor, 12, 19, 26, 34, 36, 39
Conley, Arthur
  'Sweet Soul Music', 198
Cooke, Deryk
  The Language of Music, 10–12, 13, 15
Copeland, Miles, 238n
Council of Laodicea, 68
Council of Trent, 69
Cream
  'Sunshine of Your Love', 198
Cros, Charles, 103
Crosby, Stills, Nash and Young, 192
culture, 171

dancing, 93, 95–8, 123, 135, 152, 161–2, 218
  forms of music for dancing, 41, 53–4, 103, 122, 150, 190, 198, 203, 206, 220
Danyel, John, 152, 159
Darmstadt School, 50
  see also, serialism
Davenant, William, 33
  The Siege of Rhodes, 162
Davis, Gary, 86
Debussy, Claude-Achille, 56
declamatory style in singing, 149, 159, 161
  see also, voice, monody, recitative
Defoe, Daniel, 34
De Forest, Lee, 104
Dennis, John, 34
Dionysus, 22, 64
Dire Straits
  'We are the Sultans of Swing', 205
disco music, 170–5
Dissolution of the Monasteries, the, 124, 133, 134, 140
dissonance, 12, 13, 26, 27, 48–9
  tritone ('the devil in music'), 66, 70, 71
  false relations, and dissonances of pain in madrigals, 13, 27, 73, 146, 150
  'emancipation of the dissonance', 46, 48, 77–8, 81–2

Index

dissonance — *continued*
  'reflection of social relations', 78, 82–4
  in punk and New Wave, 197, 220, 221
Dogons, 68
domestic performance, 18, 101–2, 120, 164
Doors, the, 218
Dowland, John, 119, 121, 123, 134, 152, 159–60
  First Booke of Songs, 122, 152, 156
  'Sleepe Wayward Thoughts', 156
  Lachrymae, 159
Dowland, Robert, 158, 159
  The Musical Banquet, 158
Dryden, John, 93
Duke's Theatre, the, 162
dub effects, 172, 174
  see also, reggae
Dunbar, Sly, 171, 173–4
  'Oriental Taxi', *Sly, Wicked and Slick*, 171–3
Duncan, Isadora, 96
Dunstable, John, 135
Dylan, Bob, 180, 199, 218
  'Simple Twist of Fate', *Bob Dylan at Budokan*, 202
  'Rainy Day Women', 210–11
  Bringing it all Back Home, 225

Eash, George, 108
East, Thomas, 136
Easy Rider, 231
Edison, Thomas, 103, 104
Eddy, Duane, and the Rebels, 195
Eisler, Hanns, 78, 82–4, 95
  Workers' Music Movement, 83
electric guitar, *see*, guitar
Elizabeth I, 126, 135, 144
Emerick, Geoff, 217
Emerson, Lake and Palmer, 192
equal temperament, 31
Euclid, 21
Eurythmics, 195

fancy, 158, 164
Farbenindustrie, I. G., 107
Farnaby, Giles, 126, 134
Feliciano, José, 86
Fellowes, Edmund, 120, 126, 236n
film music, 86, 87–8, 95, 114, 168, 171, 172–3, 186, 193, 229, 230–3
  see also, television, video, image
Fischer–Dieskau, Dietrich, 90
Fleming, John Ambrose, 104

folk music, 11, 54, 97, 225
Freed, Alan, 200
Freud, Sigmund, 235n
fugue, 42

Gabriel, Peter
  'Biko', 208
Gabrieli, Giovanni, 37
gammelan, Balinese, 23
Gastoldi, Giovan Giacomo, 150
Gaye, Marvin, 179, 208
  'You're a Wonderful One', 208
George, Stefan, 46
ghazal, 173, 238n
Gibbons, Orlando, 119, 126, 134, 137, 143
  'The Silver Swan', 143
Globe, the, 161
Gluck, Christoph, 100
gramophone, 103–5, 227, 233
  discs, 168, 170, 179, 230
  album, 114, 183, 199, 211–20, 229
Grant, Eddy, 228
Greece, music in Ancient, 29, 63–6, 74, 122
Gregory the Great, 66
Guido D'Arezzo,
  Micrologus, 69
Guimard, Marie-Madeleine, 97
guitar, 101, 225
  electric guitar, 102, 223–6

Hammond, Laurens, 102
  hammond organ, 102, 226
Handel, George Frederic, 42, 44
  Messiah, 35
Harris, Blind Willie, 86
Harrison, James, 35
Hasan, Kamal, 171
Hauer, Josef, 49
Hawkins, John Isaac, 101
Haydn, Franz Joseph, 17, 39, 40, 44, 99
heavy metal, 220
Helmholtz, Hermann, 60–1
Henry VIII, 134
Hickford, John, 33
Hindemith, Paul, 53, 76
Hitler, Adolf, 107
Holly, Buddy, 179
Homer, 86
Humble Pie, 192
Hume, Tobias, 160

image, 86, 115, 123

image — *continued*
  spectacle of performance, 24–5, 31, 33, 41, 80, 83, 123, 161–2
  of performers ('portraiture'), 115, 183, 195, 228, 230
  record sleeves, 87, 230
  see also, television, film music, video
improvisation, 18, 26, 54, 69, 72, 98, 100, 112, 182, 233
  improvised solos in rock numbers, 219
  Elizabethan fancy, 133, 158, 164
India, 172–3, 238n
instrumental music, 16, 21, 26, 36, 48, 159–60
ITT, 107

Jackson, Michael
  'Don't Stop till you Get Enough', 190
Jagger, Mick, 204, 205, 231
Jamaica, 174
Janet, Paul, 107
jazz, 30, 39, 53–4, 63, 86, 97, 100, 111, 191
Jefferson, Blind Lemon, 86
John, Pope, XXII, 71
Johnson, Robert, 161
Jones, Grace, 171, 228
Jones, Quincy
  'Love I Never Had It So Good', *Sounds . . . and Stuff Like That*, 208
Jonson, Ben, 162
Jubal, 26

Karyoli, Otto
  Introducing Music, 14
King, Carole
  'You Make Me Feel Like a Natural Woman', 206
King Crimson, 227
King, Martin Luther, 210
King, Robert, 33
King's Men, the, 161
King's Musick, the, 134, 159
Kirk, Roland, 86
Knight, Wilson, 10
Kraftwerk, 227
Krenek, Ernst
  Johnny Strikes Up, 53
Kristeva, Julia, 90

Lanier, Nicholas, 122, 157
Lawes, Henry, 122, 157–8, 162
Lear, William, 108
Léonin, 70
Letts, Don, 232

Lipps, Theodor, 61
Liszt, Franz, 34
Locke, Matthew, 162
Lully, Jean-Baptiste, 100
lute, 121–2, 123, 133, 160
Luther, Martin, 69
Lycurgus, 65
lyre, 202

Mace, Thomas, 33
Machaut, Guillaume de, 25
madrigals, 13, 41, 89, 119–66
Madrigal Society, 126
Mahler, Gustav, 43, 44, 46
Mannheim School, 38, 44
Marconi, 104, 107
Marenzio, Luca
  'A la Strada', 150
Marley, Bob, and the Wailers, 174, 176, 180
  'Lively up Yourself', 176, 180
  'No Woman No Cry', 180
Martin, George, 213, 217
Marylebone Gardens, 35
Marx, Karl, 80
Mason, Nick, 211
masques, 33, 41, 93, 96, 123, 135, 139, 149, 151, 159, 161–2
McCartney, Paul, 208, 213–14, 228
  'Maybe I'm Amazed', 208
McTell, Blind Willie, 86
mechanical reproduction of music, 4, 23, 25, 27, 46, 51–2, 89, 100–9, 112–14
  see also, gramophone, recording, radio
Medina, Maria, 97
Mellers, Wilfrid, 236n
mellotron, 226–7
mento, 175
  see also, reggae, ska, two-tone
Mersenne, Marin, 74
Merseybeat, 177, 197
Milhaud, Darius
  The Creation of the World, 54
Milton, John, 86, 143, 157–8
  'To Mr H. Lawes, on his Aires', 157–8
Minos, 65
minstrels, 135, 164
Mitchell, Joni, 179, 218
modes, 59, 63–5, 72, 98
modulation, 73–5
  see also, tonality
Monkees, the, 192
Monteverdi, Claudio, 37, 87
  Orfeo, 37, 87

Moody Blues, the, 227
monody, 125, 149, 159
  see also, declamatory style in singing, voice
Monson, Sir Thomas, 159
Moresque, 96
Morley, Thomas, 119, 120, 126, 134, 136, 137, 140, 144, 145, 155, 156
  Canzonets, or Little Songs to Foure Voyces, 120
  The Triumphs of Oriana, 135, 144
  The Plaine and Easy Introduction to Practicall Musicke, 138, 141–2, 148
  'Fyer! Fyer!', 150–1, 155
Mosel, Ignaz Franz von, 93
motet, 121, 138, 144, 164
Mothers of Invention, the, 195
Mousike, 20–2
Mozart, Wolfgang Amadeus, 11, 13–14, 17, 25, 38, 40, 44, 84
  Piano Concerto No. 18, 86
Muses, the, 20–1, 25
music of the spheres, 9, 21, 64–5, 66, 87, 161
  God's harmony, 142, 146–7
music publishing, *see*, notation

Negri, Cesare, 96
Newport Folk Festival, 225
Nice, the
  Five Bridges Suite, 218
Nielsen, Carl, 44
Notari, Angelo, 158
notation, 39, 51, 52, 54, 98–100, 101, 110–11, 125, 179
  Franconian system, 98
  Gregorian Neumes, 98
  music publishing, 35, 120, 135
  see also, royalty ballad
Novello, 35
Noverre, Jean-Georges, 96

Oldfield, Mike, 228
  Tubular Bells, 218
Oliphant, Thomas, 126
opera, 32, 33, 36, 41, 44, 45, 53, 72, 73, 75, 83, 86, 89, 93–5, 96, 101, 149, 158, 162, 166, 203
orchestra, 19–20, 36–40
  orchestration, 19, 40
orchestrina, 102
Orpheus, 121
Oxy and the Morons, 195

Palestrina, Giovanni, 73, 84
Panzera, Charles (Auguste Louis), 90
Pappenheim, Marie, 46, 48
Paradis, Maria Theresa, 86
Parker, Archbishop, 59
Parsons, Alan, 217
Pater, Walter, 8–10, 15
  'The School of Giorgione', 8–10
Peacham, Henry
  Minerva Britanna, 159
Pembroke, Lord, 135
Performance, 231
Peri, Jacopo, 37
Pericles, 21
Petrucci, Ottaviano, 98
Pfleumer, Fritz, 107
Philips, 108
Phonographic Performance Limited (PPL), 104
piano, 101–2
pianola, 101–2
Pilkington, Francis, 134
  Madrigals and Pastorals of 3, 4, 5, and 6 Parts, 137
Pink Floyd, 184, 195, 211, 227
  'Another Brick in the Wall', 184
  Dark Side of the Moon, 211, 213, 214–16, 217
  'Echoes', *Meddle*, 216
  'Welcome to the Machine', *Wish You Were Here*, 216
  Animals, 216
  The Wall, 216, 231
  Pink Floyd Live at Pompeii, 231
plainchant, 13, 66–7
Plank, Conny, 217
Plastic Ono Band
  'Give Peace a Chance', 184
Plato, 63, 64, 65, 66
  The Republic, 63, 64–5
  Laws, 65
Playford, John, 96, 137
Plotinus, 66
Police, the, 238n
polyphony, 37–8, 42, 69–71, 98, 133, 138, 150–1, 159
  polyphonic atonality, 47–8, 49, 69–71
Pop, Iggy, 189
Poulsen, Valdemar, 107
Presley, Elvis, 231
Prosdocimus, 73
psychoanalysis, 235n
punk and New Wave, 188, 189, 197, 199, 220–2, 230

punk and New Wave — *continued*
  DIY ('do-it-yourself'), 109, 197
  see also, dissonance
Purcell, Henry, 93, 124
Puritans, 140–1
Pythagoras, 21, 60, 66
  Pythagorean scale, 73

quadrophonic sound, 105
Queen
  'Bohemian Rhapsody', 232

radio and broadcasting, 101, 102, 104, 105–7, 112, 170, 186, 187, 193, 199–201, 203, 205, 211, 233
  programming, 216
  playlist and charts, 106, 182, 185, 193, 200–1
  radio seen in image, 88, 232
  BBC, 105–6, 198
  pirate, 105–6, 200
Ramis, Bartolomeo, 74
Ramones, the, 189
recitative, 41, 43, 119, 127, 151, 157, 159, 180, 199
  see also, voice, cantabile
recording, tape, 102, 107–9, 112, 113
  cassettes, 107–8, 168
  dolby, 108
  digital, 108
  stereo, 104, 105, 113
  multitrack, 108, 217, 228
  DIY ('do-it-yourself'), 109, 197
Reformation, 124, 140
reggae, 172, 174–5, 226
  'dub' effects, 173, 174
  see also, ska, mento
Restoration, 119, 124, 157–8, 160, 162
Reed, Lou, 180
  'Take a Walk on the Wild Side', 209
Richard, Cliff, 231
Rolling Stones, the, 177, 186
  'Get off of my Cloud', 204
  'We Love You', 204
  'Angie', 204
  Gimme Shelter, 231
rondeau, 43
Roseman, Jon, 232
Rosen, Charles, 77
Ross, Diana, 204, 231
  Lady Sings the Blues, 231
  Mahogany, 231
Rosseter, Philip, 123, 155, 159
  see also, Thomas Campion, Philip Rosseter
Rotten, Johnny, 180
round, 138
royalty ballad, 101, 103
Rushent, Martin, 217

Salinas, Francis, 74
salsa, 171, 174
Sanam Teri Kasam, 171–3
Saturday Night Fever, 171
Saussure, Ferdinand de, 7
Schlick, Arnolt, 74
Schoenberg, Arnold, 38, 45–9, 55, 75, 77, 78, 80, 81
  Three Pieces for Piano, Op 11, 46
  Erwartung, 46, 48
  Book of the Hanging Garden, 46
  Pierrot Lunaire, 48
  Suite for Piano, Op 25, 49
Schubert, Franz, 11
Scott, Edouard-Léon, 103
scratching, 227
Sedaka, Neil
  'Oh Carol', 204
serialism, 45, 48, 49–51, 55
  octave equivalence, 55
  see also, Darmstadt School
Sex Pistols, the, 195
  'Pretty Vacant', 208
  'My Way', 199
Shakespeare, William, 142–3, 161
  Richard II, 143
  The Merchant of Venice, 143
  Cymbeline, 161
Short, Peter, 122
Simon, Carly
  'You're so Vain', 204–5
Simon and Garfunkel
  'Bridge over Troubled Water', 219
Sinatra, Frank, 231
Siouxsie and the Banshees, 180, 195
Sister Sledge
  'We are Family', 205–6
ska, 175
Slits, the, 195
Smith, Floyd, 102
Smith, Norman, 217
Solon, 65
Somnium Scipionis, 66
sonata, 43, 44
spectacle, *see* image
Spandau Ballet, 195
Spohr, Louis, 39
Sprechstimme, 48, 89

Sprechstimme — *continued*
  see also, Schoenberg
Stamitz, Johann Wenzel, 38
standards, 123, 170, 198–9
  see also, composition
Steel Pulse, 174
stereo, 104, 105, 113
  see also, recording
Stigwood Organisation, the Robert, 171
Sting, 204, 231
Stradivarius, 80
  see also, violin
Strauss, Richard, 25, 38, 44, 46
  Alpine Symphony, 44
Stravinsky, Igor
  The Rite of Spring, 24
  Ragtime for 11 Instruments, 53
  Piano Rag Music, 54
Stumpf, Carl, 61
suite, 43
Sulpice Seminary, the St, 68
symphony, 41, 42–4
synoptic scores, 32, 99
synthesisers, 102–3, 191, 222–3, 226–8

Talking Heads, 195
Tallis, Thomas, 134, 135–6
  and Byrd, William, *Cantiones Sacrae*, 136
Tamla Motown, 174, 177, 182
Taylor, James, 205
technique, musical, 17, 50, 99–100, 159–60, 221
  see also, improvisation
Television, 195
television, 186, 187, 228, 230–3
  see also, film music, video, image
Temptations, the
  'Papa was a Rolling Stone', 208
Terpander, 21, 26
Terry, Sonny, 86
theatre, music in the, 9, 93–5, 120, 133, 160–2, 165, 192, 199
Them, 195
Tomkins, Thomas, 126–48
  'Music Divine', 126–32, 135, 137–48, 155
  Songs of 3, 4, 5, and 6 Parts, 135
tonality, 72–5, 76–7, 79–80, 99
  see also, modulation
Tornados, the
  'Telstar', 226
Toscanini, Arturo, 80
Tosh, Peter, 171

'Legalize It', 184
Tovey, Donald, 236n
tritone ('the devil in music'), see, dissonance
Troubadours, 122
two-tone, 174
  see also, ska, reggae

U2, 195

Vagrancy Laws, 135
Vautrollier, Thomas, 136
Verdi, Giuseppe, 100
video, 89–90, 95, 105, 113–15, 183, 199, 222–3, 229–33
  see also, image, television, film music
viols, 36, 133, 152, 160
  lyra viol, 160
violin, 36
virginals, 160
Visconti, Tony, 217
Vitry, Philippe de, 70
voice
  voice-quality, 90–2, 92–3, 179–81
  accent in performance, 164–6, 180–1
  register and dialect, 187
  see also, cantabile, recitative, Barthes: 'The Grain of the Voice'

Wagner, Richard, 9, 31, 38, 46, 93–5, 112
  Reinzi, 12
  Tannhauser, 93
  Tristan and Isolde, 48
  mystic gap or gulf, 9, 94
  Bayreuth, 9
waits, city, 133, 135, 160
Wakeman, Rick
  Myths and Legends of King Arthur, 218
Wallington, Ben, 33
Watson, Thomas
  First Sett of Italian Madrigals Englisshed, 120
Weelkes, Thomas, 119, 126, 137, 150
  'O Care, Thou wilt Dispatch me', 150
Webern, Anton von, 50, 80
  The Path to the New Music, 77
Wesley, Samuel Sebastian, 69
Who, the, 186, 195
  'My Generation', 186–8, 205, 206
  Tommy, 231
  Quadrophenia, 231
Wilson, John, 123, 161
Wilbye, John, 119, 126, 134, 137, 148

Wilbye, John — *continued*
   'Adieu, Sweet Amaryllis', 148, 150
women performers in rock music, 191,
   206–7, 221–2
Wood, Roy, 228
Woodstock, 186, 231
Wonder, Stevie, 86, 210, 228
   'Happy Birthday to You', 210
Wyatt, Robert, 179
   Rock Bottom, 211

XTC, 195

Yonge, Nicholas
   Musica Transalpina, 32, 120

Zarlino, Gioseffo, 74
Zappa, Frank, 195
   Freak Out, 213

GPSR Compliance

The European Union's (EU) General Product Safety Regulation (GPSR) is a set of rules that requires consumer products to be safe and our obligations to ensure this.

If you have any concerns about our products, you can contact us on

ProductSafety@springernature.com

In case Publisher is established outside the EU, the EU authorized representative is:

Springer Nature Customer Service Center GmbH
Europaplatz 3
69115 Heidelberg, Germany

www.ingramcontent.com/pod-product-compliance
Lightning Source LLC
Chambersburg PA
CBHW031519100426
42873CB00013B/133